# CHRISTIAN COSMOPOLITANISM

In the series *Religious Engagement in Democratic Politics,*
edited by Paul A. Djupe

FELIPE AMIN FILOMENO

# CHRISTIAN COSMOPOLITANISM

*Faith Communities Talk Immigration*

TEMPLE UNIVERSITY PRESS
*Philadelphia • Rome • Tokyo*

TEMPLE UNIVERSITY PRESS
Philadelphia, Pennsylvania 19122
*tupress.temple.edu*

Library of Congress Cataloging-in-Publication Data

Names: Filomeno, Felipe Amin, 1981– author.
Title: Christian cosmopolitanism : faith communities talk immigration /
   Felipe Amin Filomeno.
Other titles: Religious engagement in democratic politics.
Description: Philadelphia : Temple University Press, 2025. | Series:
   Religious engagement in democratic politics | Includes bibliographical
   references and index. | Summary: "Investigates whether and how
   deliberative dialogues about immigration in Christian congregations can
   perform a cosmopolitan role"— Provided by publisher.
Identifiers: LCCN 2024006692 (print) | LCCN 2024006693 (ebook) | ISBN
   9781439925980 (cloth) | ISBN 9781439925997 (paperback) | ISBN
   9781439926000 (pdf)
Subjects: LCSH: Intercultural communication—Religious
   aspects—Christianity. | Cosmopolitanism. | Christians—United
   States—Attitudes. | United States—Emigration and
   immigration—Religious aspects—Christianity.
Classification: LCC BR115.E45 F55 2025 (print) | LCC BR115.E45 (ebook) |
   DDC 261.8/38—dc23/eng/20240706
LC record available at https://lccn.loc.gov/2024006692
LC ebook record available at https://lccn.loc.gov/2024006693

Printed in the United States of America

9  8  7  6  5  4  3  2  1

# CONTENTS

# LIST OF FIGURE AND TABLES

## Figure

## Tables

# Acknowledgments

This book is an accomplishment I gladly share with those who contributed to the research and community service on which it is based. Rachel Brubaker, Jessica Berman, Joby Taylor, Devin Hagerty, Stephen Millies, Sarah Fouts, Sara Poggio, and Paul Djupe offered comments that improved and guided my work. Matthew Harrington, Hannah Jang, Annette Marin, Rehman Liaqat, and Viridiana Colosio-Martinez worked as research assistants, helping implement, transcribe, and analyze dialogues. Maryland Humanities, the Louisville Institute, the Center for the Study of Religion and the City at Morgan State University, and the University of Maryland, Baltimore County, generously provided grant support to different portions of the project. I am also thankful to the editorial team at Temple University Press, especially Aaron Javsicas, for the friendly support and efficient work. My biggest debt of gratitude, however, is to the Latino Racial Justice Circle volunteers, whose ministry inspired this project, and to the clergy and laypeople of the congregations that hosted the Honest Conversations on Immigration from 2018 to 2022.

# CHRISTIAN COSMOPOLITANISM

# 1

## Introduction

On the evening of April 15, 2022, I walked into a Methodist church in Baltimore, Maryland, to attend a Good Friday worship service. I sat on the third row of pews, where I could read the words *Ich bin das brot des lebens* in wooden relief on a table in front of the altar. Those words are German for "I am the bread of life," which, according to the Gospel of John, Jesus said to his followers (John 6:35). The walls of the church had stained glass windows with Christian motifs and the names of German families that had been members of that congregation many years ago when German immigrants populated the neighborhood. By the early twenty-first century, that neighborhood and the church had undergone many changes. The neighborhood had become an enclave of Latino immigrants, and the congregation had become a Latino faith community.[1]

The Good Friday service I attended was cohosted by a nearby Lutheran congregation, whose membership was primarily U.S.-born. The pastors of both churches presided over the service, and members of both congregations attended. The service was held in English and Spanish. A banner hung from the church ceiling, reading "One in Spirit / Uno en Espíritu." In the pews, there were Bibles in English and Spanish. It was a special occasion where ethnic communities from past and present were represented physically or through symbols and where Christians of different denominations (including myself, a Catholic) worshipped together. Diverse in language, phenotype, and faith tradition, but common in religion: "One in Spirit." This event sharply contrasted with the exclusionary images many people in the United States have come to associate with Christianity: prejudice against gender and sexual orientation minorities, fundamentalism, and White American nationalism.

I attended that Good Friday service because, a few months earlier, those two congregations had participated in one of the deliberative dialogues on immigration I had facilitated in Christian congregations since 2018. Those dialogues aimed to promote mutual understanding and collaboration between immigrants and U.S.-born people in the context of faith communities. Holding joint religious services was one of the collaborative activities that members of both congregations had planned in their dialogue. In this book, I investigate whether and how deliberative dialogues about immigration in Christian congregations can perform a cosmopolitan role. Cosmopolitanism is a normative theory (making moral claims about how the world should be) and an empirical condition (a particular type of existing social phenomena). In the normative sense, cosmopolitanism argues that all human beings are endowed with dignity and constitute a global community in relation to which one has membership, rights, and duties. Based on this moral claim, one can make judgments and prescriptions about social attitudes, behaviors, and institutions. In the empirical sense, cosmopolitanism refers to real-life interactions between diverse people through which they expand their identities and solidarities across boundaries of nationality, race, and culture toward a global community of human beings. This cosmopolitanization can happen without individuals or groups necessarily erasing their differences. Deliberative dialogues on immigration—by promoting critical thinking, mutual understanding, and collaboration across differences—could be a cosmopolitan interaction and turn Christian congregations into spaces of cosmopolitanization.

## 1.1 Religion and Immigration

Faith communities are puzzling spaces in which to investigate cosmopolitanism, because religion has been both a unifying force and a divisive force in human societies. On the one hand, religious belonging, beliefs, and behaviors can make communities cohesive; on the other hand, religion has been used to justify civil and international wars, colonialism, terrorism, genocide, and the discrimination of minorities. Religion's historical ambiguity in human relations is especially visible in its relation to immigration. From the persecution of religious minorities to colonial projects justified by religious conversion, religion has been integral to why people move. Once foreigners arrive in a new territory, religion is crucial to how they relate to long-standing inhabitants. While religious institutions have been gateways for immigrants into local communities, religion has also been a marker for local communities to discriminate against newcomers from minority denominations.

Contemporary Christianity is no exception to religion's ambiguous relation to immigration. In the encyclical *Fratelli Tutti*, Pope Francis declared, "It is my desire that, in this our time, by acknowledging the dignity of each human person, we can contribute to the rebirth of a universal aspiration to fraternity. Fraternity between all men and women. . . . Let us dream, then, as a single human family, as fellow travelers sharing the same flesh, as children of the same earth which is our common home, each of us bringing the richness of his or her beliefs and convictions, each of us with his or her own voice, brothers and sisters all" (Pope Francis 2020, 4–5). Around the same time, however, far-right nationalist and authoritarian leaders like Donald Trump in the United States, Vladimir Putin in Russia, Matteo Salvini in Italy, and Jair Bolsonaro in Brazil were using the Christian religion "as a tool of identity politics" to mobilize "feelings of belonging among the majority population" and exclude minorities, immigrants in particular (Permoser 2020, 4).

Organized religion has been an essential part of the social context of immigrant integration. Historically, immigrants have relied on faith communities in the host country to connect with local co-ethnics, sustain transnational relations with homelands, maintain cultural traditions, learn about the new country, and gain access to employment, housing, and other opportunities. If an ethnic faith community is introverted and part of a local ethnic enclave, however, its capacity to integrate immigrants into mainstream society is limited. Religious institutions have also played a more intentional role in immigrant integration, establishing dual language schools for children of immigrant families, providing charity and social services to immigrant communities, and advocating for immigrant rights. In the United States, the official stance of the largest religious denominations on immigration is generally pro-immigrant. In the case of Christian denominations, this position is often justified by the numerous biblical passages about migrants. For instance, Leviticus 19:34 says, "Any immigrant who lives with you must be treated as if they were one of your citizens. You must love them as yourself." Psalms 146:9, Malachi 3:5, and Jeremiah 7:6 reference immigrants as vulnerable people who deserve special attention. In the New Testament, Jesus states that by showing hospitality and love to the stranger, one is actually welcoming him (Matthew 25:31–45). In the United States, faith-based community organizers have drawn on theologies of inclusion to give meaning to organizing across racial, national, and ethnic lines (Flores 2020, 232). Collective religious rituals such as prayer, singing, and worship have brought together Latino immigrants and African Americans, creating common ground for community organizing (Flores 2020, 232–33).

Nonetheless, there are important variations across religious denominations in how religious organizations and communities integrate immigrants. Mainline Protestant communities and Catholic communities have established organizational structures, broad funding sources, and strong connec-tions in civil society; they have also promoted a commitment to social re-sponsibility. All of these features have enabled many of the communities to perform an active role in immigrant integration (Andrews 2011). The Cath-olic Church, in particular, currently promotes multicultural parishes as a pan-ethnic model for immigrant integration (Menjívar 2003). In many of these "shared parishes," however, Latino congregants are marginalized, with less representation in parish leadership, while Sunday masses in Spanish are as-signed to the least convenient times (Hoover 2014). Evangelical communities are comparatively newer, have narrower funding sources, are more inward-looking, and stress individual-level conversion, limiting their role in immi-grant integration (Andrews 2011). Evangelical denominations tend to integrate immigrants into smaller, tightly knit, and ethnically homogeneous congre-gations (Menjívar 2003). Among Evangelicals, theological interpretations of adherence to the rule of law have also justified opposition to immigration reform and unauthorized immigration in particular (Melkonian-Hoover and Kellstedt 2019, 159). Still, World Relief, the humanitarian arm of the Nation-al Association of Evangelicals of the United States, is active in service to im-migrant communities, and Evangelical leaders are "coming to see immigra-tion not as a threat, but as an opportunity to 'share the Good News'" (Bauman and Yang 2013, 50).

Research on the effects of religion on individual attitudes toward immi-grants and immigration policy has produced mixed conclusions and shown that the attitudes of believers can be sharply different from the official position of religious institutions (Breitkreutz 2011, 14; Bloom, Arikan, and Courte-manche 2015, 1; Paterson 2017, 37). Bloom, Arikan, and Courtemanche (2015) found that, across religious denominations, religion as a type of social iden-tity has a parochialist effect, increasing opposition to immigrants who are dissimilar to in-group members in religion or ethnicity (group self-defense), while religion as a set of beliefs has a limited cosmopolitan effect, engender-ing welcoming attitudes toward immigrants of the same religion and ethnic-ity among the less conservative devout (in-group solidarity). Other studies have found that principles such as "welcome the stranger," "love thy neigh-bor," and the sacredness of the family have motivated religious Americans to advocate for immigrant rights even if they did not share immigrants' eth-nicity (Park 1998, Hondagneu-Sotelo 2008, Freeland 2010, Houston and Morse 2017). In a study of two Catholic dialogues on immigration, Boryczka, Gude-lunas, and Gil-Egui (2015) found that when participants discussed immigra-tion from a faith-based perspective, the framing of immigrants was mostly positive. In contrast, when participants discussed immigration from a gov-ernment and institutional perspective, the framing of immigrants was pri-marily negative.

Intersectionality seems to shape the effects of religion on immigration attitudes, but research findings are complex and not fully comparable.[2] Yukich and Edgell (2020, 10) pointed out that "race shapes several specific aspects of religious identity and experience," including the connection between religion and immigration. Brenneman (2005, 25), Deitz (2014, 37), and Jones et al. (2013, 1) found that religious Black Americans are not more likely to hold restrictive opinions on immigration than religious people of another race or ethnicity. However, Brown and Brown (2017) found that the association between the exposure of congregants to clergy political discourse (including the clergy's usually pro-immigrant stance) and the attitudes of congregants toward immigration policy is contingent on race. Among White Americans, that exposure is associated with less restrictive preferences on immigration policy. Among Black Americans, that exposure is associated with preferences equally as restrictive or more restrictive on immigration policy. Brown and Brown (2017, 15) suggested that the comparatively low economic status of Black Americans (implying more vulnerability to economic competition from immigrants) might make them particularly susceptible to the narrative of immigration restrictionism.

Among White Americans who identify as Protestants, Catholics, or nonbelievers, Christian nationalism—a political-religious ideology that melds Christianity with American national identity—is a robust predictor of hostility toward immigrants (McDaniel, Nooruddin, and Shortle 2011). Once this intersectional variable is included in statistical analyses, the effects of religious affiliation on immigration attitudes are not statistically significant (McDaniel, Nooruddin, and Shortle 2011, 226). Moreover, looking not only at religious ideology but also at religious behavior, Stroop, Rackin, and Froese (2021) found that Christian nationalists who regularly attend religious services hold less negative attitudes toward immigrants than Christian nationalists who do not attend church regularly. In their study of immigration attitudes among Evangelicals in the United States, Melkonian-Hoover and Kellstedt (2019, 8) found that a large majority of White Evangelicals are on the political right and hold more restrictive opinions on immigration, whereas most Black, Latino, and Asian Evangelicals are left of center and hold less restrictive views on immigration. Brenneman (2005, 31) and Knoll (2009, 327) concluded that Jewish Americans have more positive immigration attitudes than other religious groups. Both authors explained this finding based on the minority marginalization hypothesis, according to which groups that share an experience of marginalization tend to have solidarity toward each other.

While religious institutions, communities, and identities are critical to how immigrants integrate into host societies, immigration has been integral to the transformation of the religious landscapes of host societies. Christianity arrived in what today we call the United States because of the immigration of European colonists in the late sixteenth and early seventeenth centuries. Successive waves of immigration of Christians and followers of other religions further expanded the religious landscape of the United States. In the late twentieth century, when the proportion of religiously affiliated people in the country started to decline and many Christian congregations began to shrink, immigration became even more vital to religious life in the United States. In 1972, 95% of Americans belonged to a religion, and approximately 95% of the religiously affiliated were Christian (Pew Research Center 2022, 20). By 2021, 71% of Americans belonged to a religion, and 89% of the religiously affiliated were Christian (Pew Research Center 2022, 20). While "the number of participants in congregational services has not kept up with the overall population growth," congregations—Christian and otherwise—"with large numbers of immigrants have seen steady growth" (Shimron 2022). Latino immigrants, in particular, have been crucial to U.S. Catholicism and Evangelicalism (Shimron 2022, Winter 2021). However, despite "the increasing racial and ethnic diversity of the country, the vast majority of churchgoers report that their congregations are mostly monoracial" (Public Religion Research Institute 2023, 21).

In light of the ambiguous and multifaceted role of religion discussed above, we need a better understanding of the empirical conditions under which religion—particularly Christianity—works as a unifying or divisive force in society, politics, and immigration affairs. Deliberative dialogues on immigration in Christian congregations offer a vantage point to investigate that fundamental question for several reasons.

First, immigration is the quintessential cosmopolitan challenge. How a nation, community, or organization welcomes the stranger is a litmus test of its capacity to accommodate human diversity while recognizing our common humanity.

Second, migration is intrinsic to the traditions and historical development of major world religions. In Christianity, that has been the case from the beginning. According to the Gospel of Matthew, soon after Jesus Christ was born, his parents were forced to flee their homeland for fear of King Herod's persecution. The early Christian centers were established by apostles and missionaries migrating in and around the eastern half of the Roman Empire. As I stated above, migration is a recurring theme in both the Old and New Testaments.

Third, Christians have been talking about immigration openly and intentionally (more on this in the next section). Deliberative dialogues in congregations can expose the unifying and divisive tendencies of religion. The dialogues analyzed in this book explicitly covered controversial aspects of immigration (such as illegal immigration and economic competition with immigrants), had clergy and laypeople as participants, and happened inside congregations, making them an appropriate empirical space in which to observe the conflicting tendencies of religion.

## 1.2 Christians Talking about Immigration

Immigration is one of the most contentious political topics in the United States. In 2023, only 28% of Americans were satisfied with the country's immigration level (Saad 2023), and 47% considered illegal immigration a "very big problem" (Pew Research Center 2023). Yet, Americans are far from agreeing on how to approach the issue. The proportion of Republicans dissatisfied with the level of immigration in the United States (71%) is much higher than the proportion of Democrats (19%) (Saad 2023). Views on immigration also vary significantly according to gender, age, education (Berg 2015), and, as shown in the previous section, religion. It is therefore not surprising that people are having heated, and often unproductive, discussions about immigration. As a consequence, a number of organizations—among them the Study Circles Resource Center (Scully and Leighninger 1998), now called Everyday Democracy; ARISE and the Labor Council for Latin American Advancement (LCLAA) (2011); Living Room Conversations (2021); and Welcoming America (Herzig 2011)—have tried to improve the quality of civic talk on immigration through dialogue and deliberation. This work has important implications because talking about civic issues, even if only casually, can encourage civic participation and strengthen democracy (Klofstad 2010).

Talking about immigration has also been one of the main ways Christian congregations in the United States have responded to immigration in the twenty-first century. This has taken the form of sermons about immigration; lectures and panels by immigration experts, activists, or clergy; immigrant testimonials; or direct conversations between congregants. In 2010, 32% of Catholics and 20% of Protestants who attended religious services at least once a month said they heard clergy speak out about immigration (Pew Research Center 2010, 5). The persistent centrality of immigration in public debates makes it unlikely that those proportions have diminished since then. In fact, over the past fifteen years, Christian congregations nationwide have used group-based conversations to promote mutual understanding between immigrants and U.S.-born people and to discern ways to act on immigration as people of faith. In a Web search for this type of event, I found national and regional organizations that promote congregation-based conversations on immigration and individual instances of such events.[3] Among those organizations are the Catholic Legal Immigration Network, the Evangelical Immigration Table, the Discipleship Ministries of the United Methodist Church, the Interfaith Immigration Coalition, the Lutheran Immigration and Refugee Service, the National Issues Forums, Religions for Peace, Sojourners, and the Unitarian Universalist Association. In general, these organizations justify the promotion of conversations on immigration in Christian congregations by arguing that immigration is one of the most polarizing issues in the United States and that migration is a significant religious matter discussed in scripture.

In the aforementioned Web search, I found twenty-three Christian congregation conversations on immigration that happened between 2006 and 2020 in the United States. Those events occurred in sixteen states in almost every region of the country. Mainline Protestant, Evangelical, Catholic, and nondenominational congregations hosted the conversations. Interdenominational groups organized a few of the events. While we cannot take those twenty-three events as a representative sample,[4] they illustrate how congregational dialogues on immigration have happened across the country over many years and in multiple denominations. The dialogues I studied in Baltimore were not exceptional events but activities that national and regional institutions have promoted and that various congregations have implemented.

Christians have also engaged in intentional faith-related conversations about immigration outside of congregations. Reddit—the social news aggregation, Web content rating, and discussion Website—is rife with long threads about Christianity and immigration, with titles as abstract as "Is Illegal Immigration a Sin?" (U/monk2be 2013) or as concrete as "Indianapolis Church Locks Up Mary, Joseph, Baby Jesus to Condemn Immigration Policy" (U/xmasx131 2017). Similar conversations can easily be found on Facebook. For instance, in October 2018, the news and opinion Website *Vox* posted on the social media platform an article entitled "The Bible Says to Welcome Immigrants. So Why Don't White Evangelicals?," which prompted 783 comments (many of which were replies to comments, indicating an actual exchange of ideas between users) (Vox 2018). In July 2020, Women of Welcome—a Facebook group self-described as Christian women, with 116,383 followers in March of 2022—reposted an article from *The Hill* entitled "Evangelical Group Writes to Trump Urging Him Not to End DACA," which prompted 88 responses (Women of Welcome 2020). In sum, Christians are talking about immigration, and, to the extent that conversations shape individuals and organizations, that talking has significant implications for Christian congregations, the Christian church, and immigration politics.

## 1.3 "Honest Conversations on Immigration": A Local Cosmopolitan Experiment

From 2019 to 2022, as a volunteer with the Latino Racial Justice Circle (LRJC), I designed, facilitated, and analyzed deliberative dialogues on immigration involving fourteen Christian congregations in Baltimore, Maryland. With the same organization, in 2018 I ran a pilot dialogue with twenty-eight participants from various congregations as part of an ecumenical workshop on immigration. LRJC is a nonprofit organization founded in 2015 to promote the integration of immigrants from Latin America in Baltimore. As of October 2023, the organization had a scholarship program for Latino youth, a legal aid program for immigrant families, an advocacy program for immigration policy, and the dialogue program discussed in this book.

Situated in the mid-Atlantic region of the United States, Baltimore has a diverse religious landscape with a rich history. In colonial times, George Calvert (1579–1632), 1st Baron Baltimore, saw Maryland as a possible refuge for Catholics persecuted in England. His son, Cecil Calvert (1605–1675), became the first proprietor of the province of Maryland and continued his father's legacy, turning Maryland into a haven for Catholics in North America. By the mid-nineteenth century, Baltimore had become a major port and industrial center on the East Coast of the United States. The city's prominent position attracted many immigrants from Europe from the second half of the nineteenth century to the early twentieth century. Immigrants from Germany, Ireland, Italy, Greece, and Eastern Europe—including many Jews—settled in ethnic neighborhoods and founded faith communities.

Religious institutions in Baltimore were actively involved in immigration affairs. From 1904 to 1915, the German United Evangelical Church of Christ in Locust Point maintained the Immigrant House for immigrants and sailors (Baltimore Museum of Immigration 2020). In that period, Locust Point was second only to Ellis Island as the largest port of immigration to the United States. Religion, however, was also involved in racial and ethnic segregation practices in the city. In the mid-twentieth century, residential covenants "prohibited Jewish occupancy in gentile suburbs" (Power 1996, 5). Around the same time, local White churches actively promoted segregation against Black people. In 1925, a group of Methodist, Catholic, Evangelical, and Lutheran churches "signed a property agreement binding them to prevent their properties from being used or occupied by negroes within a period of ten years" (Brown 2019, 4). Five White churches (Presbyterian, Episcopal, Lutheran, and Methodist) lobbied mayor Howard Jackson, who governed the city in 1923–1927 and in 1931–1943, in favor of racial segregation because, they argued, an inflow of Blacks into their neighborhoods would reduce their property values (Brown 2019, 5).

In the early 2000s, a new wave of immigration to Baltimore emerged, consisting primarily of immigrants from Latin America and refugees from Africa and Asia. Some of these newcomers joined existing faith communities, sometimes rejuvenating churches that had lost members in the late twentieth century as Baltimore deindustrialized and lost its population to the suburbs

(Olesker 2001, 188). Other recent immigrants founded new faith communities, including mosques and Latino Evangelical churches. Religious institutions of multiple denominations have stayed active in immigration affairs, including, for instance, the Esperanza Center of Catholic Charities, the Episcopal Refugee and Immigrant Center Alliance, the Lutheran Immigration and Refugee Service, and the Immigration Clinic of World Relief (which is Evangelical Christian). At least one denomination explicitly promoted dialogue as a tool for immigrant integration in the area. In 2011, the Baltimore Archdiocese of the Catholic Church launched a campaign urging Catholic parishes in Maryland to engage in faith-filled, prayerful, and thorough dialogue on immigration (Catholic Review 2012).

Working in a city with a legacy of diversity and segregation, LRJC aims "to educate and inspire people of all faith traditions . . . [to] recognize and then act to eliminate systemic racial injustice and everyday incidents of bias and discrimination toward the Latino community. The Circle is committed to healing the wounds of racism by seeking to understand and respect one another. The Circle also strives to change human behavior . . . [to] change the human heart" (Latino Racial Justice Circle 2015). The vision of LRJC is "to create opportunities throughout Maryland for meaningful, authentic dialogue about race relations with people of different cultures. As a result, the Circle hopes to form cross-cultural, faith-based communities focused on spiritual growth and improving social relationships" (Latino Racial Justice Circle 2015). When I started volunteering with LRJC in 2017, its leaders expressed the wish to create a program of faith community dialogues on immigration called "Honest Conversations on Immigration." As a university professor experienced in classroom facilitation, I offered to lead the program's creation as a community-based research project.[5] This book tells the story and lessons from that civic experiment, one aimed at building bridges between people at a time when physical walls between nations were being expanded.

The pilot dialogue held in October 2018 was a forty-five-minute activity in a day-long ecumenical workshop on immigration of LRJC.[6] In spring 2019, I expanded that activity into two dialogues involving four Catholic parishes. Each dialogue consisted of three sessions of one hour and thirty minutes over three consecutive weeks. One dialogue happened between LRJC volunteers (all Christian and mostly Latino immigrants) and members of a predominantly African American Catholic congregation. The other dialogue happened between Latino immigrants and White American members of three Catholic congregations. In the fall of 2020, I facilitated a dialogue between two Methodist congregations, one predominantly Latino and the other predominantly African American. This time, each weekly session was expanded to one hour and forty-five minutes, which became the standard for the following dialogues. From then until May 2022, four more dialogues happened. The language used in the dialogues depended on the language of the participants. The pilot dialogue and two dialogues were conducted only in English, while five other dialogues were bilingual (English-Spanish). Two of the five English-Spanish dialogues were entirely bilingual, with every statement being interpreted from English to Spanish and vice versa. I served as the interpreter, except when participants were bilingual and could interpret their words in both English and Spanish. Table 1.1 summarizes the profile of the dialogues and assigns each of them a code for reference throughout the book.

Since the LRJC mission is to promote not only awareness but also action on issues important for the Latino community, the "Honest Conversations

| TABLE 1.1 LRJC HONEST CONVERSATIONS ON IMMIGRATION (HC), 2018–2022 | | | | | |
|---|---|---|---|---|---|
| Date | Denomination | Predominant Racial/ Ethnic Composition | Location of Congregations | Number of Participants[a] | Code |
| October 2018 | Catholic and Protestant (various) | White American and Latino | Urban | 28 | n/a |
| February– March 2019 | Catholic | African-American, Latino and White American | Urban | 12–14 | HC1 |
| May 2019 | Catholic | Latino and White American | Suburban | 11–14 | HC2 |
| October 2020 | Methodist | African-American and Latino | Urban/ Suburban | 7–12 | HC3 |
| May–June 2021 | Catholic | African, African-American and White American | Suburban | 7–8 | HC4 |
| September 2021 | Evangelical | Latino and various other | Urban/ Suburban | 3–7 | HC5 |
| October– November 2021 | Methodist[b] and Lutheran | Latino and White American | Urban | 4–13 | HC6 |
| April–May 2022 | Catholic | Latino and White American | Urban | 12–15 | HC7 |

[a] In each of the three-week dialogues, a few participants dropped in or dropped out after the first session, resulting in a range of participant numbers for each dialogue. A large majority of participants, however, attended all dialogue sessions. I counted a total of ninety-seven participants, not including the twenty-eight participants in the 2018 pilot dialogue. The number of ninety-seven participants is approximate because it refers to participants who actually spoke during the dialogues. If a participant stayed silent during the dialogues, they were not registered in the dialogue transcripts and, therefore, were out of that count. Alternatively, I could have estimated the total number of participants based on my observation notes, where I registered the total number of participants in every dialogue session. However, in every dialogue, a few participants did not attend all three sessions (often because of scheduling conflicts). Even if I added up the number of participants in the most attended session of each dialogue, I could still be underestimating the total number of participants. A participant who was present only in the least attended dialogue sessions would not be counted. Therefore, the total number of participants may have actually been slightly higher than ninety-seven.

[b] This Methodist congregation had already participated in HC3, but only three of its congregants who had participated in HC3 joined the program again to engage with members of the Lutheran congregation in HC6.

on Immigration" dialogues included a deliberation among participants about future collaboration across differences of nationality, ethnicity, and race. Therefore, from every dialogue (except the pilot) emerged a follow-up collaborative project involving some of the participants and other members of their communities. I either participated in these projects or later checked in with participants to know if and how the collaborative projects transpired. To analyze the dialogues and collaborative actions, I adopted a methodological strategy combining an entry survey to register participants' demographic data, a content analysis of dialogue transcripts, and participant observation of collaborative actions. The analysis considered not only the thematic substance of what participants said but also how the participants interacted with each other during the dialogues.

In Appendix A, I describe the methodological strategy in detail, including how I developed the *LRJC Guide for Honest Conversations on Immigration* (which is presented in Appendix B). Overall, I tried to strike a balance between, on the one hand, being systematic and objective (for instance, by using quantification of transcripts to suggest where patterns could exist in the qualitative data) and, on the other hand, being attentive to the complexity and uniqueness of each dialogue (for instance, by delving into specific exchanges between participants that were particularly illustrative or puzzling). This effort is visible to the reader in the empirical chapters, where I analyze specific participant interactions and the topics they discussed. After introducing a type of interaction or a conversation topic, I discuss how it varied across dialogue demographic makeup and the race/ethnicity of individual participants. I weave into that discussion excerpts from the dialogues to illustrate those interactions, topics, and variations. This format appears in Chapters 3, 4, and 5. While discussing the findings in those chapters, I often refer to their quantitative aspects by using either adjectives (as in "most agreement happened between participants of different race/ethnicity") or numbers (as in "immigrant participants accounted for 62% of statements about discrimination"). In Appendix A, sections A.1 and A.2, the reader will find tables with the quantitative data that assisted the qualitative analysis. Wherever I present specific numbers they should be seen as descriptive statistics, because the number of participants and dialogues, the nonindependence of data, and other characteristics of the data do not allow for inferential statistics.

Looking at all dialogues (except the pilot), the survey showed participant diversity regarding national origin: on average, 46% of the participants were immigrants. Diversity was more limited in other aspects, with the participant profile tending toward older adults, women, liberal-leaning, and college-educated people.[7] A large majority of immigrant participants were from Latin America. A few were from Asia or Africa. The resulting conversations were likely affected by this condition and should be interpreted as such. While the mission of LRJC was the main reason for the program's focus on Latino immigrants, that choice also had analytical advantages. In 2018, immigrants from Latin America and the Caribbean accounted for 50% of the foreign-born population of the United States (Budiman 2020). Latinos have also become the largest racial/ethnic minority among Christians in the United States. As early as 2014, 16% of Christians identified as Latino, while 13% identified as Black and 66% as White (Pew Research Center 2015). Yet, significant barriers have limited the inclusion of Latino immigrants in U.S. Christianity. As Hoover (2021) pointed out, institutionalized racial and ethnic inequality, especially of the anti-Hispanic kind, is ubiquitous in Catholic congregations. In Evangelical denominations, where Latinos are the fastest-growing group (Winter 2021), White Christian nationalism is a major ideological force (Whitehead and Perry 2020, x).

The dialogues I facilitated were not all moments of easygoing or superficial exchanges. For instance, when I approached clergypeople to promote the dialogue program, one priest refused to have his congregation participate for fear that conversations on immigration would jeopardize the positive relations between Latinos and White Americans that had recently emerged in his parish. Interestingly, three years after this happened, I heard from a fellow volunteer who worked with Latino members of that congregation that Latino people had been leaving that parish because the priest was "a bit dogmatic" and "did not know how to balance the unique needs of intra-parish communities." When I implemented the program in another parish, a participant questioned why I was bringing up controversial topics like unauthorized immigration: "What's the fruits of the discussion? In the sense that, if you agree or disagree with any given point, . . . what does that discussion engender, in terms of concrete action moving forward?" When we did talk about those topics, some participants made culturally offensive comments, such as claiming that being born in the United States makes one a Native American, which risked derailing the conversations into an angry debate.

## 1.4 The Argument

This book contributes to overcoming several limitations of scholarship on religion, cosmopolitanism, and dialogue. As stated by Melkonian-Hoover and Kellstedt (2019, 162), we need much more research on "the extent and effects of social engagement with immigrants in congregations." While the scholarship on cosmopolitanism (including religious cosmopolitanism) is mostly philosophical, the present study combines normative theories of cosmopolitanism with empirical analysis of real-life experiences of cosmopolitanization (the LRJC Honest Conversations on Immigration). Normative theories of cosmopolitanism provide ideal types for the political and moral organization of society that I use here as analytical categories to examine con-crete conversations and collaboration. The scholarship on dialogue has both a philosophical and an empirical branch. However, most empirical assess-ments of intergroup community dialogues are of dialogues among college students and rely on participants' self-reported attitudes and reflection with-out systematic analysis of the content of dialogues or collective action by dia-logue participants. Studies on intergroup community dialogue have also not considered the effects of religious beliefs, behaviors, and belonging on the pro-cesses and outcomes of dialogues. Although a large amount of literature on interfaith dialogues considers the effect of religion on dialogues, few studies look at the effect of religion on dialogues that are not primarily about religion. This is even though religion continues to be an important sphere of civic life in the United States.

Based on the present study, I argue that Christian community dialogues that bring together immigrants and U.S.-born people to share personal sto-ries, feelings, and thoughts about immigration; to reflect on differences and commonalities between them; and to deliberate on collaborative action in order to advance common interests and shared values can unleash the cos-mopolitan potential of the Christian religion. Unleashing this potential takes the form of mutual understanding and collaboration, not necessarily the sup-pression of differences. For instance, in one dialogue, an African American woman criticized Latino immigrants for speaking only in Spanish in shops in ethnic enclaves, even when serving English-speaking customers. However, after listening to Latino participants talk about why the use of Spanish persists in those communities and further discussing the issue of language differences, she aligned Latinos with African Americans by saying that, like Latinos, Af-rican Americans are discriminated against for not speaking the "King's Eng-lish." At another dialogue, a White American man, who spent most of the dialogue expressing concern about immigration to the United States in light of the economic and cultural anxieties of the country's middle class, said he was moved after listening to the stories of two Latina participants about their efforts to get a college degree and to educate children who can speak English.

This is not to say that Christian community dialogues on immigration have a necessary or uniform cosmopolitan effect on participants' attitudes, behaviors, and communities. As I show, there are important variations in the dialogues, and some of these variations can be traced back to the inter-section of religion with participants' race, ethnicity, and political ideology. In any given dialogue, multiple structures of social stratification intersect, and participants engage with each other from their positions in those intersec-tions. The study focuses on the role of race and ethnicity because these di-mensions of social stratification capture the immigrant-native divide that is the center of the book.[8] There are also limitations related to the type of congregant those dialogues tend to attract and the type of collaborative action they tend to pursue afterward. Moreover, conversational shifts among participants might not correspond accurately or permanently to changes in attitudes or identities.

I wrote this book not only to present original scholarly knowledge on Christian cosmopolitanism and dialogue but also to promote dialogue as a cultural practice that can help diverse communities (or communities undergoing diversification) overcome segregation and become socially cohesive. This is especially important for Christian congregations in North America, which have become more diverse over the past decades. As Ammerman (1997) showed, congregations must adapt to changing environments in order to survive and prosper, facing challenges openly and working through conflicts over program, leadership, and identity. A church that cannot mediate the relations between immigrant and native-born people neglects essential biblical principles and becomes vulnerable to internal strife, loss of membership, and a decline in relevance as an institution of social cohesion. I hope the book will inspire faith leaders, local governments, and community development practitioners to use dialogues in faith communities to promote mutual understanding and solidarity across differences.

After this introduction, the book is divided into five chapters. In Chapter 2, I present the study's theoretical framework, weaving together its central themes of cosmopolitanism, Christianity, and dialogue. In this chapter, I also connect the theoretical framework to key features of the LRJC dialogues. Chapters 3, 4, and 5 roughly follow the thematic sequence of the dialogues, which started with participants discussing cultural, economic, and legal tensions over immigration (Chapter 3), moved to participants talking about similarities and differences between immigrants and U.S.-born people (Chapter 4), and finished with participants envisioning collaboration (Chapter 5). In the last chapter, I summarize the findings, discuss their theoretical and practical implications, and explore avenues for future research.

# 2

# COSMOPOLITANISM, CHRISTIANITY, AND DIALOGUE

The theoretical framework of this study connects the central themes of cosmopolitanism, Christianity, and dialogue. In this chapter, after a critical review of theories of cosmopolitanism, I discuss (1) cosmopolitanism and Christianity, (2) cosmopolitanism and dialogue, and (3) Christianity and dialogue. In the last section, I explore how key elements of the theoretical framework were represented in the LRJC dialogues.

## 2.1 Cosmopolitanism

One dictionary defines the cosmopolitan person as "free from local, provincial, or national ideas, prejudices, or attachments; at home all over the world" (Dictionary.com 2020). From this perspective, parochial attachments are backward residuals of traditional societies or arbitrary attributes given mainly at birth. When understood in such universalist terms, cosmopolitanism makes sharp distinctions between the global and the local, unity and diversity, humanity and community, favoring the first of each pair over the second. Universalist cosmopolitanism has "the merit of highlighting what all peoples share in common," but it perpetrates "an injustice by negating precisely those factors that confer on diverse groupings their identity," such as ancestry, heritage, history, community, religion, and nationality (Healy 2011, 158). By upholding universal justice and membership to the human community, universalist cosmopolitanism does not do "justice to difference" (Shapcott 2001, 31). Moreover, when the polity, culture, and moral standards of the powerful are upheld as the universal polity, culture, and moral standards, universalist cosmopolitanism becomes an elitist ideology. If the powerful happen to belong to a single ethnicity, then universalist cosmopolitanism also becomes ethnocentric. The polity, culture, and moral standards of subaltern groups or minorities come to be seen as local, backward, or inferior.

Immanuel Kant is the most influential philosopher of universal cosmopolitanism (Mendieta 2009, 244; Healy 2011, 158). Mendieta (2009, 247) argued that Kant's cosmopolitanism is imperial because Kant uncritically assumed that "white Europeans were the most developed instantiation of humanity" and that "Western institutions represented . . . the highest accomplishment of what humans make of themselves through the enlightened use of reason." Kant could not "admit of the contributions of other cultures, or the excellence of other races"; his lectures "are replete with the reproduction and transmission of some of the worst prejudices of the seventeenth and eighteenth century" (Mendieta 2009, 246).

Karl Marx also articulated universalist cosmopolitanism in his theory of capitalism. According to Marx, there is a dialectic between the imperial cosmopolitanism of the European bourgeoisie and the emancipatory cosmopolitanism of the proletariat. Through colonization and exploitation of the world market, the bourgeoisie gives a "cosmopolitan character to production and consumption in every country" and promotes the "universal inter-dependence of nations" (Marx and Engels 1984, 16). As a consequence, "National one-sidedness and narrow-mindedness become more and more impossible, and from the numerous national and local literatures, there arises a world literature" (Marx and Engels 1984, 16). Eventually, however, the globalization of capital would bring the "workers of different localities in contact with one another" and strip them from "every trace of national character," opening the way for revolutionary global working-class solidarity (Marx and Engels 1984, 20).

Mignolo (2000) found in successive imperial projects historical expressions of universalist cosmopolitanism. Spanish and Portuguese imperialism corresponded to the cosmopolitanism of the Christian mission; French and English imperialism corresponded to the cosmopolitan mission of civilizing the barbarians; U.S. neocolonial imperialism corresponded to the cosmopolitan mission of modernization (Mignolo 2000). Hobsbawm (2013) used the term "imperialism of human rights" to refer to the intervention of the United States in Iraq in the early 2000s, which the U.S. government justified as an effort to protect the human rights of the Iraqi people. Western imperialism has conflated "the universal" with Western notions of human rights based on individualism and liberalism (Adami 2013, 49).

Acknowledging that nonrecognition or misrecognition of difference "can inflict harm [and] be a form of oppression, imprisoning someone in a false, distorted, and reduced mode of being" (Taylor 1994, 25), some scholars of cosmopolitanism have emphasized cultural diversity and championed the historical emergence of multicultural societies. I refer to these theories as particularist cosmopolitanism. They propose a peaceful coexistence of cultures, "where the cultural relationship is largely co-operative, but not necessarily devoid of conflict arising from different interests.... Cultures co-exist through the creation of frameworks for solidarity and integration" (Delanty 2011, 646, 651). Particularist theories of cosmopolitanism risk essentializing social identities and, by assumption, set a low bar for how much community and solidarity diverse people can achieve through peaceful social interaction. As stated by Healy (2011, 163), "By over-accentuating the differences between standpoints, [one] could easily mislead us into thinking that we could never really understand another, construed as so very different from ourselves." Moreover, "the pursuit of difference may be at the cost of the pursuit of equality or may result in some kind of cultural segregation of social groups or atavistic nationalism" (Delanty 2011, 634). For Healy (2011, 161), the problems of universalism "cannot be resolved simply by reverting to a one-sidedly particularistic orientation as this would simply perpetrate an imbalance in the opposite direction, emphasising difference to the point of excluding commonalities."

Given the critiques of universalist and particularist cosmopolitanism, contemporary scholars have formulated theories that balance unity and diversity and promote intercultural relations. Appiah (2019) argued that cosmopolitanism carries an inherent tension between universalism and particularism that does not have to be solved by choosing one of the two. Mendieta (2009, 242) argued that "cosmopolitanism is the dialectical interplay between singularity and universality, placedness and displacement, rootedness and rootlessness, home and homelessness, stationariness and mobility." For Appiah (2019, 24), genuine cosmopolitanism argues that people's identities and bonds of solidarity should and can be organized not only as rhizomes, spreading horizontally (toward other social groups), but also as taproots (delving deep into one's primary groups). Mendieta (2009) and Jordaan (2009) referred to these theories as dialogical cosmopolitanism, but because dialogue can also be present in universalist and particularist projects, I prefer to call them diversal cosmopolitanism. Diversality is a concept used, with some variation, by Édouard Glissant, Walter Mignolo, Patrick Chamoiseau, and others to reconcile unity with diversity. As stated by Alcoff (2007, 98), diversality "maps differences as coconstitutive and as potentially integrated, in the way that a bicultural identity can shift between multiple frames of reference without collapsing the differences but also without organizing them into hierarchies." Figure 2.1 shows how the three types of cosmopolitanism vary in their emphasis on unity or diversity among people.

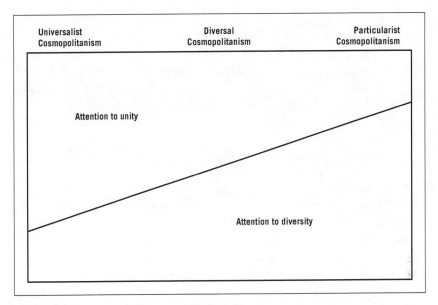

| Universalist Cosmopolitanism | Diversal Cosmopolitanism | Particularist Cosmopolitanism |

Attention to unity

Attention to diversity

**Figure 2.1** Varieties of Cosmopolitanism

Diversal cosmopolitanism "does not seek a global culture and nor does it seek diversity for its own sake, but rather cultivates an attitude of critical deliberation and ways of imagining new ways of living" (Delanty 2011, 641). Appadurai (2017) found a historical expression of diversal cosmopolitanism while studying marginalized communities where culturally diverse people had to collaborate to survive. Those communities displayed a "vernacular cosmopolitanism" that "begins close to home and builds on the practices of the local, the everyday and the familiar, but . . . builds towards global affinities and solidarities through an irregular assortment of near and distant experiences and neither assumes nor denies the value of its universality" (Appadurai 2017, 2). For Delanty (2011, 634), "Cosmopolitanism is a reflexive condition in which the perspective of others is incorporated into one's own identity, interests or orientation in the world" through exchange, dialogue, and encounters. Diversal cosmopolitanism assumes that identities are historically and socially constructed and prescribes an open-ended expansion of the boundaries of identity and solidarity without expecting people to shed their more parochial bonds.

The distinction between universalist, particularist, and diversal varieties of cosmopolitanism is important not only for philosophical and historical reasons. If Christianity, through congregation dialogues on immigration, is to build positive connections between diverse people, what should the outcome look like in reality: the elimination of group differences, with everyone adopting a superordinate identity (as in universalist cosmopolitanism), the establishment of peaceful relations between separate groups (as in particularist cosmopolitanism), or something in between? And, regarding process, what kind of conversation between participants would generate the desired outcomes? As I show in Section 2.3, those three varieties of cosmopolitanism inform different approaches to dialogue, down to the type of questions a facilitator should ask participants to discuss.

## 2.2 Cosmopolitanism and Christianity

Religion "has conventionally been considered oppositional to cosmopolitanism, the former often bound to parochialism, tradition, and intolerance, and the latter with secularism and worldliness" (Bower 2016, 238). There is some justification for this understanding, as individuals attached to their immediate social locale are more subject to the influence of norms that encourage religious participation, and local religious organizations offer settings where informal, communal relations can develop (Petersen and Takayama 1984, 98). Furthermore, much research has emphasized how religious identity and traditions can be manipulated to trigger, legitimize, and sustain violence between ethnic and national groups (Abu-Nimer 2018, 10; Kadayfici-Orellana 2013, 151). Religion, especially in its fundamentalist expressions, has also been identified as one of the main motivations for terrorism (Juergensmeyer 2000; Rapoport 1984; Stern 2003).

The association of religion with the national state is often seen as potentially violent. Religion has provided a "cultural glue" for producing everyday rituals and communal organizations to sustain nationhood (Turner 2001, 132). As states expanded, so did their religions; conquered peoples tended to adopt the conquerors' religion. For example, as the Christian and Muslim armies were victorious, so Christianity and Islam spread (Swidler 2013, 3). According to Fox (2004, 715), in the early 1980s, religious nationalist ethnic groups started to be "responsible for increasingly more violent conflicts in comparison to non-religious nationalist groups." Christian nationalism in the United States and Hindu nationalism in India are contemporary examples of anticosmopolitan associations between religion and national politics.

Religious actors have, therefore, remained relatively absent from cosmopolitan studies or have been depicted as countercosmopolitans (Krause 2011, 420). This relative absence, however, results from a downplaying of the cosmopolitan roles that religion has played in society. Using the typology of universalist, particularist, and diversal cosmopolitanism, we can better understand the association of religion with cosmopolitanism. Universalist religious cosmopolitanism often articulates "a theology centered on a universalistic ethic suggesting that national boundaries, racial/ethnic divisions, and even religious divisions are artificial constructions meant for organizing capital and power" (Brown and Brown 2017, 5). As stated by Van Zanten (2011, 2), the "Christian concept of the universal community is not based on ethnic identity, skin colour, gender, rationality, literacy, social status, modernization, or even religious affiliation, all of which have been used throughout history to define what it means to be human." In this sense, the Kingdom of God is the aspired cosmopolis.

Universalist religious cosmopolitanism, however, can function as an imperialist ideology with paradoxical affinities with religious nationalism. For Namsoon (2013, 4), Christianity and the Enlightenment were intertwined in constructing and universalizing a monolithic "we" behind imperial powers. The history of Christianity is replete with examples of Christians playing the role of "a globalizing oppressor of women, Jews, Moors, pagans, infidels, and heathens . . . through crusades, inquisitions, witch burnings, and holocausts" (Namsoon 2013, 6–7). The connection of religious cosmopolitanism with imperialism is more evident in the history of the Portuguese and Spanish Catholic empires, but it has some parallels in the present. For instance, Burity (2013, 75) showed that some transnational missions of Evangelical churches embody a cosmopolitanism in conflict with outside differences, trying to globalize the churches' boundaries through evangelization.

Particularist varieties of religious cosmopolitanism advocate for the peaceful coexistence of groups deemed as radically different. For instance, Angus Ritchie, a priest in the Church of England, argues for "deep pluralism" as "a settlement in which no particular worldview has a foundational role. . . . The motivation for denying any worldview that foundational role is not the relativistic conviction that every worldview is equally valid [but] that citizens cannot agree on which of the contending worldviews is true" (quoted in Rougeau 2017, 1357). Meintel and Mossiere (2013, 61) found in Montreal a historical situation somewhat similar to particularist religious cosmopolitanism: "Among the hundreds of those involved in religion . . . who have been interviewed for our research . . . none expressed negative reactions about religious minorities and their practices. . . . It seems as if the religiosity . . . of our informants, as well as the mobility between religions that so many have experienced . . . allows them to be at ease with the religious belonging and practices of others." However, in this case, the mobility of people across religions suggests that intergroup boundaries were less rigid than a strictly particularist perspective would assume.

Diverse varieties of religious cosmopolitanism balance the recognition of the universal moral dignity of human beings with respect for their diversity, promoting interconnection across group boundaries and leaving open the possibility for people to have multiple and shifting affiliations. In Christianity, a theological foundation for diverse religious cosmopolitanism can be found in the writings of Saint Paul. In his letters to the Corinthians, Ephesians, Galatians, and Romans, Saint Paul argued that in Christ there is "neither Jew nor Greek," "neither slave nor free," and "neither male nor female." While this can sound like an erasure of people's identities in favor of unity, Saint Paul also valued the diversity of the Body of Christ, saying, "Even so the body is not made up of one part but of many. Now if the foot should say, 'Because I am not a hand, I do not belong to the body,' it would not for that reason stop being part of the body. And if the ear should say, 'Because I am not an eye, I do not belong to the body,' it would not for that reason stop being part of the body. If the whole body were an eye, where would the sense of hearing be? If the whole body were an ear, where would the sense of smell be?" (1 Corinthians 14–17). As Gehrz (2017, 3) pointed out, "Paul went to great lengths to articulate the inherent interconnectedness and interdependence that exists among the diversity of gifts within the Body of Christ." Neuman (2011, 145) argued for a diversal religious cosmopolitanism when he said that we should "cultivate inter-epistemic fluencies, establish systems of mediation, and explore spaces of encounter that promote mutual recognition, respect, and nonviolent contention," something different "from paradigms like pluralism . . . which stress the equal validity of all religions and uphold tolerant coexistence while tending to reify existing identity formations." In the encyclical letter *Fratelli Tutti*, Pope Francis envisioned a culture of dialogue and encounter that would turn humanity into a "many-faceted polyhedron whose different sides form a variegated unity. . . . The image of a polyhedron can represent a society where differences coexist, complementing, enriching and reciprocally illuminating one another, even amid disagreement and reservations" (Pope Francis 2020, 109). According to this image, humanity is neither a monolith nor an aggregate of independent elements; the sides of the polyhedron are different, but they influence each other and cocreate a whole. Moreover, what connects one side of the polyhedron to another is different from what connects it to the other sides.

Regarding lived experiences of diversal religious cosmopolitanism, Burity (2013) and Wardell (2018) found examples in Evangelicalism. According to Burity (2013), in their encounters with cultural differences, some "Pentecostal and charismatic missionaries [from Latin America] have not only drawn and reinterpreted doctrinal and ritual aspects of their faith, but also learned from experience. They have felt compelled to make sense of experiences by sharing their message with strangers. . . . More often than not these encounters have triggered various levels of reflexivity about, for instance, what is the core of the Christian message and the cultural baggage that can be safely discarded" (Burity 2013, 76). While studying Evangelical youth workers in Uganda, Wardell (2018) found that those workers had to care for cultural others as a Christian duty to universal solidarity. In doing so, they acknowledged similarities and connected with care recipients, but "grounding themselves and much of their care labour in geographically and culturally specific locales" (Wardell 2018, 182). The resulting outlook "resonates with an image of cosmopolitan care emerging in the real world as layers of connection, obligation, and affect, that extend outwards to both neighbours and strangers to different and varying degrees" (Wardell 2018, 182).

In Catholicism, the experiences of pilgrims in the Virgin Mary's apparition sites examined by Halemba (2011) also resemble diversal religious cosmopolitanism. Pilgrims understood those sites as meaningful for national culture and transcendent connections with the world, the sacred, and pilgrims from other cultures. Those sites can invoke differences and relationality at the same time (Halemba 2011). Another example is Hoover's (2014) ideal model of the "shared parish," in which two or more cultural communities share a parish that gives space for each community to cultivate their language and faith traditions while also providing common experiences that build connections across cultures and help the multiple communities feel and operate like one church.

## 2.3 Cosmopolitanism and Dialogue

In many theories of cosmopolitanism, dialogue is a communication process through which cosmopolitanism becomes real. However, different varieties of cosmopolitanism imply different varieties of dialogue. In the most common sense, *dialogue* is a conversation between people. The word originates from Greek and combines *dia* ("through") with *legein* ("speak"). It carries slightly different meanings from one national culture to another, including assumptions about the interlocutors' attitudes (sincerity, openness, etc.), relationships (political opponents; employer vs. employee, etc.), and patterns of communication (formal vs. informal; competitive vs. cooperative, etc.) (Carbaugh 2013). In the philosophy of dialogue, however, dialogue is a specific type of communication centered on the goal of mutual understanding. Dialogue has been used in both elite and grassroots settings, such as community development and organizing, civic talk, activism, social work, government-citizen relations, diplomacy, reconciliation, peacemaking, and corporate management (Isaacs 1999, Saunders 2001, Cramer Walsh 2007, Dessel 2011, Ganesh and Zoller 2012, Westoby 2014).

Participants in dialogue are expected to improve their understanding of themselves, each other, and the subject matter of the dialogue (Bohm 2002). They should think together based on a shared pool of knowledge about each other and the world, thereby creating a "participatory consciousness" (Bohm 2002, 30–32). Through dialogue, participants may also generate a new relationship or transform an existing one (Maddison 2015, 1015). Yet, dialogue does not have to culminate in agreement or unity between participants. An outcome of "accurate disagreement" is better than the persistence of disagreement based on stereotypes or misunderstanding (Blakenhorn 2018). From an agonistic perspective, dialogue between groups with profound identity-based differences can result in a transition from violent conflict to non-violent "passionate democratic contestation" (Maddison 2015, 1015).[1] Theorists and practitioners of dialogue have converged on structures and procedures that encourage interlocutors to engage in dialogue—including, most commonly, a small number of participants (around fifteen), the presence of a skilled facilitator, open-ended questions that invite critical thinking, ground rules, and a sequential organization of conversation themes (Filomeno 2019, 153–54).

Empirical studies have shown that dialogues can indeed generate mutual understanding. Research on the intergroup dialogue model, pioneered by Janet Rifkin and developed at the University of Michigan, shows that intergroup dialogues produce cross-group communication skills and intergroup cooperation on social justice issues (Edwards 2017). In an assessment of dialogues designed according to the sustained dialogue model of the diplomat Harold Saunders, Diaz and Perrault (2010, 41) suggested that participants became more intellectually curious, cognitively sophisticated, emotionally empathetic, and skilled at communicating across differences. Research on study circles, a dialogue model that originated in Sweden in the early twentieth century and was promoted in the United States by Everyday Democracy, suggests that study circles increase participants' membership in volunteer boards and their capacity to solve public problems (Scully and McCoy 2005).

Many dialogue models pose that "personal-psychological transformation accompanies social-relational transformation" (Dezerotes 2018, 37). If dialogue makes participants suspend assumptions about themselves and the world, it can allow them to see the world as historical and prone to transformation, which opens space for creative agency (Freire 1974). Participants experience a change in relationships and learn to "design political actions and interactions that can change their larger" political organizations, such as local and national governments (Saunders 2001, 6). The intentional practice of dialogue can support deliberative democracy by promoting mutual recognition and connection between people across differences (Wolfe 2018). However, one should not assume that changes in attitudes, behaviors, and relationships among dialogue participants will necessarily generate changes in participants' communities or society at large. Kadayfici-Orellana (2013, 161) pointed out the "re-entry challenge," which happens when participants return to their communities after a dialogue. If there are no follow-up measures, such as meetings or collaborative actions, participants risk falling back in line with prevailing social norms of prejudice and antagonism.

Hammack and Pilecki (2015) distinguish between two approaches to dialogue: coexistence and confrontation. The coexistence approach is informed by social contact theory (Allport 1954) and common in-group identity theory (Gaertner and Dovidio 2000). Social contact theory claims that "interaction between members of two different groups will result in a reduction of misconceptions and prejudice and consequently lead to the formation of a positive attitude toward members of the target group" (Berg 2015, 28). Intergroup contact is more likely to result in positive mutual understanding in the presence of certain conditions, such as institutional support for the interaction, the pursuit of common goals, and the repetition of interactions in multiple settings (Allport 1954, 281; Pettigrew 1998). Common in-group identity theory proposes that members of different groups can be induced to conceive of themselves as part of the same group. This could be achieved, for instance, through engagement in cooperative tasks, which would lead participants to recategorize people from "us versus them" to "we." Therefore, the goal of coexistence dialogues is to minimize differences and foster a common identity among participants.

The confrontation approach is informed by social identity theory (Tajfel and Turner 1986). According to this theory, people derive pride and self-esteem from belonging to social groups. They tend to divide the world into "us" and "them," often through stereotyping that exaggerates differences between in-group members and out-group members while inflating the similarities between in-group members. Like the agonistic perspective on dialogue, the confrontation approach seeks to raise awareness of intergroup differences and power asymmetries to promote collective action by or with oppressed groups. In this view, dialogue is hardly as "casual, quotidian" and "secondary to the real workings of power" as commonsense views often assume (Appadurai 2017, 5). Participants in historically dominant social positions of gender, class, ethnicity, or another form of social stratification tend to exercise authority in a conversation. If this tendency is unchecked, the conversation will turn into "a centralized power system" in which "a single voice" speaks "the only truth that can exist, without challenge or interplay. Dialogic speech [by contrast] always involves a multiplicity of speakers and a variety of perspectives; truth becomes something negotiated . . . rather than something pronounced from on high" (Klages 2012, 23).

In addition to influencing who tends to control a conversation, power asymmetries imply differences in how interlocutors understand intergroup relations affectively, analytically, and practically (Nagda et al. 2012). Affectively, members of "high-power groups tend to be less emotional and more cognitive in their understanding of intergroup conflicts and to emphasize interpersonal connections" (Nagda et al. 2012, 211–12). Yet they tend to experience frustration, shame or guilt, and fear of appearing prejudiced in intergroup dialogue (Nagda et al. 2012, 211–12). Members of low-power groups tend to bring into intergroup dialogue the emotional burden of past experiences of discrimination and can feel resentment or anger during intergroup dialogue (Nagda et al. 2012, 211). Analytically, members of high-power groups tend to identify as individuals rather than as group members, subscribe to colorblind ideologies, and favor individualistic or ideological explanations to explain intergroup inequalities (Nagda et al. 2012, 212). Members of low-power groups, by contrast, think of intergroup inequalities in terms of the fairness and legitimacy of social structures (Nagda et al. 2012, 211). Practically, members of high-power groups tend to advocate change in intergroup conflict through prejudice reduction on the individual level. In contrast, members of low-power groups typically propose policy and structural changes (Nagda et al. 2012, 213).

I call coexistence dialogues *unity-focused dialogues* (because they often seek more than just peaceful coexistence of different groups) and confrontation dialogues *diversity-focused dialogues* (because they do not necessarily involve confrontation). Hammack and Pilecki (2015, 375) and Saguy (2019) found that unity-focused dialogues reproduce power asymmetries already existing in society and minimize the voices of oppressed groups. Participants from dominant groups are generally motivated to explore cross-group commonalities, whereas members of oppressed groups are interested not only in discussing commonalities but also in critically examining power imbalances (Dessel 2011, 177; Saguy 2019, 8). Unity-focused dialogues, while striving for cooperation across differences, can degenerate into co-optation dialogues, in which state, corporate, or other powerful actors organize a dialogue to give members of low-power groups an illusion of influence over collective matters in exchange for conformation with the views of the powerful (Ganesh and Zoller 2012, 74). Intergroup encounters that emphasize commonalities while neglecting power asymmetries can result in frustration, disappointment, and demobilization among members of disadvantaged groups and will likely not improve their out-group attitudes (Saguy 2019, 9).

Unity-focused dialogues are aligned with universalist theories of cosmopolitanism and carry the same risks as those theories. When dialogue seeks too much mutual understanding, "one party's deepest convictions [might] become the measure of common ground. This is the way in which false universalisms can erase true differences" (Appadurai 2017, 6). For Adami (2013, 50), "paternalistic notions of universality generally accompany a traditional view of dialogue as leaning towards universalism where the rational is equalized with dominant narratives of 'truth claims.'"

Diversity-focused dialogues are aligned with particularist theories of cosmopolitanism. In Pearce's (1989) particularist theory of cosmopolitan communication, interlocutors try to create mutual understanding without denying that there are multiple ways of "achieving coherence and mystery, without deprecating those other ways of achieving coherence and mystery, and without constantly changing the way in which one creates coherence and mystery" (Lulofs 1994, 13). In this view, people's stories are largely incommensurate and their practices largely incompatible (Lulofs 1994, 4). When dialogues offer participants the opportunity to explore their differences and conflicts, the outcome can be greater recognition of difference rather than a greater sense of unity, an overarching identity, or common ground (Cramer Walsh 2007, x). This is not necessarily a problem. Awareness of in-group identity and group-based hierarchy among members of disadvantaged groups can lead to collective action against social injustice (Saguy 2019, 10). Moreover, as Tropp, Ulug, and Uysal (2020, 8) demonstrated, "The more members of advantaged groups . . . communicate with members of disadvantaged groups about group differences in power, the more likely they are to recognize their own privilege and the ways in which members of disadvantaged groups are discriminated against . . . and the more willing they should be to take action to promote intergroup equality." In a study of sustained dialogues in Ethiopia, Svensson and Brounéus (2013) found that participants increased the importance of ethnic identity and the perception of discrimination while also experiencing increased trust in people of other ethnicities. After studying conversations between Mexican immigrants and White Americans and conversations between Israelis and Palestinians, Bruneau and Saxe (2012) concluded that the attitudes of the dominant groups (White Americans and Israelis) toward the minority groups (Mexican immigrants and Palestinians) improved significantly after the former (dominant) did the conscious and intellectual work of taking the viewpoint (perspective-taking) of the latter (minority). In turn, members of the minority groups developed more positive attitudes toward the dominant groups when they had the chance to give their perspectives (perspective-giving). Sonnenschein (2019) concluded that intergroup dialogue that is focused on power asymmetries between groups increases participants' capacity to manage conflicts through dialogue, empathy, active listening, and critical thinking (including critical reflection about one's group identity, position in power relations, and social responsibility).

There are also mixed dialogue models that lie between unity-focused and diversity-focused approaches, allowing participants to grapple with the tensions between unity and diversity, commonalities and differences, and cooperation and conflict. I call them diversal dialogues. Wolfe (2018), for instance, proposes a model of dialogue that assumes that group identities are protean, permeable, context-dependent, and socially constructed. Without necessarily culminating in the formation of an overarching identity or complete agreement, dialogue could make invisible social identities visible, facilitate connections across previously hidden social identities, and open opportunities for new constructions of collectivity (Wolfe 2018, 8–9). In diversal dialogues, participants "co-create a *community of diversity* in which each participant is free to experience and express both individuality and interconnection" (Dezerotes 2018, 35). These dialogical encounters should promote sensitivity to intergroup power imbalances while not undermining potential harmony between groups (Saguy 2019, 14).

Diversal approaches to dialogue are consistent with diversal theories of cosmopolitanism. As Beck (2008, 794) stated, the "core meaning of cosmopolitanism is the acknowledgment of otherness as at the same time different and equal." In diversal dialogues, the other is approached both as a "generalized other" (a human being like me) and a "concrete other" (a situated human being with a history and identity different from mine) (Healy 2011, 160). Interlocutors in diversal dialogues should therefore acknowledge the diversality of each other. Dialogue is central to diversal cosmopolitanism because it allows people to reflect on their perspectives and the perspectives of others mutually, learn about the various ways of being human, explore multiple claims to universality, and, maybe, reshape their attitudes and moral loyalties. As stated by Linklater (1998, 41), dialogue "is a mechanism . . . to achieve universality and to protect those who are regarded as different from marginalization or oppression." For Koczanowics (2009, 148), the "dialogical approach [to cosmopolitanism] does not presuppose an outcome of the conversation; its main principle is to find more and more complicated relationships between divergent points of views. . . . Neither the achievement of uniformity nor the persistence of difference are presumed outcomes. The 'emerging whole' [of dialogue] will more likely be a 'limited or contextual universalism'" (Koczanowics 2009, 148).

## 2.4 Christianity and Dialogue

Dialogues in Christian congregations may differ from those in other religious contexts or in secular spaces. Christianity can affect dialogue through the beliefs, values, organizations, rituals, traditions, and spaces that constitute it as a historical social institution. At least in doctrine, Christianity promotes beliefs and values that encourage dialogical attitudes. Dialogue requires people to suspend assumptions about themselves, others, and the world, loosening attachments to beliefs, ideas, and identity constructions (Gadamer 1975; Bohm 2002; Westoby 2014, 72). Humility helps one to suspend assumptions. It has been found to reduce the likelihood of one responding to disagreement in aggressive, defensive, or derogatory ways (AlSheddi 2020). Many biblical passages focus on humility. In the Sermon on the Mount (Matthew 5, 6, and 7), Jesus said, "Blessed are the poor in spirit" and "Blessed are the meek." Christianity also promotes charity and hospitality, which allow one to recognize in another person a potential source for growth and to see in dialogue a potential occasion for growth (Cornille 2013, 28). For Archbishop Brunett, in dialogue, "We are compelled to make our language understandable, acceptable and well chosen so that we can be both truthful and charitable to one another. . . . [Dialogue is characterized by] clarity, an outpouring of thought, meekness, humility, kindness, patience, generosity, prudence and trust" (Brunett 2001, 1). The Christian ideal of communion (the mutual communion of believers with each other and Christ) is also supportive of dialogical efforts (Knitter 2013, 146). As Hinze (2006, 209) observed, dialogue "provides the path of discovery in the ways of love and friendship with God and with other human beings, and is the indispensable means of individual differentiation and communion."

However, a dogmatic attachment to Christian beliefs is a significant obstacle to interactive critical thinking and the serious consideration of other viewpoints that characterize dialogue. In defense of Evangelical fundamentalism, for instance, Jerry Falwell said, "The danger of tolerance is that ultimately the [Evangelical] movement will lose its identity and will begin to drift toward the position of the people with whom it carries on a dialogue" (Falwell 1981, 176). According to Lulofs (1994, 9), in Evangelical Christianity, when "dialogue falls, and when others fail to be 'converted' to the conservative Christian view, there is a retreat into dogma as a place of safety." Dogmatism and the goal of converting others to one's beliefs will likely push a dialogue to extreme versions of diversity-oriented dialogue (with groups staying attached to their truths and, at best, learning about each other and how to coexist peacefully) or unity-oriented dialogue (with a dominant group trying to assimilate the other group into its truth).

The hierarchical organization of major Christian institutions can also limit or distort dialogue. For Bakhtin (1981), polyphony—a diversity of simultaneous voices—should characterize dialogical communication. By contrast, the reaction of the Catholic Church to the Protestant Reformation, the rise of modern science and liberal ideology emphasized one-way hierarchical communication within the church and polemical communication with those outside of the church (Hinze 2006, 6). That approach began to change with the Second Vatican Council (1962–1965), when Catholics started to participate in multiple types of dialogical encounters: "small, basic Christian community movements, justice and peace outreach groups, women's groups, parish and diocesan councils, special diocesan synods, episcopal and regional synods, as well as the more obvious dialogical settings of ecumenical and inter-religious encounters" (Mallon 2008, 494). Many conservative Catholics, however, still see dialogue as a threat to the traditional authority of the church hierarchy (Hinze 2006, 1).

The participation of clergy in dialogues where most participants are laypeople can be a double-edged sword. On the one hand, it can encourage laypeople to engage in dialogue and to trust in the process. Institutional support is one of the conditions Allport (1954) identified for positive intergroup contact. On the other hand, it can lead congregants to favor politeness over authenticity, to self-censor ideas they think will be contrary to clergy opinion (a form of social desirability bias), and to limit speaking time to make room for clergy to speak (Christians are used to listening to sermons and to speaking only reactively during worship services). In the Catholic Church, gendered structures and behaviors, which lack reciprocity and egalitarianism, also tend to restrict dialogue (Tentler 2011). As Coco (2015, 2) pointed out, "Asymmetrical power relations are supported symbolically by images of the Holy Family and Catholic household. The preferred and legitimated interpretation of the Catholic household favours communication patterns that are authoritarian and paternalistic." Moreover, in some Catholic settings, the expression of strong negative emotions, such as anger, is sanctioned or neglected (Coco 2015, 5). This can lead individuals, especially women and members of other historically marginalized groups, to repress their feelings and stay quiet.

Some religious traditions and rituals can work synergistically with dialogue. Incorporating spirituality into communication processes makes "new modes of relationship, new social, economic and political structures, and thus new ways of understanding the human situation" possible (Sacks 2002, 136). The reference to religious beliefs, the use of religious symbols and vocabulary, and the practice of religious rituals such as prayer and chanting can give legitimacy and efficacy to faith-based dialogues (Kadayfici-Orellana 2013). As collaborative activities, they can set the tone for dialogue and allow participants to build relationships. Rituals "are special contexts conducive to the symbolic transformation of identity and the framing of conflict toward sustainable, coexisting relationships" (Schirch 2001, 154). They "may be particularly critical for transcending into the spiritual realm as well as nurturing an important affective dimension of dialogue" (Neufeldt 2001, 350).

Sacred spaces, like the participation of clergy in dialogues, can have ambiguous effects on dialogue. Congregants are familiar with the church hall and, to the extent that they consider it part of a sacred space, may feel moved to speak with respect and charity, two dialogical virtues. However, congregants may think that a church hall is not a place for disagreement and conflict, which would undermine authentic dialogue. They may also feel that a sacred space is not the place to discuss specific topics (such as politics or sexuality), which could restrict the thematic scope of a faith-based conversation.

Outside forces can also shape Christian institutions and communities in ways that impact dialogue. While globalization has created pressures for the Catholic Church hierarchy and laity to engage in dialogue among themselves and with others, the political polarization associated with the so-called culture wars has made "some Catholics, liberal and conservative alike," retreat "into enclave communities of like-mindedness where diatribe is more the case than" reasoned debate (Mallon 2008, 491). Some Catholics even perceive dialogue as a liberal strategy that could undermine a distinctively Catholic identity (Mallon 2008, 491), a parallel to the attitudes of many Evangelical Christians toward dialogue.

In Chapter 1, I mentioned that Christian conversations on immigration have happened across the United States for many years. I came across individual events held at congregations as well as national and regional organizations that created dialogue guides to promote those events to congregations. How do the defining elements of dialogue and religion appear in those programs? Table 2.1 summarizes the key features of each dialogue guide, which I discuss in further detail in the remainder of this section. I present the guides as an illustrative set, not as an exhaustive list.

The two most common justifications for creating these guides are the political polarization on immigration in the United States and the religious significance of immigration. The latter is expressed in religious teachings on immigration, the migration history of some religious peoples, and the role that religious communities and institutions have historically played in immigrant integration. Regarding the structure and procedures, the guides usually recommend conversations in small groups bound by ground rules, following thematic stages, with open-ended questions posed by a facilitator. For instance, the conversations based on the JustFaith Ministries' guide go from exploring U.S. immigration history to discussing the immigrant experience and immigration policy to envisioning immigrant advocacy (JustFaith Ministries 2021). The program of the North Carolina Council of Churches sequentially covers the life of Christ, Bible stories, the economy, laws in the Bible, immigration enforcement, and the Bible on citizenship (Liu-Beers, Salata, and Gustine 2011). Common ground rules include active listening, keeping an attitude of curiosity and nonjudgment, and disagreeing respectfully. The guides vary substantially in terms of the length of the programs. The Evangelical Immigration Table, for instance, states a preference for a "long game" with "multiple conversations over an extended period of time" (Evangelical Immigration Table 2022). The program of the Discipleship Ministries of the United Methodist Church has only one session (Discipleship Ministries of the United Methodist Church 2016).

While reading each guide, I took note of the elements (rules, discussion questions, etc.) that aligned with unity-focused, diversity-focused, or diversal dialogue models. I then reviewed those notes to determine if a guide leaned toward any of those models. The guides show a variety of approaches to dif-

## TABLE 2.1 GUIDES FOR CONGREGATION CONVERSATIONS ON IMMIGRATION

| Guide | Rationale | Main Activities | Length | Ground Rules (Examples) | Religious Dimension | Approach |
|---|---|---|---|---|---|---|
| Discipleship Ministries of the United Methodist Church (2016) | n/a | Opening and closing prayers Listening circle Discussion Guest speaker | One session (90 min.) | Active listening Curiosity Limit individual speaking time | Faith-based ground rules Prayer | Diversal |
| Evangelical Immigration Table (2022) | Political polarization on immigration Religious significance of immigration | Opening prayer Reading Discussion Personal storytelling | Multiple sessions over extended period | Active listening Charitable discourse Curiosity | Religious rationale Faith-based ground rules Prayer Questions on religion and immigration Scripture reading | Unity-focused |
| Interfaith Immigration Coalition (2013) | Failures of the U.S. immigration system Religious significance of immigration | Opening and closing prayers Discussion Story circles Instruction on immigration policy Personal testimonies Deliberation | One session (approx. 2 hrs., 30 min.) | n/a | Religious rationale Prayer Questions on religion and immigration | Diversal |
| JustFaith Ministries (2021) | Political polarization on immigration Religious significance of immigration | Prayer Reading Discussion Deliberation | Eight sessions (2 hrs. each) | Active listening Holy dialogue | Religious rationale Prayer Faith-based ground rules Scripture reading | Diversity-focused |

| Organization | Topics | Format | Duration | Norms | Religious elements | Diversity |
|---|---|---|---|---|---|---|
| Lutheran Immigration and Refugee Service (2021) | Critical need to integrate refugees<br>Political polarization on immigration<br>Religious significance of immigration | Opening and closing prayers<br>Reading<br>Discussion<br>Deliberation | Three sessions | Active listening<br>Generosity<br>Keep an open mind | Religious rationale<br>Prayer<br>Questions on religion and immigration<br>Scripture reading | Diversal, leaning unity-focused |
| National Issues Forums Institute (London and Rourke, 2018) | Political polarization on immigration<br>Religious significance of immigration | Prayer<br>Discussion<br>Deliberation | One session | Active listening<br>Civil disagreement<br>The golden rule | Religious rationale<br>Faith-based ground rules<br>Prayer | Diversal |
| North Carolina Council of Churches (Liu-Beers, Salata, and Gustine, 2011) | Religious significance of immigration | Opening and closing prayers<br>Reading<br>Discussion<br>Deliberation | Six sessions (approx. 1 hr., 15 min. each) | Active listening<br>Mutual learning | Religious rationale<br>Faith-based ground rules<br>Prayer<br>Questions on religion and immigration<br>Scripture reading | Diversal, leaning unity-focused |
| Religions for Peace (2020) | Political polarization on immigration<br>Religious significance of immigration | Reading<br>Discussion<br>Video screening<br>Deliberation | Eight sessions (1 hr. each) | Active listening<br>The golden rule<br>Try to see the best in others | Religious rationale<br>Faith-based ground rules<br>Questions on religion and immigration<br>Scripture reading | Diversal |
| Sojourners (Wallis et al., 2015) | Failures of the U.S. immigration system<br>Religious significance of immigration | Reading<br>Discussion<br>Deliberation | Four sessions | n/a | Religious rationale<br>Questions about religion and immigration | Diversal, leaning diversity-focused |

(continued)

**TABLE 2.1 GUIDES FOR CONGREGATION CONVERSATIONS ON IMMIGRATION** (*continued*)

| Guide | Rationale | Main Activities | Length | Ground Rules (Examples) | Religious Dimension | Approach |
|---|---|---|---|---|---|---|
| Sojourners (Berger, 2008) | Religious significance of immigration | Opening and closing prayers Reading Discussion Follow-up actions | Six sessions (90 min. each) | Allow time for individual reflection Civil disagreement Limit individual speaking time | Religious rationale Prayer Questions on religion and immigration Scripture reading | Diversal, leaning diversity-focused |
| World Relief (Soerens and Yang, 2021) | Religious significance of immigration | Video screening Reading Discussion Deliberation Closing prayer Follow-up actions | Six sessions | Active listening Civil disagreement | Religious rationale Prayer Questions on religion and immigration Scripture reading | Diversal |
| Unitarian Universalist Association (Hicks, 2010)[a] | Increasingly multicultural world | Opening and closing rituals Reading Discussion Deliberation | 24 sessions (2 hrs. each) | Curiosity about others Keep an open mind Use "I" statements | Religious rituals Questions on religion and immigration | Diversity-focused |
| United Church of Christ (n.d.) | Religious significance of immigration | Reading Discussion | One session | n/a | Religious rationale Questions on religion and immigration Scripture reading | Diversal |

*Note:* n/a = not available
[a] Focused on race/ethnicity, but covering immigration.

ferences and inequality between social groups, but most are consistent with diversal cosmopolitanism. The Evangelical Immigration Table adopts a unity-focused approach, advising people to emphasize commonalities between conversation partners and immigrants and to frame immigrants as people created in God's image, people of faith, and with family values (Evangelical Immigration Table 2022). By contrast, JustFaith Ministries adopts a diversity-focused approach, encouraging participants to discuss the specificity of the migrant experience and to criticize the immigration policy status quo (Just-Faith Ministries 2021). Somewhere in the middle is the Discipleship Ministries of the United Methodist Church, which recommends that participants acknowledge each other as equals (which could undermine discussions of diversity and inequity) but also encourages them to express emotions and fears about immigration and to consider all views and information, even if those views and information conflict with the participants' assumptions (Discipleship Ministries of the United Methodist Church 2016).

Several guides explicitly apply Christian beliefs and values to dialogue. The Evangelical Immigration Table, for example, recommends that participants of conversations on immigration engage in "charitable discourse" and "God-honoring discussions," "model Christ-like love" not only in the message they share but also in the way they engage with each other, and frame immigrants as people created in God's image, people of faith, and with family values (Evangelical Immigration Table 2022). Quoting 1 Peter 2:17, the Evangelical Immigration Table also tells participants to "Show proper respect to everyone" (Evangelical Immigration Table 2022). Similarly, the JustFaith Ministries' guide for conversations on faith and immigration justice invites participants to engage in "holy dialogue" (JustFaith Ministries 2021, 2). The North Carolina Council of Churches' guide for conversations on immigration asks participants to remember that they are a loving family of brothers and sisters in Christ who have something to learn from others and should listen to each other intently (Liu-Beers, Salata, and Gustine 2011, 2).

The guides often include Christian rituals as part of the dialogue programs. Reflections on biblical passages about migration and the stranger, such as the parable of the Good Samaritan, are common. Prayer is prescribed in almost all guides. The Discipleship Ministries of the United Methodist Church, for example, offer a list of prayers that specifically invoke unity and humility to overcome pride and self-righteousness (Discipleship Ministries of the United Methodist Church 2016). The Evangelical Immigration Table recommends Psalm 139:23–24: "Search me, God, and know my heart; test me and know my anxious thoughts. See if there is any offensive way in me, and lead me in the way everlasting" (Evangelical Immigration Table 2022).

Lastly, several of those dialogue guides assign to participants the task of deliberating on collective action on immigration. Simply put, they ask participants, "What will you do after this conversation in response to immigration?" We already know from previous research that not only structured community dialogues but also casual civic talk can encourage collective action. However, we also know that the move from deliberative dialogue to collective action is neither necessary nor automatic. We have no reason to expect dialogues about immigration in congregations to be different. Congregational response to change—including changes brought by immigration—depends on the will and skill of congregants to mobilize resources (Ammerman 1997). There is also the question of what kind of action will emerge. On the one hand, as Harris (1994, 61–62) concluded, "Both for whites and blacks, religion performs as a resource for political action" by providing organizational resources and psychological motivation. With immigration being a highly politicized topic, one could expect civic or political actions to emerge from the dialogues. On the other hand, based on several studies of congregations in Chicago, Livezey (2000, 20) found that congregations often respond to change not through action in the public sphere but through service to their members. One could, therefore, expect follow-up collaborative actions to be mostly internal to congregations and not political in nature. I will return to this issue in Chapters 5 and 6.

## 2.5 The LRJC Dialogues

Dialogue is central to cosmopolitan efforts at reconciling unity with diversity in the human experience. Significant variations exist, however, in how unity and diversity are balanced in such efforts, which can range from imperialist endeavors to unify society under a single culture to multicultural projects that risk siloing identity-based groups. This is true of cosmopolitan efforts inspired by religion. Table 2.2 summarizes the approaches to dialogue, cosmopolitanism, and religion discussed in this chapter and in the previous chapter, showing their correspondence across each line.

Considering the pitfalls of unity-focused and diversity-focused approaches, the LRJC dialogues followed a diversal approach that sought to promote

| TABLE 2.2 CORRESPONDING APPROACHES TO COSMOPOLITANISM, RELIGION, AND DIALOGUE | | |
|---|---|---|
| Varieties of Cosmopolitanism | Varieties of Religious Cosmopolitanism | Varieties of Dialogue |
| Universalist cosmopolitanism | Universalist religious cosmopolitanism | Unity-focused dialogue |
| Particularist cosmopolitanism | Particularist religious cosmopolitanism | Diversity-focused dialogue |
| Diversal cosmopolitanism | Diversal religious cosmopolitanism | Diversal dialogue |

faith-based diversal cosmopolitanization, represented at the bottom line of Table 2.2. The LRJC dialogues did not privilege similarities between immigrants and U.S.-born people (which could lead to unproductive conformation between participants), nor did they privilege differences between immigrants and U.S.-born people (which could lead to useless confrontation between participants). Instead, both similarities and differences, harmony and tensions, between immigrants and U.S.-born people were considered. Each dialogue ended with a deliberative and decision-making moment in which participants proposed and discussed actions they would take together to help materialize a vision for excellent intergroup relations in their communities. Participants were tasked with identifying one issue of common interest on which they would collaborate, but they freely determined the issue and the level of collaborative engagement. The LRJC dialogues also included prayer and faith-based reflection. Based on the theories and empirical research synthesized in this chapter, we can reasonably expect that dialogues in line with the LRJC model will move congregations toward mutual understanding and collaboration on the issue of immigration.

Did the diversal approach of the LRJC dialogues avoid the pitfalls of unity-oriented and diversity-oriented dialogues? A basic approach to answering this question is to verify whether immigrants or U.S.-born participants tended to dominate conversations. We know from the literature that members of high-power groups prefer discussions of commonalities, while members of low-power groups tend to favor discussions of diversity and inequality. A diversal dialogue, by combining both types of questions, should prevent domination by either group. The relative number of words uttered by immigrant participants in a dialogue can indicate how much space immigrants took in the dialogue compared to U.S.-born participants and, therefore, can be an approximate indicator of domination. I conducted a quantitative content analysis of dialogue transcripts and found that neither immigrants nor U.S.-born participants tended to dominate the LRJC dialogues. Even when segments that focused on similarities and common goals were compared to segments that focused on differences and tensions, no pattern of domination emerged. In Appendix A, I describe the procedures and results of this quantitative content analysis.

What about the role of clergy members in the dialogues? Clergy worked as gatekeepers of their congregations (allowing or not allowing the program to take place) and assisted in implementing the dialogues (helping recruit participants and making physical space available). In my conversations with them, various reasons for their openness to the program surfaced: previous experience as the pastor of a predominantly Latino congregation, previous work in immigrant advocacy, a desire to build relationships with Latino congregations, the interest of congregation members in immigration affairs, and so on. They also participated in the conversations in most dialogues (HC2, HC3, HC5, HC6, and HC7). Using the same procedures to verify possible domination by immigrant or U.S.-born participants, I found no evidence that clergy took a disproportionate amount of space in the conversations (see Appendix A for procedures and results). In the following chapters, I explore in greater depth how participants interacted with each other.

The LRJC Honest Conversations on Immigration tried to leverage religion for dialogue in three ways: (1) by starting each session with a prayer, (2) by connecting ground rules to faith traditions, and (3) by connecting faith traditions to immigration. At the beginning of each session, participants said the Prayer of Saint Francis of Assisi, which, like dialogue, emphasizes an orientation to the other. This prayer is presented in Appendix B. In the first session of every dialogue, I asked participants to create ground rules for dialogue (in HC1 and HC2, I suggested a list of ground rules as a starting point). Various participants engaged in this decision, usually by adding rules to the list one after another, sometimes building upon what others had proposed and never in disagreement. Most commonly, they asked participants to allow everyone to speak; to respect others, even when in disagreement; to listen to others without judgment; and to not make generalizations about a whole group of people. Starting with HC3, after participants had agreed on a set of rules, I asked them to connect each rule to specific values, beliefs, or practices of their faith tradition. Most often, they spoke of the duty to love one another, called others to see God in every person and respect their dignity even in moments of disagreement, and follow the Golden Rule (Do unto others as you would have them do unto you).

In every dialogue, I also asked participants what their faith tradition says about immigration. In the exchanges that followed that question, participants engaged mainly in agreement (primarily through corroboration of what other participants had said) and in interactive critical thinking (with participants sequentially assessing the logic and evidence of arguments). Regarding thematic patterns, the exchanges focused on religious values, beliefs, and institutions. Participants connected religious values and beliefs to immigration, usually by invoking biblical calls to welcome the stranger and the image of Jesus and other biblical figures as migrants, foreigners, or refugees. In HC1, for instance, an African American woman said, "All are welcome," to which another African American woman agreed: "Right. We are all God's children. . . . So it's a matter of opening your arms and loving your people." In HC2, a moment of interactive critical thinking started when a White American man recalled Pope Francis's exhortation for European countries to accept refugees. Another White American man qualified that by saying that while the United States should accept "bona fide" asylum seekers, the pope should be tougher on the "yahoos" and "dictators" that rule Mexico, Central

America, and Africa, causing people to move away. Two White American women then questioned what might be Americans' responsibility for that displacement, considering "Who is buying the drugs [from Latin America]?" and "What we, the United States, [have] done to just absolutely undermine and facilitate violence there." The participant who had criticized Pope Francis then acknowledged the merit of those points. Interestingly, across the dialogues, no participant—not even those who had expressed conservative opinions—invoked faith traditions to justify government authority, the rule of law, the enforcement of immigration law, or national borders. This suggests that religious beliefs and a religious framing of immigration tend to engender welcoming attitudes toward immigrants, as argued by Park (1998); Hondagneu-Sotelo (2008); Freeland (2010); Bloom, Arikan, and Courtemanche (2015); Boryczka, Gudelunas, and Gil-Egui (2015); and Houston and Morse (2017). Even among Christian nationalists, exposure to religious discourse tends to mitigate anti-immigrant sentiment (Stroope, Rackin, and Froese 2021).

When participants brought up religious institutions, they framed them largely as institutions that welcome and celebrate diversity or promote solidarity toward immigrants. In HC3, a Latino man stated that all are welcome in the Methodist Church; an African American woman agreed with this, saying, "One of the things I love about the United Methodist Church in general is the effort that's made to celebrate our diversity." This suggests that, as pointed out by Brown and Brown (2017), religious people heed the generally pro-immigrant message of religious institutions but do not necessarily acquiesce to it (as exemplified by the participant in HC2 who criticized Pope Francis for supposedly not addressing responsibility for the root causes of immigration). In HC1, participants engaged in critical thinking about the Christian church. A White American woman argued that "religion is really a mixed bag when it comes to how people treat each other. . . . You can take the Bible and see places where people are stoned and we are chosen, special and wonderful. . . . Religion can be wonderful, or religion can be really destructive." Several participants agreed.

When talking about religious institutions, religious values, beliefs, or other topics in this segment of the conversations, participants across all dialogues articulated cosmopolitan ideas. There was broad agreement around the cosmopolitan religious value of welcoming the stranger. Among the statements that leaned toward a specific variety of cosmopolitanism, most were aligned with diversal cosmopolitanism. In HC5, a Latino man balanced unity and diversity while arguing, "We are called to love the foreigners . . . embrace them, welcome them. . . . One of the main problems . . . is that when immigrants come and they don't have any introduction to the country . . . they come and bring their own traditions and thoughts. . . . There should be a way to teach them . . . the games of society . . . rules and ways of connecting. This is not to erase their cultural backgrounds, but something to bring their cultures together." A few other statements were aligned with universalist cosmopolitanism. In HC1, an African American woman said, "We're all God's children, and there should be no barriers amongst us. It's like people are trying to separate each other. What we need to be doing is pulling ourselves together. . . . We are all God's people. . . . We have to put our prejudices aside, all of our discrepancies, and come together as one." Yet, there was also critical thinking about universalist religious cosmopolitanism, when a White American woman in that same dialogue pointed out that "you can find a White male European medieval system that says 'Go out and get all the souls you can get. You'll get credit for it. If they don't cooperate, it's okay to kill them.' . . . I mean, it [Christianity] is really a mixed bag." No participant made a statement evidently aligned with particularist cosmopolitanism.

In the following chapters, I analyze the relational and thematic patterns that emerged in conversations about tensions over immigration (Chapter 3), similarities and differences between immigrants and U.S.-born people (Chapter 4), and collaboration with immigrants (Chapter 5), connecting them to theories of cosmopolitanism, Christianity, and dialogue. In Chapter 5, I also analyze the follow-up collaborative projects that emerged from participants' deliberations.

# 3

## Navigating Tensions over Immigration

Immigration is a transformative process for both immigrants and the communities where they settle. From a cultural perspective, immigration can be seen either as enriching or as threatening to local cultures as new traditions, customs, and languages arrive. From an economic perspective, immigration can promote growth in receiving communities by expanding and diversifying the workforce. However, immigration may also put a strain on local public services and intensify competition for some types of jobs and other economic resources. If immigrants enter or stay in the country illegally, some community members will be concerned by the vulnerability of immigrants to abusive landlords or employers, while others will be worried about the lack of immigration law enforcement. Even when immigration is low, it can draw public attention (both positive and negative). Long-standing members of a predominantly White congregation will quickly notice when an African refugee family starts to attend worship service.

In the United States, immigration has become the most polarizing issue in public debates (USC Annenberg, Golin, and Zignal Labs 2022, 2), making the peaceful and reasoned navigation of tensions over immigration all the more important for U.S. civic life. In every dialogue, I asked participants if they had experienced or observed tensions in their communities around immigration: cultural tensions (over language, traditions, and ways of life), economic tensions (over jobs, housing, and welfare), and legal tensions (over unauthorized immigration). In the first two dialogues, I also asked participants what had made it difficult for them to feel included in situations where they were outsiders, a question that also pointed to intergroup tensions. In this chapter, I analyze those segments of the dialogues to understand how participants interacted while talking about tensions over immigration and to comprehend their perspectives on those tensions.

## 3.1 Participant Interactions

From a relational perspective, the dialogue segments about tensions over immigration were marked by agreement, perspective-giving, and perspective-taking. Agreement happened in nineteen exchanges across six of the seven dialogues (HC1, HC2, HC3, HC4, HC6, HC7). The large majority of occurrences of agreement involved corroboration—when a participant followed the statement of a previous participant with additional evidence or reasoning—indicating that participants were not simply acquiescing to what others had said. No instance of agreement was classified as a possible case of domination (in which a participant of a historically marginalized social group acquiesces without justification to a proposition of a participant from a historically dominant social group).

The distribution of instances of agreement across the dialogues does not suggest an association with the demographic makeup of dialogues. Agreement was especially pronounced in HC2 and HC7 and relatively sparse in HC3 and HC5. While HC2 and HC7 were Catholic dialogues between mostly Latino and White American participants, this is probably a spurious explanation for their high incidence of agreement. HC1 and HC4 were Catholic dialogues but had lower levels of agreement than HC2 and HC7. HC6 happened between mostly Latino and White American participants but had a lower level of agreement than HC2 and HC7. There is no theoretical reason to expect the intersection of the Latino-White American racial/ethnic makeup with the Catholic denomination to produce high levels of agreement. HC3 and HC5, in turn, do not share a demographic profile that distinguishes them from the other dialogues and explains their lower incidence of agreement.

On the level of individual participant identity, agreement happened across differences of race, ethnicity, or nationality and between participants of the same race, ethnicity, or nationality. There was no remarkable discrepancy between the distribution of instances of agreement according to participant race/ethnicity and the distribution of speakers according to participant race/ethnicity in the dialogue segment as a whole. For instance, the modal types of agreement according to participant race/ethnicity in the segment on tensions were agreement between Latino participants (present in ten exchanges) and agreement between White American participants (present in ten exchanges), which is consistent with Latino and White American participants being the modal racial/ethnic identities of speakers in that dialogue segment (twenty-eight and twenty-two speakers, respectively).

Perspective-giving—someone showing people of other social groups how they have experienced the world—happened sixty-five times across six of the seven dialogues (HC1, HC2, HC3, HC4, HC6, HC7). It happened to the most extent in HC3 and HC7 and the least extent in HC4 and HC5. This distribution does not indicate a variation according to the demographic makeup of dialogues. HC3 and HC7 have quite different demographic makeups (Methodist vs. Catholic; mostly liberal vs. mostly conservative, etc.), and the same applies to HC4 and HC5 (Catholic vs. Evangelical; mostly liberal vs. mostly conservative, etc.). There was, however, a pattern in terms of participants' individual identities. Latino participants tended to give perspective more often than U.S.-born participants. They accounted for a proportion of perspective-giving instances higher than their proportion among dialogue speakers (58% vs. 41%). Latinos shared experiences of dealing with language differences, suffering discrimination, living without regular immigration status, and adapting to new rules and social norms. In HC2, for example, a Latina participant said, "I have beautiful neighbors, but some people I know you say 'hi' and [they] never say 'hi' back. . . . It's difficult sometimes." African American participants gave perspective roughly as often as their proportion among dialogue speakers would suggest (21% vs. 19%). They usually shared experiences of being discriminated against on the basis of race. In HC3, an African American man said, "Whether you're at a car dealership, or you're looking for a house, or even sometimes in the store . . . people wanna make sure that you know how much stuff costs because they think you can't afford something." In contrast, White Americans tended to give perspective much less often than their proportion among dialogue speakers would lead one to expect (15% vs. 32%). They usually talked about experiences of contact with immigrants in family, church, work, or community life. White American and African American participants usually expressed sympathy for immigrants for the challenges they face. In HC1, a White American woman described her experience teaching in New Jersey: "That [school] was mainly the African American, Hispanic, Puerto Rican. . . . We said we're not gonna stand for [students of different race/ethnic groups] coming in at separate times and eating at separate times. . . . We said, instead of us going separately to outside for gym class, . . . let the kids play [together]. . . . And nobody killed each other."

Perspective-taking—someone considering how people of another social group have experienced the world—was also a common relational process, but it happened about five times less often than perspective-giving (thirteen instances across five of the seven dialogues: HC1, HC2, HC3, HC6, HC7). It happened to the largest extent in HC1 and HC7 and the smallest extent in

HC4 and HC5. The distribution of instances of perspective-taking across the dialogues does not suggest an association with the demographic makeup of dialogues. For example, HC1 and HC7 have in common the Catholic denomination, but so does HC4. HC4 and HC5 have quite different demographic makeups. There was a pattern, however, in terms of participants' individual identities. White American participants and African American participants accounted for all instances of perspective-taking. While White Americans were 32% of the active speakers in that segment, they accounted for 69% of instances of perspective-taking. African Americans were 19% of the speakers but accounted for 31% of instances of perspective-taking. In almost all of these instances, White and African Americans considered how immigrants experience challenges such as displacement, discrimination, labor exploitation, and landlord abuse. In HC1, for instance, an African American man said, "In their own community, they [immigrants] are afraid to talk or speak out [about labor exploitation] because they fear something is going to happen to them."

The different relative engagement of immigrant, White American, and African American participants in perspective-giving and perspective-taking is consistent with the pattern of communication that, according to Bruneau and Saxe (2012), is conducive to equity through dialogues: members of historically marginalized groups giving perspective more often (and taking perspective less often) than members of dominant groups. Immigrant participants gave perspective more often, White American participants took perspective more often, and African American participants both gave and took perspective (consistently with their marginalized racial position and their dominant national position, respectively). According to Tropp, Ulug, and Uysal (2020), this pattern of communication is also conducive to members of dominant groups recognizing their privilege, acknowledging the discrimination suffered by members of disadvantaged groups, and becoming more willing to take action to promote intergroup equality.

In a dialogue segment about intergroup tensions, one could expect disagreement and interactive critical thinking to be prominent relational processes. Questions about controversial topics, such as illegal immigration or competition between immigrants and U.S.-born people in the job market, could have elicited the expression of divergent opinions, which in turn could have led to a scrutinizing of those opinions based on logic and evidence. Although exchanges like that did happen, they were much less common than occurrences of agreement (which is the comparable relational process among the top relational processes identified in this dialogue segment, because each instance of agreement consists of multiple rather than single utterances). Disagreement happened in seven instances across four dialogues (HC1, HC2, HC3, HC5); participants disagreed on several topics. There were no moments of confrontation (vitriolic disagreement) in the dialogue segments on tensions over immigration. No clear pattern of variation emerged when we looked at the distribution of instances of disagreement according to the demographic makeup of the dialogues. Moreover, while one could expect dialogues between mostly liberal participants or dialogues between mostly conservative participants to yield more agreement than dialogues between participants of different political orientations, that was not confirmed in the segment about tensions over immigration. Among the least politically diverse dialogues (HC1, HC3, HC4, HC5, HC6), agreement did not happen more often than disagreement in two out of five (HC3, HC5). Among the most politically diverse dialogues (HC2 and HC7), disagreement was absent in one (HC7) and happened less often than agreement in the other (HC2).

What about variation of disagreement according to individual participant identity? Disagreement happened across differences of race, ethnicity, or nationality and between participants of the same race, ethnicity, or nationality without a clear pattern regarding participants' identities. Disagreement occurred most often in HC2, including two instances of opposition (in which a participant of a historically marginalized social group challenged a proposition of a participant from a historically dominant social group). In both cases, a White American woman challenged a White American man (opposition across genders) who had expressed opposition to undocumented immigrants. The man said, "I consider myself a Native American because I was born and raised here. . . . My ancestors came from Germany and Poland . . . legally. I have a lot of problem with people coming here illegally." In response, the woman said, "The United States was founded on bloodshed and destruction by invaders from Europe. . . . The idea of calling someone illegal disturbs me . . . the rhetoric that is spoken about [immigration] is racist." An instance of opposition also happened in HC1, when a Latina participant disagreed with the suggestion by an African American woman (opposition across nationality) of focusing immigration reform on undocumented children who crossed the border. According to the Latina participant, immigration reform should be comprehensive and should not privilege one group of immigrants.

Interactive critical thinking—in which interlocutors assessed propositions on the basis of logic and evidence—happened in twelve exchanges across four dialogues (HC1, HC2, HC3, HC6). Participants discussed various topics related to tensions about immigration, including American identity, U.S. immigration policy, and immigrants' economic standing (access to social services, payment of taxes, etc.). Interactive critical thinking was especially pronounced in HC1, HC2, and HC6, which does not indicate a connection with the demographic makeup of dialogues. Interactive critical thinking happened across differences of race, ethnicity, or nationality and between participants of the same race, ethnicity, or nationality. There was no salient discrepancy between the distribution of instances of interactive critical thinking according to participant race/ethnicity and the distribution of active speakers according to participant race/ethnicity in the dialogue segment as a whole.

Solidarity across differences is a major indicator of cosmopolitanization because it means that diverse participants not only understand each other but also acknowledge shared interests and express a mutual commitment. There were eight instances of solidarity across differences in the segment on tensions, which does not place it as a top relational process but is not irrelevant either, considering how high the bar is to classify a statement in this relational category. Those eight statements were all in HC1 and HC3, which were the two dialogues between mostly African American and Latino participants. In those dialogues, all but one of the statements articulating solidarity across differences consisted of an African American participant expressing solidarity toward Latino immigrants (usually regarding labor exploitation). In Section 3.2, I analyze the key substantive themes of conversations about tensions over immigration with references to the relational processes discussed in Section 3.1.

## 3.2 Conversation Themes

What was the substance of participants' conversations about the cultural, economic, and legal tensions that immigration may bring to communities? In five out of the seven dialogues (HC1, HC2, HC4, HC5, HC6), various participants shared stories, feelings, or ideas consistent with cosmopolitanism. Statements with stories, feelings, or ideas consistent with cosmopolitanism appeared most often in HC4 and least often in HC3 and HC7. This suggests no clear connection between those statements and the demographic makeup of the dialogues. HC3 and HC7 have very different demographic makeups, and the only trait that distinguishes HC4 is the absence of Latino immigrants, which is not a reasonable explanation for the larger incident of cosmopolitan statements. Regarding individual participant identity, White Americans made statements consistent with cosmopolitanism much more often than Latino or African American participants. White Americans were 32% of the speakers but made 65% of cosmopolitan statements. Latinos were 41% of the speakers but made only 19% of cosmopolitan statements. African Americans were 19% of the speakers but made only 10% of cosmopolitan statements. However, the high representation of White American participants in statements consistent with cosmopolitanism does not seem to be associated with their racial/ ethnic identity but with an extensive discussion among White American participants of HC4 about cosmopolitan efforts and challenges at their congregation. These and other themes that were present in cosmopolitan statements (such as cosmopolitan critiques of government policies or characterizations of the United States as a cosmopolitan nation) were also articulated by Latino and African American participants.

In HC1, HC2, HC5, and HC6, different participants offered cosmopolitan critiques of individuals and institutions (especially educational, political, and religious organizations). For example, in HC5, a Latino participant said, "I have a lot of Mexican friends that despise African Americans because they have been hunted down and beat up [by African American robbers]. . . . I've met a lot of White people that are really nice, and they love Latinos because they are honest and hard workers. At the same time, I've met some that don't like us or the immigrant community because they think that we want to cut into the system and take advantage of it. . . . I think that their shortsightedness [is in not] being open-minded to everybody being different and . . . judging . . . one whole ethnic group by one person." In HC1, a White American participant criticized schools for segregating students in the past, while two African American participants criticized educational institutions for not supporting educators to serve immigrant students. In that same dialogue, two African American women (including one of the participants mentioned in the previous sentence) eloquently criticized U.S. immigration policy: "We are supposed to be as humanitarians. . . . I don't care what Trump says [about immigrants], once you cross the border, you are now one of us, and we are taking . . . care of each other"; "I think it goes beyond once they cross the border. I think the gate should not be closed. How did we get here!? . . . We crossed. Somebody scored us. . . . So now you're going to take ownership of the borders and say, 'I'm letting you in, I'm not letting you in'? . . . People, this is the land of refuge." In HC2, a White American man criticized the U.S. government for not being welcoming to immigrants, and another White American man argued the U.S. government had not done enough to help Central American countries solve their problems.

In HC1, HC4, HC5, and HC6, various participants brought up the obstacles and accomplishments of cosmopolitanism in specific congregations. Overall, they had learned from experience that "religion can be helpful [in bringing people together, but] it can also be a hindrance" (White American woman in HC1). Latino and White American participants criticized religious parochialism, especially in the form of long-standing White American congregants refusing to cede control over a congregation's identity and practices to newcomers of a different racial/ethnic background. In HC6, a White American man discussed how local congregations founded by previous generations of European immigrants reacted negatively to the arrival of Latino immigrants, who eventually became the majority in those congregations. He said there was "anxiety" and "anger" on the part of long-standing congregants over who belonged in a congregation and who controlled that congregation. In that same dialogue, a Latino man argued that people with power tend to see new groups as a threat to their privileges, and he criticized the existence of ethnic churches: "There are churches of Black people and churches of White people; there are churches of Italians, churches of Hispanics, and [divisions] even inside the same denomination, and why?!" Another Latino participant in the same dialogue claimed that the leadership of his religious denomination had discriminated against Latino clergy. In HC3, a Latina participant talked about how she felt excluded in her previous congregation, being the only Latino member: "Every time I opened my mouth . . . I was told, 'Oh, you know the protocol' . . . , so I felt like I was only used . . . to be a greeter and to clean the bathroom. I was good enough for that."

In other instances, participants gave perspective on more positive experiences in their congregations. In HC3, the Latina who was mentioned in the previous paragraph as feeling excluded because she was the only Latina in her previous congregation said, "Coming to [her new congregation] was a blessing because we [are] all the same. . . . I allowed God to heal me . . . , and he released me to come to [the new congregation]." In HC5, a Latina participant said that, in her church, White Americans and Hispanics "live together" and "have been able to blend with our brothers and sisters and share some commonalities." According to her, for that to happen, the White American members had to become aware of their privilege of class (for being generally more educated) and of nationality (for having citizenship status). In HC4, several participants shared their views on the history of intergroup relations at their congregation, which was the result of a top-down merger of congregations of different racial/ethnic compositions. Some long-standing members were very resistant to the merger, and a few are said to still resent that event. As a White American man in that dialogue said, "The most frustrating part . . . was when the old White folks would also be pissed off that 'these people [of another congregation and racial/ethnic group] are changing . . . the way things have always been.'" The participants said the congregation had come a long way in integrating diverse members, partly thanks to a pastor who listened and worked with parishioners rather than ruling the congregation from the top down. According to the White American man cited just above, engaging in dialogue with older White congregants was also helpful: "When we feel the resistance of the people who have always had control . . . I've tried to see why that [change and integration] bothers them and [it] makes it easier to talk to them . . . to bring them into the culture we're trying to create, which is . . . everybody belongs here . . . we not only want to tolerate people and their differences, we kinda like to celebrate them."

However, the food bank of the congregation in HC4 revealed intergroup challenges that remain. The COVID-19 pandemic dramatically increased the need for food on the part of low-income congregants while also increasing the availability of congregants who could work in the food bank because their physical workplaces had shut down. Both the beneficiaries and the staff of the food bank were diverse. The food bank had bilingual telephone operators and material translated into the main languages of the congregation. Still, miscommunication happened, and a facilitator was brought in to mend relationships and help people build trust. According to a participant, their food bank is now much better because of "the consistency, and continuing to do the ministry, and not stopping, and trying to reach out [to diverse members] continually." These statements about parochialist and cosmopolitan experiences in congregations suggest that an acknowledgment of privilege on the part of long-standing congregants, their willingness to let go of privilege, and intercultural competence on the part of congregants and pastors (especially a capacity to listen to others' concerns) are key for the making of a cosmopolitan faith community.

A theme that was associated with cosmopolitan thinking among participants was the state of migrant-sending countries, which appeared in three of the seven dialogues (HC1, HC2, HC6). The majority of references to that theme were made by Latino speakers, followed by African American speakers, and, lastly, by White American speakers. Latino participants talked about migrant-sending countries, usually while giving perspective about positive or negative conditions in their homelands. In contrast, when African American and White American participants talked about migrant-sending countries, they engaged in interactive critical thinking about the root causes of migration to the United States (poverty, violence), the U.S. responsibility over those causes (through foreign policy or demand for illicit drugs), or the U.S. responsibility to help migrant-sending countries solve their problems. Acknowledging the root causes of migration seems to have elicited expressions of cosmopolitan solidarities. In HC1, for instance, an African American woman said, "Global warming is killing; they [people abroad] have no food, they have nowhere to live, so they have to come. So, as humans, we have to be willing to open up and take care of them." In HC2, a White American man said, "We should be helping these countries deal with their own population problems in regards to jobs and security."

Only a few times did participant statements align neatly with a specific variety of cosmopolitanism. For example, how the aforementioned Latina participant of HC5 described intergroup relations at her church resembles religious diversal cosmopolitanism. She said her congregation has White Americans and Hispanics who acknowledge their differences (especially the privilege enjoyed by White Americans) but also "live together" and "have been able to blend with our brothers and sisters and share some commonalities." In HC2, a White American man articulated a diversal cosmopolitan perspective on U.S. nationhood, pointing out that "America is a hodgepodge of immigrants" but that the English language was "one of the [few] things that create

'Americans.'" In his view, by speaking English in the public sphere while maintaining homeland languages within family life, immigrants to the United States showed "the value of speaking a common language while maintaining your ethnic identity." In HC5, an African man expressed a universalist cosmopolitan perspective: "What we have discovered is that you have white, you have black, you have green, you have yellow, whatever the color. . . . When it comes to some basic necessities in life, we are all the same . . . as human beings." No participant statement, however, was clearly aligned with particularist cosmopolitanism. In the Cultural Tensions, Economic Tensions, and Legal Tensions sections below, I discuss further how cosmopolitanism and parochialism surfaced in exchanges specific to the cultural, economic, and legal tensions raised by immigration.

## Cultural Tensions

When I asked participants about cultural tensions over immigration, they focused on language differences, which were discussed in six of the seven dialogues (HC1, HC2, HC3, HC4, HC6, HC7). The topic appeared most frequently in HC3 and HC7 and least frequently in HC2 and HC5, which does not indicate a clear association with the demographic makeup of dialogues. HC3 and HC7 have very different demographic profiles. HC2 and HC5 share a predominance of conservative participants, but so does HC7. What about variation according to individual participant identity? Immigrants made comments about language slightly more often than African American participants, who, in turn, were more likely to make such comments than White American participants were. Immigrants (Latino and African) made 58% of statements about language while accounting for 49% of speakers. African Americans made 22% of statements about language but accounted for 19% of speakers, a roughly proportional representation. White Americans made only 20% of statements about language while accounting for 32% of speakers. The centrality of the language barrier in the immigrant lived experience probably explains this discrepancy in emphasis, as I discuss in the next three paragraphs. Statements on tensions related to language coalesced into three themes: (1) the assumption of English as the national language and an associated discomfort with immigrants speaking other languages in public; (2) the persistence of limited fluency in English and of attachment to homeland languages among immigrants; and (3) the experience of minor tensions over language differences, but with sympathy for immigrants' lack of fluency in English.

The first theme was rare, appearing only in the segment on tensions in HC2 and HC3. In HC2, a White American man quoted in the previous section argued that "America is a hodgepodge of immigrants. The only thing that brings them together is [the English] language." His argument reflected a diversal cosmopolitan notion of U.S. nationhood, combining language diversity in the family or community life with a common language in public life. In HC3, an African American woman articulated a more parochialist view of language in the United States: "I have a problem with . . . Little Havana in Miami. . . . Shopkeepers there do not speak English. . . . If I go to Cuba, I could understand [people not speaking in English]. . . . But I do have a problem here in the United States with that." Her argument prompted interactive critical thinking with immigrant participants, whose responses fell under the second theme.

The persistence of limited fluency in English among immigrants and their attachment to homeland languages was the most pervasive theme about language. It often appeared when immigrant participants gave perspective on their struggles with language differences. On the one hand, immigrants presented several justifications for not speaking in English, often corroborating each other's statements: anxiety or shame over speaking "broken English," family and work responsibilities leaving no energy or time to take English classes, preference for language that feels comfortable, the need to feel connected to co-ethnics through language, and the absence of an official language in the United States. On the other hand, immigrants acknowledged that language differences can be a barrier to opportunities or can be grounds for discrimination by intolerant U.S.-born people. In HC7, for example, a Latino participant reported the story of a Latino friend who worked in landscaping and could "do more" but kept being assigned simple tasks because his lack of fluency in English hampered communication with clients. A Latina participant in the same dialogue shared the story of a friend from Puerto Rico who "was told in her face from a [potential employer] that she would not be taken as a worker because she has an accent. . . . And she has all the papers. . . . Then, there is a moment where you think that 'I have education, I can do it, but because [of] my accent, being Latina or . . . the way I look is an impediment to get the same than other people.' . . . So, you ended up having an education but working in a store, or retail or something like that." Also in HC7, another Latino participant said he had taken English classes, but economic hardship prevented him from continuing to learn the language: "It is harder to concentrate because you are focused on working, making money, and supporting your family. . . . I had a lot of depression. I couldn't [study] anymore with the job and everything else." These stories showed U.S.-born participants that economic hardship and language barriers could reinforce each other and lock low-income immigrants in a marginalized social position: unable to learn English because of overwork, unable to move up in the workforce because of limited fluency in English.

The third theme (the experience of minor tensions over language differences) was not widespread across dialogues, appearing in HC1, HC4, and

HC6 when White American and African American participants gave perspective on how they have dealt with language differences. In HC6, for instance, a White American man said, "When I am out and see someone who appears to be from Central or South America, I always hesitate, just thinking, 'Do I engage with them in Spanish or that will be offensive?' Because they could be someone who's never learned Spanish, and I am just judging by appearances." In HC1, an African American man said, "As an educator, having the opportunities of having other cultures to be in the classroom, the [school] system doesn't provide you with the support to really kind of work. . . . I try to learn a little bit of their language to try to communicate . . . , but the system itself doesn't provide any support a lot of times . . . , so there's like really no way to . . . make the [immigrant] child really feel that you're there for them." Overall, U.S.-born participants tended to be sympathetic toward immigrants who face a language barrier, and their statements suggested cosmopolitan attitudes. They were somewhat divided, however, on who has the primary responsibility in overcoming the language barrier: Is it immigrants who must learn English (an assumption implicit in statements by three participants), or is it institutions that must become multilingual through the translation of materials, hiring of bilingual personnel, and so on (an assumption implicit in statements by four participants)?

The only instance in which participants discussed tensions over language differences in the context of a faith community was in HC4. As discussed in the introduction of Section 3.2, the congregation of HC4 had seen not only tensions over language differences (such as miscommunication between parishioners working with the food bank) but also cosmopolitan efforts to overcome those tensions (such as holding a bilingual mass in Spanish and English, translating informational materials to different languages, having the pastor learn Spanish, and adding songs in multiple languages to the choir repertoire).

In HC2, a few White American participants expressed feelings of cultural anxiety. They all voiced conservative opinions throughout the dialogue. One of them, a White American man, said, "It's also having your culture change. A culture, you're a part of that, that changes while you're within it, and you find yourself now feeling outside of it." In HC3, HC4, and HC6, participants did not express cultural anxiety but recognized it in White American people, usually with a negative assessment. For example, in HC6, a White American woman criticized U.S.-born people who feel threatened by immigrants' ties to homeland cultures, seeing those ties as "a rejection of what America is or should be."

In discussions of cultural tensions over immigration, participants often talked about youth (especially children). This topic appeared in six of the seven dialogues (HC1, HC2, HC3, HC5, HC6, HC7), most often in HC1, HC3, and HC7 and least often in HC4, HC5, and HC6. Given the significant variation in demographic makeup within the high-incidence group (HC1, HC3, and HC7) and within the least-incidence group (HC4, HC5, and HC6), one cannot point out a pattern of variation. In terms of participant individual identity, African Americans made statements about youth more often than Latino participants, who, in turn, talked about youth to a greater extent than White American participants. African American participants made 41% of statements about youth while accounting for only 19% of speakers. Latinos made 38% of the statements about youth while accounting for 41% of speakers. White Americans made only 21% of the statements about youth but accounted for 32% of speakers. Indeed, the two main themes about youth that emerged in those conversations—which I discuss starting just below—were articulated primarily by African Americans and Latinos, respectively.

The first theme was the need to educate children about antiracism, which was articulated mostly by African American participants. As an African American participant in HC1 argued, "You need to be designed [to] educate your students to appreciate diversity. That gives the opportunity to change the mindsets of generations and communities." The second theme was Latino children's experiences of adaptation, intergroup tensions, and self-segregation at schools (including discrimination between Latino children of different nationalities). Exchanges about this theme involved perspective-giving by Latino participants. In HC5, for instance, a Latino participant said, "Sadly, my own ethnic group did not like me when I was in middle school. . . . I was shunned upon because I was not from Central America, I was from South America." In HC7, a Latina participant recalled, "I remember the first time when I went to drop her [daughter] off at school. . . . The teacher approached her and asked her name in English. So she answered and reached her hand. But, it got my attention that the children in the back started laughing. I left with that thought and said, 'Poor girl.'" Overall, participants saw youth from a perspective of compassion and hope.

## Economic Tensions

The most salient topic in the conversations about tensions over immigration was the discrimination, abuse, or exploitation of historically marginalized people (African Americans, Native Americans, but mostly immigrants), which appeared in all dialogues. The discrimination against immigrants specifically was discussed in all dialogues and, generally, in direct proportion to the relative number of immigrants in each dialogue. This topic was discussed to a greater extent in HC6 and HC7, both of which had a high proportion of immigrant participants (70% to 75%), and to a lesser extent in HC2 and HC4, both of which had a low proportion of immigrant participants (21% to 25%).

What about variation according to individual participant identity? Immigrant participants (Latino and African) accounted for 72% of statements about discrimination, abuse, or exploitation of immigrants while accounting for only 49% of speakers. In most of these statements, immigrants gave perspective by telling stories of experiences of discrimination, abuse, or exploitation in the economy (the job market, housing, or the workplace).

In HC3, a Latino participant said, "[One time] My family and I went to a store. My wife saw a group of Hispanic people . . . looking for something in the pharmacy. . . . One of the guys was bleeding. . . . We asked . . . if they need some help. . . . There was this guy who have a hole in his hand. . . . We take him to his apartment and patched him up, and he was saying that his boss was upset with him and took . . . the nail gun, and put a nail in his hand. [I have also heard of] guys [employers] asking to the [immigrant] girls to sleep with them, and if they don't sleep with them, they will fire them." Later he argued, "It's like slavery all over again." In HC6, a Latino participant said, "A painter . . . has to be paid forty-five dollars per hour [according to regulations], and the company that hires him, they put forty-five dollars on the paper but to the worker they pay only eighteen, fifteen dollars." Such stories often led to expressions of sympathy or solidarity on the part of U.S.-born participants. In HC6, for example, a White American man said that the exploitation and abuse of undocumented immigrant workers "is a type of slavery, paid slavery. Because there is this class of people who do not have rights here. So they cannot do or say anything against people in power. So for the government, for the corporations, it's okay to have these people here."

Only one immigrant participant (an African man in HC5) denied the significance of discrimination against immigrants in the economy, saying, "When I think the White population discriminates against me economically . . . I don't think this is true. . . . If you follow the rules, you can create your own . . . economic power. . . . I've seen a lot of people . . . from God's grace . . . people who go from nowhere and truly climb the ladder of success. . . . The beauty of this society of the American way is personal effort." This understanding of economic justice as each person being rewarded according to their personal responsibility and effort appeared elsewhere only in HC2 when a White American woman criticized "African and Hispanics" going to the hospital only at the time of needing emergency assistance and relying on charity or government assistance to "pick up the tab for everything."

In four of the seven dialogues (HC1, HC2, HC4, HC6), participants also discussed competition between Latino immigrants and U.S.-born people in the job market. The topic appeared most commonly in HC1 and HC2 and least commonly in HC3, HC5, and HC7. This distribution does not point to a clear association between the topic and the demographic makeup of dialogues. For instance, HC1 and HC2 share the Catholic denomination, but so does HC7. In terms of participant individual identity, African Americans tended to speak more than White Americans about immigrant-native competition in the job market. Latinos were even less likely than White Americans to speak about this topic. African Americans accounted for 30% of statements about competition with immigrants in the job market while accounting for only 19% of speakers. This variation is largely associated with exchanges in HC1 and HC2, which I discuss below.

A few participants pointed out that immigrants undercut or take jobs from U.S.-born workers. In HC1, an African American man said, "Immigrants come in and work for lower wages. . . . I don't think it's a feeling like it's taking jobs [from us], but it kinda undercuts or undermines [African American workers] because [employers] say, 'Hey, I can get him for this amount, when you want this.'" In HC2, two White American men argued that U.S.-born people are anxious because of the rate of technological change. As one said, "If somebody comes up here from El Salvador or something, they know how to operate a computer, they're going to take my job." Other participants then engaged in critical thinking about those arguments. In HC1, two African American men shifted the blame from immigrants onto business corporations. One said, "I think it's globally . . . Corporate America in general just saying, 'It's gonna cost us less to outsource some of these jobs'"; the other man said, "Corporate America doesn't realize it's feeding into all of that. . . . We get angry and upset with [immigrants] for taking our jobs, but I'm not sure if it's them taking our jobs or if it's just they're looking in terms of survival." These two statements indicate a cosmopolitan solidarity based on the recognition that both African American and Latino workers share class interests in relation to business corporations. In HC2 and HC6, Latina participants argued that immigrants are capable people who make contributions to the U.S. economy: "Immigrants help a lot in economics in this country. If you go to a hospital, a lot of doctors, nurses, they are from Latin America or Asian countries" and "Clearly there are conflicts [over jobs], but I don't see it that way, certain communities believe that we come to steal the jobs . . . but we have the same capacities . . . our children also want to go to college . . . and help the economy of this country."

In response to the question about economic tensions over immigration, participants also talked about taxes. This topic appeared in four dialogues (HC1, HC3, HC6, and HC7), indicating no association with their demographic makeup. All but one statement about taxes came from immigrant participants, including several statements in which they explained how and why they pay taxes (for instance, to have a driver's license or to help with the regularization of immigration status). Lastly, a few participants expressed feelings of economic anxiety because of immigration, competition in the job market, and technological change. They were all conservative-leaning White American participants of HC2.

## Legal Tensions

In five out of the seven dialogues (HC1, HC2, HC4, HC6, HC7), participants discussed the legal tensions brought by illegal immigration. There was no pattern across dialogue demographic makeup, but there was a pattern regarding participants' individual identities: Latino speakers engaged in those discussions to a greater extent than White American speakers, who, in turn, spoke relatively more than African American speakers. Latinos made 55% of statements about legal tensions while accounting for only 41% of speakers. White Americans made 36% of the statements about legal tensions while accounting for 32% of speakers, a roughly proportional representation. African Americans made only 7% of the statements about legal tensions over immigration while accounting for 19% of active speakers. Examining the substance of those exchanges can help readers understand this variation. Conversations about legal tensions over immigration coalesced into three themes: (1) the criticism of undocumented immigrants for not playing by the rules while crossing the border or living in the United States (largely by White American participants); (2) the hardship that undocumented immigrants experience because of their immigration status (largely by Latino participants); and (3) the rights of immigrants, not only in the immigration system but also in housing and labor (by a mix of participants). Most participants articulated the second and third themes, which is consistent with many of them (47%) having a liberal political orientation (the remainder self-identifying as moderates or conservatives).

The first, second, and third themes were present emblematically in HC2 through disagreement, perspective-giving, and interactive critical thinking between participants. The exchange started with a White American man, quoted earlier in this chapter, saying, "My ancestors came here legally. . . . I have no problem with anybody coming here legally. I have a lot of problem with people coming here illegally." Two White American women opposed that stance by considering other aspects of the legality of migration. One of them said, "The first European settlers here; there was no legal system. So are they illegal? I think that's helpful to consider what makes a person illegal. There's the 'dreamers' [whose parents brought them as children across the border without authorization]. . . . There are people who are considered illegal now who are seeking asylum. . . . Legal/illegality is very nuanced." The second woman (also quoted earlier in this chapter) then added, "The idea of calling a person illegal disturbs me. . . . It's a complicated [immigration] system to navigate. . . . Asylum is a whole other issue. That's something . . . that we agree as part of the United Nations, to accept asylees, but that conversation doesn't seem to happen on the news." Later in the conversation, another White American woman shifted back to the first theme, pointing out that some undocumented immigrants take advantage of the health system. At last, a White American man who had expressed conservative opinions during the dialogue proposed a compromise between cosmopolitan international law, national sovereignty, and Christian values: "[To] bona fide asylum seekers, we have a legal obligation under international treaties. . . . Mass deportations, I think, is inhumane. . . . On the other hand, we are a sovereign nation . . . , and one of the aspects of sovereignty is that you establish borders. . . . We can't allow people . . . to just come across. . . . There has to be some control. . . . But once again, we are a nation of immigrants. We're a constitutional republic. . . . We stood for the proposition 'in God we trust' [and] God wants us to be opening . . . and compassionate."

In other dialogues, discussions of the legal tensions over immigration leaned much more toward the second theme (the hardship that undocumented immigrants experience) and the third theme (immigrant rights). These themes often appeared in statements about immigrant vulnerability to economic exploitation (which I discussed in the section above on Economic Tensions) and about barriers for immigrants to access resources and services. While several nonimmigrant participants (both White and African American, in HC1, HC3, and HC6) acknowledged those hardships in sympathy for immigrants, it was immigrant participants who discussed them to a greater extent through perspective-giving and mutual corroboration. For instance, in HC6, a Latina participant said, "We don't have an identification document like that of someone who was born here, and we don't have the same opportunities to buy a house. . . . many immigrants are living in dwellings with up to ten people in it. In a bedroom, there are five, six people of a single family." In the same dialogue, another Latina participant told the story of taking her sick mother to the hospital. After giving her initial care, the hospital staff reportedly said, "There isn't anything else we can do for you because you don't have health insurance." In HC7, a Latina participant said she was offered an internship opportunity but could not take it because she did not have a Social Security number. In that same dialogue, two other Latina participants shared stories of immigrants of color who had their rights allegedly violated by law enforcement. They were stopped by law enforcement on the street because of supposedly broken taillights and then were profiled and questioned about their immigration status. Several other stories were about undocumented immigrants being vulnerable to crime or scams. In HC7, a Latina participant reported, "I experienced deportation proceedings. . . . When I came to this country, I came here ignorant about the laws, and my sisters told me to go to a lawyer, but he was not a lawyer; he was a notary that filed immigration proceedings. . . . He didn't make things right. [I ended up] detained . . . eleven months . . . , and my daughters had to stay with my sister."

While sharing their stories, several immigrant participants revealed connections between the economic and legal tensions around immigration. Like the Latino participant of HC6 who was quoted earlier, who pointed out that employers take economic advantage of the fragile legal status of undocumented immigrants to underpay them, a Latina participant of that dialogue claimed that "If a Latino . . . is given a job [and] he demonstrates he can do more . . . then the employer gives him more work, but with the same pay. . . . There is abuse of power on the part of bosses. . . . The Latinos, we don't have vacations. . . . We are working all the 365 days of the year." The same participant said, "We don't have an identification document like that of someone who was born here, and we don't have the same opportunities to buy a house. . . . I have dreams but the system does not allow me to accomplish them. The system puts a limit and a barrier, the difference that having or not having a social security makes. I cried to my daughter, saying, 'Mom wants to do more for you, but I cannot.'"

## Intergroup Awareness of Shared Marginality

While discussing tensions over immigration, several African American and Latino participants connected their experiences as historically marginalized people in the United States. This awareness of a shared condition often emerged as they corroborated each other's stories about discrimination and, typically, in the dialogues in which African American and Latino participants were the majority. Not only immigrants but also African American participants took advantage of questions about tensions over immigration to talk about the discrimination they have endured. Discrimination against African Americans was a prominent topic in HC1 and HC3, which had a high proportion of African American participants (50% and 64%, respectively). African Americans spoke more about racism than White Americans and Latinos. They gave perspective through storytelling on experiences of racism in schools (all involving racial bias among educators), churches, retail establishments, neighborhoods, and interactions with the police.[1]

While giving perspective on experiences of discrimination, abuse, or exploitation, Latino and African American participants used their own stories to reinforce points made in the stories of other participants. In HC3, for example, a Latino man told a story of a White woman who was afraid of his sister because she was Mexican and "Mexican women are dangerous." Two African American women followed by complaining about the stereotyping of Black women in the United States: "One of the questions that has been asked of me . . . continues to be 'Why are you so angry?' That just gets me upset"; "That's the first thing that a lot of times people will think when they see a Black woman. They think she's angry or has an attitude."

Even when African American participants discussed the competition between African American and Latino workers in the job market (in HC1), there was awareness of a shared marginality. An African American man quoted earlier in this chapter started the exchange about intergroup competition by saying that "Black Americans have come a long way in being able to get where they are now so far as making the money or being able to work in the positions that we hold now or the opportunities. They've traded a long way in being able to do that. I think what we've seen now, or the thought is, the immigrants come in and work for lower wages and do all the grunt work, and I say that in a similar way that a lot of Black Americans or African Americans feel we have graduated way from at doing that." In other words, the participant saw in immigrants today the overexploited labor force that African Americans were in the past. Also in HC1, an African American woman said, "I really get angry about the situation with the immigrants. . . . What is being done to them was done to us [African Americans]. Nobody talked on our behalf. And I will not be a party to that kind of treatment to anybody. . . . If we don't speak out, we, in essence, are supporting that kind of conduct. That's us. That was us. Same thing."

An awareness of shared marginality also surfaced in statements about neighborhoods as spaces where tensions over immigration might develop, which appeared in five out of the seven dialogues: HC1, HC2, HC3, HC5, HC6 (most extensively in HC1, HC3, and HC6; least extensively in HC4 and HC7). This distribution does not suggest a clear association with dialogue demographic makeup. For instance, HC4 and HC7 share the Catholic denomination, but so does HC1. While a few participants recalled positive interactions between immigrants and U.S.-born people in neighborhoods, participants of various racial/ethnic identities discussed neighborhoods as sites of negative intergroup contact. As in the discussion about churches as spaces of intergroup tension, several participants criticized long-standing White American residents who expressed resentment against local demographic shifts caused by the arrival of African Americans or Latinos. To illustrate, in HC1, an African American woman described the experience of moving into a predominantly White neighborhood: "I was like the second African American family to move there, and there was a bit of racial tension. . . . There would be little things [written] on the stop sign. . . . Certain children weren't playing . . ." A Latina participant then corroborated with an analogous experience: "When I moved to Baltimore, my husband and I lived in . . . a predominantly orthodox Jewish neighborhood. . . . In the grocery store . . . people don't talk to each other. They bump into each other, and they don't say excuse me. . . .

It's really disturbing." This was another moment when a Latina and an African American participant acknowledged a shared experience of discrimination and marginality.

Four participants (each in a different dialogue: HC2, HC4, HC6, HC7) understood the discrimination faced by immigrants of color as intersectional, resulting from the combination of nativism and racism. Three of those four participants were immigrants of color, and one was a White American woman with family ties to immigrants of color. For instance, an African woman in HC4 said, "They are being racist to you. . . . [The White males in the workplace] don't want to listen to you because you're female, you're Black, you're an immigrant." In HC2, a White American woman quoted in the previous section said, "The idea of calling a person illegal disturbs me. . . . The rhetoric that is spoken about that is racist."

The dialogue segment on tensions over immigration was modeled after diversity-focused dialogues. According to Dessel (2011), Hammack and Pilecki (2015), and Saguy (2019), these dialogues favor participants from oppressed groups, who tend to be especially interested in critically examining power imbalances between groups. As I state in Chapter 2, Section 2.5 (The LRJC Dialogues) and explain in Appendix A, immigrant participants (members of an oppressed group in terms of nationality) did not take more speaking time than U.S.-born participants in the segment on tensions, which would have been in line with theoretical expectations about diversity-focused dialogues. However, the emergence of an awareness of shared marginality between immigrant and African American participants in that segment is qualitative evidence supporting those theoretical expectations. The findings about shared marginality are also consistent with previous research that shows that emphasizing salient experiences of intergroup discrimination promotes positive relations between groups that share a dimension of identity (such as two different minority groups) (Cortland et al. 2017, 547). In the literature on religion and immigration attitudes, this argument has appeared in the form of the minority marginalization hypothesis, according to which groups that share an experience of marginalization tend to have solidarity toward each other. As stated in Chapter 1, Brenneman (2005, 31) and Knoll (2009, 327) applied that hypothesis to explain why Jewish Americans have more positive immigration attitudes than other religious groups. Here, we see evidence of that mutual understanding and solidarity between Black and Latino Christians.

This is not to say that expressions of sympathy or solidarity toward immigrants came only from African American participants in discussions of tensions over immigration. In HC1, a White American woman told the story of a Mexican family that cleaned toilets at a nearby school without being given any gloves or protective attires. She criticized the employer for an "I got mine, you get yours" individualistic mentality and said, "For me, that's very pain-ful. . . . Unless we realize . . . that we're all in this together, we're gonna go down the tubes." In HC6, a White American woman said, "People who are undocumented are really vulnerable to crime and violence, uhm, . . . with hous-ing, [the] slum lord situation, not caring for the people the way they should, not doing their basic kind of rights as a landlord." In HC7, a White Ameri-can woman argued that "immigrants as a labor force here are exploited, and they can't complain, and they can't organize . . . because they have the prob-lem [of being] immigrants and they have [immigration] statuses not totally resolved, so they are subject to exploitation and injustices." These statements, however, did not come from a lived experience of discrimination, exploita-tion, or abuse as a member of a historically marginalized group.

## 3.3 Conclusion

Table 3.1 summarizes the main thematic and relational patterns found in the dialogue segment about tensions over immigration. The salience of agreement, perspective-giving, and perspective-taking suggests the conversations were dialogical in the sense of being marked by mutual understanding between participants. It is concerning, however, that, even in a segment about inter-group tensions, agreement was much more common than disagreement. This may have resulted from a lack of diversity of opinions within some dialogues or from participants self-censoring potentially controversial opinions dur-ing the conversations. At least, most occurrences of agreement consisted of participants corroborating others' statements with logic or evidence rather than just rephrasing them or acquiescing without justification.

**TABLE 3.1 THEMATIC AND RELATIONAL PATTERNS OF SEGMENT ON TENSIONS OVER IMMIGRATION**

| Thematic Patterns | Relational Patterns | |
|---|---|---|
| Critique of religious parochialism | Agreement | Mostly through corroboration |
| Critique of ethnic siloing in diverse congregations | | Between and within groups |
| Anxiety and discomfort of US-born people about immigration | Perspective-giving | Mostly by immigrants |
| Discrimination, abuse, and exploitation of immigrants | Perspective-taking | Mostly by U.S.-born participants |
| Black-Brown awareness of shared marginality | Domination by U.S.-born or immigrant participants (word count) | No |

The exchanges on tensions over immigration displayed one of the advantages attributed to diversity-focused dialogues: the opportunity for members of historically marginalized groups to voice their grievances about discrimination, exploitation, or abuse in U.S. society. Latinos and African American participants gave perspective more often than White American participants. White American and African American participants took perspective from Latino participants. Moreover, there was evidence of solidarity between participants of different groups, with Latino and African American participants bonding over shared experiences of marginalization in the United States. Talking about tensions over immigration allowed immigrant participants to give perspective to U.S.-born participants, to validate the perspectives of other immigrant participants through corroboration, and to develop feelings of solidarity with African American participants.

Many of the feelings, ideas, and stories shared by participants were aligned with cosmopolitanism. Several participants criticized individuals and organizations from a cosmopolitan perspective (even if not using this term), with special attention to faith communities. Most participants attacked the parochialism observed in some congregations; some were able to single out conditions that favor the emergence of a cosmopolitan congregation: long-standing congregants need to acknowledge their privilege and be willing to cede control over the identity and practices of the congregation, and congregation leaders and members need to develop competence in intercultural communication. Cosmopolitan thinking also emerged in discussions about the conditions of migrant-sending countries. Latino participants talked about living conditions in their homelands, while U.S.-born participants discussed the root causes of migration and U.S. responsibility for those causes (which points to cosmopolitan solidarities).

The discussions of specific tensions brought by immigration (cultural, economic, legal) revealed two broad framings of those issues by participants: On the one hand, the anxiety or discomfort that U.S.-born people feel in the face of immigration. Some U.S.-born participants—largely conservative White Americans—expressed those feelings, while other participants (both U.S.-born and immigrant) acknowledged the presence of those feelings in their communities. On the other hand, the discrimination, exploitation, and abuse of immigrants. Many immigrant participants told stories about those issues, and many U.S.-born participants either acknowledged those issues or expressed solidarity toward immigrants. Even conservative participants expressed appreciation for the hard work ethic of Latino immigrants and criticized their exploitation in the economy. Thus, as a whole, participants oscillated between looking at the tensions from the perspective of U.S.-born people (their economic interests, laws, and cultural preferences) and looking at the tensions from the perspective of immigrants (their discrimination, exploitation, and abuse). What people understand as "tensions over immigration" depends on whose perspective they take.

The analysis of the conversations showed evidence that dialogue and deliberation helped bridge those different perspectives. Three exchanges mentioned earlier illustrate this process well. In HC1, bridging happened over economic tensions. Through interactive critical thinking, participants shifted from "Latino workers undercut African American workers in the job market" to "corporations exploit workers globally." In HC2, bridging happened over legal tensions. After disagreement and critical thinking about illegal immigration, a conservative participant synthesized a compromise between international asylum law, national sovereignty, and the Christian value of compassion. In HC3, an African American participant criticized Latino immigrants for speaking Spanish in public business interactions, prompting Latino participants into interactive critical thinking and perspective-giving. As I show in Chapter 4, the African American participant later argued that both African Americans and Latinos share an experience of linguistic discrimination for not speaking the "King's English." In these three examples, we see participants stretching their bonds of identity and solidarity, indicating that deliberative dialogues on immigration can unleash the cosmopolitan potential of Christianity in congregations.

# 4

## Exploring Similarities and Differences with Immigrants

The 2020 Census of the United States showed that the country had become more racially and ethnically diverse since the previous census of 2010. The proportion of non-Hispanic Whites in the population decreased from 63.7% in 2010 to 57.8% in 2020 (Jensen et al. 2021). This demographic shift has been observed within Christian congregations. According to Dougherty, Chaves, and Emerson (2020, 651), racial and ethnic diversity within congregations increased substantially between 1998 and 2019, and the proportion of all-White congregations among all Christian congregations in the country declined. Much of this change resulted from immigration, which has slowed the decline of religious life in the United States since the late twentieth century. Skirbekk, Kaufmann, and Goujon (2010) argue that the decline of religion in the country will eventually level off, largely because immigrants, who "comprise a historically high and rising share of the U.S. population," tend to arrive from religious countries of the Global South (Kaufmann 2019).

Yet, conversation about racial differences and inequalities is often avoided or discouraged even in diverse congregations, with congregation diversity being displayed in merely performative ways (Dougherty, Chaves, and Emerson 2020, 660). Although more than "three-fourths of [U.S.] churchgoers" said in 2022 that "their church does somewhat or very well discussing racial justice and hatred toward immigrants (77% and 76%, respectively)," Democrat and non-White churchgoers were less likely than Republicans and White Americans, respectively, to report that their church does a good job discussing those issues (Public Religion Research Institute 2023, 25). This discrepancy may suggest, as Dougherty, Chaves, and Emerson (2020, 660) argued, that conversations about those issues are more performative than critical of the status quo. What happens, then, when diverse members of Christian congregations talk explicitly about differences in race, ethnicity, and nationality?

Informed by diversal cosmopolitanism, the LRJC dialogue model seeks to build communities that balance unity and diversity. This requires people to understand the similarities and differences between groups (including differences in power). By identifying and understanding similarities, people can find common ground and shared goals, without which they cannot exist as a community. By identifying and understanding differences, communities can allow individuals and groups to maintain particular cultural traits and redress the inequalities and power imbalances that might exist between them. Integrating both processes should protect communities from the extremes of segregation and uniformity. The LRJC dialogue included questions that encouraged participants to explore the similarities and differences between immigrants and U.S.-born people. In the first session of the dialogues, I asked participants if they had ever felt like an outsider in a given social situation. In the second session of the dialogues, I asked them to discuss similarities and differences between immigrants and U.S.-born people, especially concerning why people move from one place to another and the problems people face in the United States. In HC1, HC2, and HC3, I also asked participants what it means to be an American, which implied considering what might distinguish Americans from people of other nationalities.[1] In this chapter, I analyze the dialogue segments on similarities and differences in order to understand how participants interacted with each other and the ideas they articulated about what unites and distinguishes immigrants and U.S.-born people.

## 4.1 Participant Interactions

While talking about similarities and differences, participants tended to engage mostly in agreement, in perspective-giving across differences, and in perspective-taking across differences. Agreement happened in forty-one exchanges on multiple topics across all dialogues, but most often in HC2 and HC5 and least often in HC4, HC6, and HC7, which does not indicate a clear pattern in terms of the racial/ethnic, gender, or denominational makeup of the dialogues. The high proportion of conservative participants could explain the high levels of agreement in HC2 and HC5, but participant convergence in political ideology did not necessarily lead to high levels of agreement (HC4 and HC6 had a high proportion of liberals but two of the lowest levels of agreement).

Agreement on issues relating to similarities and differences between immigrants and U.S.-born people was characterized by mutual understanding across differences much more than domination by participants of high-power groups. Of the dialogue passages coded as instances of agreement, 78% were cases of corroboration, in which a participant added logical reasoning or evidence in support of what another participant previously said. Most occurrences of agreement (66%) happened between participants of different racial/ethnic identities. Between immigrant and U.S.-born participants specifically, 46% happened. Immigrants led a majority of the instances of agreement with U.S.-born participants (53%) by making original statements that U.S.-born participants then followed or elaborated, which is commensurate with the proportion of immigrant speakers in the dialogue segment on similarities and differences (48%).

Only 34% of instances of agreement happened between participants of the same race/ethnicity, and 78% of those instances took place in HC2 between White American participants. As I show in further detail in Appendix A, in every session of HC2, U.S.-born participants (all White Americans) spoke relatively more than immigrant participants. As a facilitator, I had inadvertently let older White American males dominate that dialogue (and they tended to agree with each other). Only 7% of the instances of agreement were possible instances of domination, in which a participant of a historically marginalized group simply acquiesced to a statement made by a participant of a historically dominant group. They all happened in HC5, once between an African man and a Latina woman (domination across gender) and twice between a White American man (who also happened to be the pastor of one of the congregations) and immigrant participants (domination across nationality). Another instance of possible domination did not involve a participant of a historically marginalized group directly acquiescing to something that a participant of a historically dominant group had said, but it could be an instance of implicit domination. It happened in HC2. A White American man who had expressed several conservative opinions about immigration during the dialogue told a story about a group of children from the same school, several of whom were Spanish-speaking and a few African American. According to him, the Spanish-speaking children would only speak in Spanish while sharing a space with the African American children. By the end of the school year, the African American children had learned how to speak some Spanish, but the Spanish-speaking children continued to speak only in Spanish. He then said, "When I talk to them [Latino children], they look at me like they hardly understand what I'm saying." The Latina participant followed with this: "My whole house is talking in Spanish, [but] my house is talking English outside. Because sometimes, I'm talking to my children and tell them 'Don't talk in Spanish in front of other people, only English. You need to respect people outside of the house, you need to talk in English to understand everybody.' I think for respect . . . that is good in a public space. Speaking the same language. Everybody." It is hard to verify whether the Latina participant said that because she genuinely believed in it or in order to gain the approval of the White American participant. This nondialogical type of interaction, however, was rare.

Perspective-giving—in which someone conveys to people of other social groups how they have experienced the world—happened very often in the dialogue segment on similarities and differences. There were 152 instances of perspective-giving in all dialogues together. Perspective-giving happened to a similar extent across the dialogues, with the exception of HC7 (where it took place significantly more often) and HC6 (where it took place significantly less often). This distribution of instances of perspective-giving across dialogues does not indicate an association with the demographic makeup of dialogues. HC7 participants had, on average, a lower level of formal education than the participants of other dialogues, but that, in itself, should not lead to higher levels of perspective-giving. I found a better explanation for the higher level of perspective-giving in HC7 in my observation notes, where I noted that Latino immigrant participants of that dialogue had shared many emotionally charged stories about challenging migration and settlement experiences in the United States. For example, a Latina participant in that dialogue talked about her border-crossing experience in the following terms: "I want to tell you, taking this road is not easy, not easy at all. On our way here, we didn't shower for like ten days. She [daughter] got lice. You have no idea what it is." U.S.-born participants seemed to have been humbled by those stories. When asked about similarities and differences between their experiences and those of immigrant participants, they simply could not identify similarities because several of the immigrant stories were too heart-wrenching to compare to their lives as U.S.-born citizens. This was an extreme version of a pattern observed across the dialogues in the segment on similarities and differences: immigrant participants gave perspective much more often than U.S.-born participants. While immigrants (Latino, African, Asian) were only 48% of speakers in that dialogue segment, they accounted for 77% of the instances of perspective-giving. U.S.-born participants were 51% of the speakers but accounted for only 23% of perspective-giving. This indicates an equitable pattern of communication centered on the voices of members of a historically marginalized group.

Most occurrences of perspective-giving happened in response to questions about previous experiences of feeling like an outsider, reasons to migrate to the United States, and problems that immigrants face in the United States. Participants—most of them immigrants—gave perspective usually by telling short stories about family, work, school, or, to a lesser extent, church life. When U.S.-born participants gave perspective, they sometimes did so while comparing their experiences with immigrant experiences, resulting in a combination of perspective-giving and perspective-taking. This happened in HC1, HC2, HC3, HC4, and HC5 by a total of seven U.S.-born participants. While comparing life experiences, some U.S.-born participants emphasized the similarities between themselves and immigrants, while others emphasized the differences. By way of illustration, in HC1, an African American woman said, "I think the biggest thing they [immigrants] face is prejudice, discrimination, and biases, and it makes their way hard. . . . As Black people, we've had the same experience, so we truly can identify with what that means. And it just is not a thing that happens in this instant, and then, as you get better, things improve. That kind of stays with you." In contrast, in HC5, a White American man argued that "mainly because of, maybe economic [reasons], like, people [abroad] don't have access to travel as easily in their place of birth as we do as Americans. I can hop on a plane, and I can pretty much . . . afford to fly anywhere . . . , so there is a lot of mobility and access." Perspective-giving by U.S.-born participants rarely articulated feelings of resentment against immigrants. It happened only in the cases of an African American participant in HC1 and two White American participants in HC2. In the latter dialogue, for example, a White American man said, "When we hear people from another country speaking their language, we don't understand it. And when they're out in public, you know, we get suspicious: 'Are they talking about me?' . . . 'Are they planning something against me?' I think that's a typical American feeling when people are talking a different language." His statement was the last in a long exchange about language that involved several participants.

Perspective-taking—in which someone considers how people of another social group have experienced the world—was also a common relational process, but it happened half as frequently as perspective-giving (sixty-two instances). Still, participants took perspective in all of the seven dialogues, to the greatest extent in HC1 and HC2 and to the least extent in HC5, HC6, and HC7. This distribution of instances of perspective-taking across the dialogues does not suggest an association with the demographic makeup of dialogues. For instance, HC1 and HC2—which had high levels of perspective-taking—were held in Catholic congregations, but so was HC7—which had one of the lowest levels of perspective-taking. There was, however, a pattern in terms of participants' individual identities. U.S.-born participants (White American and African American) accounted for 95% of the instances of perspective-taking while being only 51% of the speakers in that dialogue segment. In contrast, immigrant participants (Latino, African, and Asian) accounted for only 5% of the instances of perspective-taking while being 48% of speakers in that dialogue segment. This is also indicative of an equitable pattern of communication centered on the experiences of a historically marginalized group: immigrants.

Most perspective-taking happened after the questions about why people move to the United States (and how that might be different or similar for people who move within the country) and about problems that immigrants face in the United States (and how that might be different or similar for people who are born in the country). In relation to the first issue (reasons to move), some U.S.-born participants made connections between immigrant experiences and family histories of migration (within the United States or to the United States by immigrant ancestors). In HC2, for instance, a White American woman referred to her grandparents from Poland: "So they spoke mostly Polish, they, you know, struggled with English, and it wasn't until their children that that language barrier diminished." Others discussed the root causes of migration. For example, in HC1, a White American woman said, "Given the situations throughout our world . . . and God knows there are many more countries with difficulties and strife, uhm, I would say that, yes, they [immigrants] come for their children, et cetera, but I think it's survival in capital letters for many, many people."

In relation to the second issue (problems immigrants faced in the United States), a White American man in HC6 argued that "the education system is different but also the system of professional licenses. . . . They [some immigrants] are well-educated people, with experiences, with skills to share . . . , but they cannot easily or immediately work here in this country. This makes it very difficult for them to support their families." However, while taking perspective from immigrants, three African American participants (two in HC1, one in HC4) connected more deeply with them by considering their shared marginality in U.S. society. In HC4, an African American woman argued, "If you look at the media . . . when it comes to Black and Brown people, education really isn't viewed to be the same way as though [for White people] [it] is nowhere in their [media] agenda . . . , so I would say that would be a similarity." This participant conveyed that media coverage of Latinos and African Americans does not portray them as people invested in education. White American participants could not speak of an experienced shared marginality, but four of them (in HC2, HC4, and HC6) did point out that African Americans and immigrants of color are discriminated against by law enforcement.

The statements of U.S.-born participants in response to the questions about reasons for immigrants to come to the United States and the problems they experience in the country usually included careful and empathetic language typical of perspective-taking, such as "I can understand where she is coming from," "I would say that . . . ," "Perceived [rather than experienced], obviously, . . . ," "I would think that . . . ," "I would imagine that . . . ," and "I can understand it, but I can't relate to it as having [it] happened to me."

For three participants in HC3, one participant in HC5, one participant in HC6, and one participant in HC7, taking perspective from immigrants led to an acknowledgment of the privileges that come with being born in the United States. In HC3, an African American woman said, "You know, from learning to talk to people that came from other places [you become] grateful to . . . things that we . . . take for granted, I think, a lot of times as Americans . . . your safety of your family . . . whether you're gonna have a meal . . . a roof over my head. . . . I don't have a whole lot, but I'm grateful for what I do have." In the same dialogue, a White American woman argued that "if I get very, very sick, I know that I will be okay because I have the healthcare providers around me that could take care of me but not everybody has that and that could be reason enough to migrate." Later in that dialogue, another African American woman talked about the prison pipeline to describe the plight of African Americans in the U.S. criminal justice system but acknowledged that, unlike immigrants who get detained, "we're not sent back to Africa, 'cause most of us have been born in this country." In HC5, a White American man said, "As a native, it isn't even on my radar to think that 'Oh, wait, people can't get health care because of their immigration status,' wow!" In HC6, a White American man pointed out that "the challenge of those that are undocumented is never ever kind of having a sense of security or permanence in place, so there is this kind of baseline anxiety . . . that never goes away. . . . There is no guarantees, there is no rights, there is no privileges. . . . on one level, if you are a citizen of the United States, some of that anxiety just doesn't exist because you do have certain rights and protections." Similarly, in HC7, a White American woman commented that "when you are in another country, where everyone has a different language or different social conventions, you are so vulnerable. . . . But being born here is an automatic security of, just like inherited understanding of knowing [the language and social norms]." These cases of privilege-acknowledging perspective-taking attest to the potential of diversal dialogues to promote critical reflection on intergroup power imbalances.

The concentration of perspective-giving among immigrant participants and of perspective-taking among U.S.-born participants indicates equity in the dialogue and, as stated in Chapter 3, is conducive to members of dominant groups recognizing their privilege, acknowledging the discrimination suffered by members of disadvantaged groups, and becoming more willing to take action to promote intergroup equality. However, solidarity across differences was not a salient relational process in this dialogue segment. We could expect solidarity to have emerged in this segment because it covered similarities between immigrants and U.S.-born people and finished with a discussion of shared interests. Yet, there were only ten instances in which participants of one group expressed a feeling of mutuality and commitment toward participants of another group. To the extent that solidarity did emerge in this segment, it was largely in HC1 between Latino and African American participants (eight of the ten occurrences). By way of illustration, in HC1, an African American man made an eloquent call for intergroup solidarity that expanded from Black-Brown to multiethnic appeals: "In this country, . . . a lot of animosity that has occurred is because the powers that be want the Blacks to be separate from the Hispanics. They want the Hispanics to feel separate from the Blacks. They want poor Whites to feel that they're better than anybody else, and they maintain this because, politically, it's advantageous to those in power. . . . There needs to be some work to get other people involved and understand that we are all human, we all have commonalities, and that if we could join forces, politically, as well as socially, we could move mountains. . . . But things that we've been told, trained [to believe], that we're different, and they're like this, and we're like that, and this other group is like this, that, it's like, you almost fight against one another instead of working together with one another to make a difference." In Section 4.2, I analyze the key themes of this segment of the dialogue, pointing out how agreement, perspective-giving, perspective-taking, and other relational processes were associated with their discussion.

## 4.2 Conversation Themes

When talking about similarities and differences between immigrants and U.S.-born people, participants made statements that aligned ideologically with universalist, diversal, and particularist varieties of cosmopolitanism or that described real-life situations that embodied one of those varieties of cosmo-politanism. Perhaps because of the diversal design of the dialogue—which had participants consider both similarities and differences—most partici-pants gravitated around diversal cosmopolitanism. For instance, in HC4, an African woman criticized the melting pot model of immigrant integration for its homogenous results: "You become nothing, frankly." Instead, she said she had educated her children to see immigrant integration more like a "tossed salad," so "even though you are tossed together, with a nice sauce, you still retain your original [culture], you get something from everybody else, but you retain your original [culture]. . . . You don't have to choose either or."

On the one hand, the discussion of similarities between immigrants and U.S.-born people allowed participants of historically marginalized groups (African American, immigrant, and, to a lesser extent, female participants) to connect their experiences and even express solidarity toward each other. On the other hand, the discussion of differences led U.S.-born participants (even those of historically marginalized groups) to acknowledge the privi-leges of being born in the United States. Throughout these discussions, par-ticipants were also able to think critically about what it means to be an Amer-ican and unpack the diversity and tensions that exist within immigrant communities. This indicates the existence of a process of diversal cosmopolitanization in the dialogues, through which participants of different racial/ethnic groups developed mutual understanding, empathy, and solidarity across differences while heeding the singularity of each group's experiences and the power asymmetries that exist between them.

Expressions of universalist cosmopolitanism were not predominant but they were common. In HC1, for example, an African American woman articulated a universalist cosmopolitan understanding of the U.S. Constitution. She argued that the Constitution preamble stated that all men and women are created equal and that certain human rights apply to all people, "that has nothing to do with citizenship." Universalist cosmopolitan statements, however, came largely from White American participants, who also tended to talk about the marginalization of certain groups of people as an abstract or historical social problem rather than as an observed or lived experience. As an example of a universalist statement, a White American woman in HC1 said that "as common ground, we can all find that place of agreement where we like dignity, respect, the fair wages . . . and decent education . . . and the same with housing . . . no matter what color or where they [tenants] are from." In HC2, a White American woman claimed that a broad common interest was "freedom from discrimination, but that's every individual . . . that's something I think we all have to struggle with." As I argued in Chapter 2, cosmopolitan solidarity, when understood in such universalistic terms, can overlook intergroup asymmetries to the detriment of marginalized groups as, in reality, not everyone struggles with discrimination to the same extent or in the same way.

Particularist cosmopolitanism surfaced several times in the conversations on similarities and differences, even if less frequently than diversal or universalist cosmopolitanism. In HC3, for example, a White American participant and a Latino participant argued that immigration-driven diversity is the defining feature of the United States as a nation. In that same dialogue, an African American woman called for a refounding of the nation through people embracing their differences. In the remainder of this chapter, I elaborate on the discussion of thematic patterns found in the conversations about similarities and differences between immigrants and U.S.-born people with a focus on six topics around which those conversations coalesced: (un)belonging, discrimination, language differences, legally defined boundaries, economic problems, and family.

## (Un)belonging

Conversations about similarities and differences between immigrants and U.S.-born people started with participants sharing stories of moments in which they felt like outsiders who did not belong in a specific context. Most stories were passed at schools, churches, workplaces, or in the neighborhoods. While giving perspective through storytelling, participants revealed how, where, and when they experienced social boundaries and what kind of social boundaries were more salient in their experiences. In those exchanges about social identity and belonging, there was no clear variation across dialogue demographic makeup or the race/ethnicity of individual participants, with one exception: the stories shared by White American participants referred to only sporadic and superficial experiences of feeling like an outsider, usually in the context of travel for tourism or work. In HC2, a White American man even said, "I don't have any problems interacting with anybody, friend or stranger. I find the best way to break the ice is with humor," an attitude that is probably easier for someone in a dominant social position to hold. In contrast, the stories shared by African American and immigrant participants referred to repeated and deep experiences of feeling like an outsider because of differences in race and ethnicity. In HC4, an African American woman reflected on the long-term effects of this condition: "Very often, when you are viewed as a marginalized person, and you go into a situation wondering, 'Are these people who want to appreciate who I am? Or are these the people who won't appreciate who I am?' . . . It is a very difficult way to live, you know?" In HC7, a Latina participant said, "In the first months that I was in this country, I felt like I was the only immigrant. I felt very lonely, I cried, even though I had my husband and children with me."

Many participants' stories about (un)belonging referred to churches. Participants across all dialogues (with the exception of HC1) talked about situations in which churches or church-affiliated institutions performed a cosmopolitan role, allowing immigrants to build community and get help while settling in the United States. Those stories revealed a range of congregation approaches to cultural diversity. On one end were the ethnic congregations, which are typically aligned with either parochialism or particularist religious cosmopolitanism. For example, the aforementioned Latina participant of HC7, who reported crying and feeling like the only immigrant in the country, said, "Then . . . I started to go to church, and I felt like, over there, I began to feel peaceful, like they embraced me . . . and my healing process began." A condition for that, she pointed out, was that "in the church, there were a lot of Hispanics." Hers was a Latino Catholic congregation that held masses in Spanish but existed in a parish shared with an old White American congregation. Moving toward diverse religious cosmopolitanism, but probably still within particularist religious cosmopolitanism, was a Vietnamese American Catholic congregation that an Asian participant of HC2 had belonged to. She appreciated that the mass was bilingual (Vietnamese and English) so that both U.S.-born and foreign-born congregation members could participate. The multicultural congregation of HC4 participants also seemed to be within particularist religious cosmopolitanism but had started to make efforts toward diversal religious cosmopolitanism. An African participant in that congregation reported having a positive experience in that community. Upon her arrival in the United States with two children, she felt "quite vulnerable" in what was, for her, a "very scary" situation, in which she was not surrounded by people committed to her because of family or friendship bonds. At the congregation, she found a "family from church," "a diverse church," where people were "so nice and warm." In HC5, an African man expressed appreciation for a congregation he previously attended, which seemed to fall under diversal religious cosmopolitanism. He described it as a "rainbow church" because there "we find [people of] all corners" and "they really welcomed the foreigners" and "helped them navigate the system."

White American participants did not report experiences of feeling like an outsider in a congregation, but a few of them demonstrated an awareness of the implications of different approaches to cultural diversity in congregation life. In HC2, a White American man argued that, in the early twentieth century, ethnic churches established by immigrants used non-English languages in their schools and liturgy, which might have contributed to their internal sense of belonging but discouraged intercultural relations outside of the ethnic community. In HC4, a White American woman talked about how her congregation's collective decision-making on a capital fundraising campaign taught her that the various opinions expressed by congregants often came down to their national origin: "I was, like, kind of being schooled.... For some [national groups of congregants] the most important thing [in the capital campaign] was the heart [the emotional meaning] of giving a gift.... For others, it was knowing 'Are we raising the money [we need]?'" She also stressed the need for translation in those collective discussions. Less often, participants shared examples of parochialist behaviors observed in churches or church-affiliated institutions where participants worshipped, worked, or attended school. By way of illustration, in HC3, an African American woman reported feeling isolated in church events where most other women were White. In the same dialogue, a Latino participant said that in a previous congregation he had felt uncomfortable as a homosexual person. Altogether, the stories of belonging and marginalization in churches suggest different ways through which historically marginalized people can feel like they belong in a congregation: descriptive racial/ethnic representation in the demographics of the congregation, mutual help between immigrants and U.S.-born members, linguistic representation in religious services, and opportunity to influence congregation decisions. Yet, when that inclusion takes the form of ethnic churches, particularist religious cosmopolitanism or even parochialism can emerge, with the potential negative implications discussed in Chapter 2, such as the essentializing of social identities.

At times, U.S.-born participants took perspective on the outsider experiences of participants of historically marginalized groups. In HC4, for instance, the White American woman mentioned in the previous paragraph told the story of an immigrant friend whose child was discriminated against at a Catholic school and expressed feeling "just so sad" because of that problem. In HC6, a White American man argued that his immigrant and African American neighbors experience a "lack of . . . assurance and recognition that who they are matters and that they have a place here, that there is something permanent for them." Such realizations often came from previous experiences of intergroup contact, through which U.S.-born participants learned about the lives of immigrants and developed feelings of empathy (although certainly not all experiences of intergroup contact reported in the conversations were positive or conducive to empathy). For African American and female participants, however, discussions about the un(belonging) of immigrants in social spaces often involved the drawing of parallels with their own experiences of marginalization. In HC1, for example, an African American woman said, "That reminds me of racism for African Americans," after listening to a Latina participant talk about how she and her sister felt isolated at a school where they were a minority. This intergroup awareness of a shared marginality became clearer in exchanges about discrimination.

## Discrimination

The topic that recurred most often in conversations about similarities and differences between immigrants and people born in the United States was the exploitation, abuse, or discrimination of historically marginalized people. About half of the statements about exploitation, abuse, or discrimination were about the experiences of immigrants specifically. Exploitation, abuse, or discrimination was discussed to the greatest extent in HC1, HC3, and HC4, and to the least extent in HC2, HC6, and HC7. This distribution across dialogues indicates a possible pattern of variation across the demographic composition of dialogues: HC1 and HC3 were between largely Latino and African American participants, while HC2, HC6, and HC7 were between mostly Latino and White American participants. This might reflect the mutual understanding and solidarity that can emerge between Latinos and African Americans when they discuss marginalization in U.S. society. No other pattern of variation according to the demographic composition of dialogues was evident from the distribution of participant statements on exploitation, abuse, or discrimination of historically marginalized people. For instance, HC1, HC3, and HC4 had an above-average proportion of liberal-leaning participants who—because of the social justice concerns typical of this political orientation—might have focused on the exploitation, abuse, or discrimination of historically marginalized people. However, HC6 had the highest proportion of liberal-leaning participants and yet the lowest proportion of statements about the topic.

Conversations about exploitation, abuse, or discrimination showed a clear pattern in terms of the race/ethnicity of individual participants. While participants of historically marginalized racial/ethnic groups (African Americans, Latinos, Asians, and Africans) were 65% of speakers in the segment on similarities and differences, they accounted for 83% of statements on exploitation, abuse, or discrimination. Narrowing down to immigrant participants, these were only 48% of the speakers but made 54% of statements about that topic. White American participants, by contrast, were underrepresented in statements about exploitation, abuse, or discrimination (accounting for 34% of the speakers but making only 17% of the statements on the topic).

Most statements about exploitation, abuse, or discrimination were about race or ethnicity (a few were about gender). When participants discussed the discrimination against African Americans, they focused on race. African American participants shared many personal stories of experiences with racism, especially in the workplace, in the job market, and, to a lesser extent, in schools or while in contact with law enforcement. As an example, in HC4, an African American woman talked about having to give her young son "an education of driving while Black, and [that] if someone [a cop] stops you, that you truly need to call your parents. . . . You can't do everything that maybe some of your [White] friends are able to do." When participants talked about the discrimination against immigrants of color, they focused on ethnicity, emphasizing that not only phenotype but also language has been a marker to discriminate against immigrants. Several immigrant participants shared stories about discrimination in the workplace (mistreatment and unequal pay): "I remember that when I came to the United States, I was working at a warehouse because this is the only place that you can work if you don't have the documents. So I remember this lady who used to work in the office [saying] things like 'This little Mexican,' 'Why she doesn't learn English,' 'She's trying to take my job'" (Latina participant in HC1). Less often, immigrants told stories about discrimination at schools, in experiences of contact with law enforcement, and, rarely, at churches.

Some immigrant stories surfaced mechanisms for responding to discrimination. During the segment on tensions over immigration, in HC2, a Latina participant had already articulated a coping mechanism (which she developed while dealing with a bigoted neighbor): politeness ("I tell my kids to keep saying 'Hi!' to him"). In the segment on similarities and differences, immigrant participants mentioned two other mechanisms: hiding sadness or anger as a way of presenting as a strong person, and showing pride in cultural heritage. The Latina participant of HC1 who was discriminated against while working at a warehouse said, "I used to go to the restroom, you know, and cry because, I mean, you're human . . . even though you don't express your feelings. So I used to go to the restroom and say [to myself] 'She won't see me cry.'" In HC4, an African woman said that her son once came home from school complaining that an African American student had been teasing him by calling him "African boy." She recalled telling her son, "You should say 'Yes, I am an African boy. I'm proud of being an African boy.'" Only two immigrant participants invoked religious beliefs in their coping with discrimination. In HC5, for instance, an African man said, "Because of the color of my skin, they [law enforcement at the airport] are going to be a little bit more strict, but just [asking] more questions about where you work or where you live, and then [they say] I'm good to go. That's why I said, we need to be . . . church [loving and understanding] in that kind of experience."

In HC1, HC3, HC4, and HC5, conversations between African American and Latino participants about similarities and differences led to them establishing parallels between their experiences with exploitation, abuse, and discrimination in the United States and, sometimes, expressing solidarity toward each other. For instance, an African American woman in HC1 commented about her work in health care: "They [immigrant health care workers] get all the heavier patients, you know, they get a larger patient load. . . . And it's total discrimination because we know it happened to us [African Americans]." In that same dialogue, a Latina participant argued that "a lot of the issues that immigrants face are very similar to the issues that people experiencing poverty face. . . . And one of the things that always sticks in my head is why we don't have the dialogue specifically between the Latino community and the African American community because all of the issues that the African American community has faced and continues to face are issues that the Latino community faces and continues to face, and how much power there would be in a united community." In HC3, an African American woman claimed that "many [White] folks are afraid of the browning of . . . our nation. And so a lot of the pushback is out of their own fear that they will lose privileges. . . . And I think that this [dialogue] is a great opportunity for us to know each other and be committed to embrace our differences and embrace each other." This sentiment was echoed in HC5 by a Latina participant: "White people are growing more fearful, and they are losing space, [fearful] that they can become a minority, in what they think is their own country." These expressions of intergroup solidarity were rare but not unremarkable because they emerged out of a broader context where misunderstandings and even animosity exist between Latinos and African Americans. In HC1, African American participants talked about resentment toward immigrants in their community because Latinos accept to work for lower wages, Koreans own the corner shops, and refugees receive government financial assistance. In HC1 and HC5, Latino participants talked about resentment toward African Americans in their community because Latino workers are often victims of robberies by African Americans in the streets of Baltimore. Solidarity based on shared marginality is not the default relationship between African Americans and Latinos.

## Language Differences

Language was among the most common topics in conversations about similarities and differences between immigrants and U.S.-born people. Participants tended to see language differences as a major reason to feel like outsiders in a social situation. Exchanges about language happened in all the dialogues, but most frequently in HC2 and HC7 and least frequently in HC5 and HC6. This does not indicate a clear pattern of variation according to the demographic composition of the dialogues. HC2 and HC7 happened in Catholic congregations, mostly between White American and Latino participants, and with a relatively large proportion of conservative-leaning participants, but this was most likely a coincidence for several reasons: (1) HC1 and HC4 were also in Catholic congregations but showed lower amounts of discussion on language; (2) HC6, like HC2 and HC7, happened mostly between White American and Latino participants but had one of the lowest amounts of discussion on language; (3) HC5, like HC2 and HC7, had a relatively large proportion of conservative-leaning participants but one of the lowest amounts of discussion on language; and (4) I have no theoretical reason to expect the combination of Catholicism, White American-Latino composition, and a conservative majority of participants to lead to more discussion about language. What about variation according to individual participant identity? The distribution of statements about language was approximately even across the race/ethnicity of participants. This was unlike conversations about other issues that can marginalize people, which tended to have an overrepresentation of immigrant and African American participants.

Several immigrant participants expressed feelings of not belonging in mainstream spaces because of the language barrier and gave perspective on being discriminated against because of language differences in various settings, such as the workplace, school, or the airport. For instance, in HC7, a Latina participant talked about how she felt excluded at her previous school because U.S.-born Latino students would make fun of her problems with English: "Even though they were Hispanics born here, they pushed me aside for not knowing English. . . . Yeah, so I received, I am going to call it bullying, for not knowing English." In HC5, an African participant said, "With respect to discrimination, I would get discriminated against by another Black man, particularly an African American. Most of the time, when I speak, it is an African American who says he does not understand my accent. An average White American can understand my accent. So you can see something there."

Many immigrant participants pointed out the language barrier as an obstacle for immigrants to access resources (like health care and education) and opportunities (like jobs and travel). They gave perspective from personal experience. In HC6, for instance, a Latino participant said, "When I arrived here [in the United States], nothing was easy; because of the language. . . . It was a shock." A few participants—all immigrants—claimed that the language barrier makes immigrants vulnerable to people with bad intentions, such as abusive landlords: "Housing, people take advantage of immigrants. You're not familiar with the laws, you're not familiar with your rights as a tenant. And so a lot of people end up living in rundown houses. And they're threatened by their landlords. . . . Language plays a huge issue in why a lot of these issues come about" (Latina participant in HC1).

U.S.-born participants generally saw discrimination on the basis of language as a distinct immigrant experience (one exception was an African American woman in HC3, who argued that both immigrants and African Americans are singled out for not speaking "the King's English"). In HC2, for instance, a White American woman said that "immigrants are more likely to face discrimination . . . language-wise, it takes time for, uhm, the English language to be assimilated even by native-borns." Some U.S.-born participants also took perspective from immigrants by acknowledging that the language barrier is also a barrier to resources and opportunities. In HC2, for example, a White American man argued that "in employment, this area [Baltimore] isn't what it was, and it doesn't present the same opportunities [as it did in the past]. . . . It's [affecting] everybody, but it's going to hit immigrants even harder because they're already fighting a language barrier in a lot of cases."

A few White American participants expressed resentment against immigrants speaking non-English languages in public spaces, a feeling grounded in the understanding of English as the national language. In HC2, a White American man argued that "historically, the one thing that united everyone was a common language, but, you know, uh, celebrating our cultural experience is a wonderful thing. And we do that privately. We do it as a family." Another White American man corroborated, saying that "in America, the language of commerce, which drives the train, okay, is English. . . . If you're out there in the business world and we have to transact business . . . it's gotta be in English." Yet, many participants, including some of those who had expressed discomfort with immigrants speaking non-English languages in public, stressed the benefits of bilingualism: "It's very important to try to teach the kids to speak two languages or more . . . because it makes the country richer than others. . . . It is a parent's responsibility because this is going to give these kids more opportunities, job opportunities" (White American woman, HC2). For immigrant participants, bilingualism was also seen as necessary in order for immigrant youth to be connected to their families and their cultural heritage: "I have five children, and sometimes they get together and speak only in English. They know their mom does not speak. . . . It is very frustrating. . . . I was very obstinate that [my daughter] needed to talk [in Spanish], not only because I didn't speak English but [because] I wanted her to learn my language" (Latina participant, HC7).

## Legally Defined Boundaries

Among the challenges that participants also recognized as unique to immigrants were the need to navigate a complex immigration system that is impermeable to many, the risk of deportation, and the limited access to the national welfare system. Most of these challenges are based on legal distinctions within the immigrant population (naturalized citizens, permanent residents, unauthorized immigrants, etc.) and between immigrants and U.S.-born citizens. Indeed, issues related to law and citizenship were prominent in conversations about similarities and differences between immigrants and U.S.-born people. The topic was discussed most often in HC1 and HC5 and least often in HC2, HC3, and HC4, which does not suggest an evident pattern according to the demographic makeup of the dialogues. The demographic compositions of HC1 and HC5 are quite different, as are the demographic compositions of HC2, HC3, and HC4. There was, however, a clear pattern of variation according to the racial/ethnic identity of individual participants. Immigrant participants (especially Latinos) were more likely to discuss issues related to law and citizenship than U.S.-born participants. Immigrant participants were only 48% of the speakers in the dialogue segment on similarities and differences but accounted for 65% of the statements about law and citizenship. U.S.-born participants, who were 51% of the speakers in that segment, accounted for only 35% of statements on the topic.

Several participants in HC1, HC2, HC5, and HC7, both immigrant and U.S.-born, referred to the rule of law as a distinct characteristic of U.S. society. In HC1, for example, a White American woman talked about "the freedom that, you know, many other people [in foreign countries] don't have, because we have laws." In HC2, when I asked about common interests between immigrants and U.S.-born people, a White American man singled out the rule of law as a "personal favorite of mine." A few immigrant participants pointed out that immigrants often arrive in the United States with little knowledge of the country's laws (not only immigration law but also tax, employment, and housing law): "We come [to the United States] ignorant about the laws of this country. We don't know about the laws, and sometimes, because we don't know them, or have a guide, we also make mistakes" (Latina participant in HC7). These participants stressed that immigrants should learn the law of the land as part of their integration into U.S. society. As suggested in the above comment by the Latina participant of HC7, the lack of knowledge about U.S. law among immigrants is not necessarily willful ignorance. As a few participants pointed out, it can also come from a country-of-origin culture lacking the rule of law. In HC1, a White American woman shared that a friend of hers who is from El Salvador told her, "The advantage that you have in the United States and that I had when I lived there [is that] you have the laws and they are respected for the most part."

Yet, by and large, discussions of the legal dimension of the similarities and differences between immigrants and U.S.-born people revolved around the legal barriers that immigrants (especially undocumented immigrants) face in accessing resources (such as health insurance) and opportunities (such as formal employment). Immigrant participants led exchanges on this topic by giving perspective based on their personal experiences or based on what they had observed in their communities. In HC6, for instance, a Latino participant pointed out that "the pandemic, right from the start, has opened our eyes to the situation of the Hispanic community that is undocumented, who have not received help from the government, no stimulus check, no help for rent past due . . . in comparison to those who have social security, who have received help from the government. . . . Our community works on their own, independently, for a daily, weekly, or biweekly wage. They don't have any secure job. So the country stopped, the work stopped for them. . . . The only help we've gotten is from the food banks, right? . . . But the rent, the energy, the phone, who pays for that?" Several U.S.-born participants sympathized with undocumented immigrants by taking perspective. For example, in HC1, an African American woman recalled that "undocumented aliens were allowed to get a driver's license . . . but they [the government] are changing the driver's license laws . . . where you have to bring like five different documents to prove your identity before they will issue a driver's license. So that's knocking a whole lot of people out of mobility." In HC5, a White American man picked up the same issue: "There's a certain driver's license that says you can't go into federal facilities."

A few participants also noted that immigrants who are uneducated about U.S. law or are excluded from its protections because of immigration status are especially vulnerable to abuse by landlords and employers. For example, in HC7, a Latina participant shared that she "worked for a year cleaning an attorney's office. They [the employer] were paying cash because we didn't have a work permit. . . . [Then] there was an increase in the salary. They were [going to start] paying $12.65 [per hour]. The guy [employer] told us he could not give us a raise because he was paying us in cash. And he said to the ones that have the papers [that] he would pay what it was [the increased salary]. . . . And we were cleaning twenty-seven floors between eight people!" In HC5, HC6, and HC7, some immigrant and U.S.-born participants pointed out a basic level of anxiety that undocumented immigrants experience due to their immigration status, which other immigrants and U.S.-born people do not experience. Taking perspective from undocumented immigrants, a White American man in HC6 argued that "part of the challenge of those that are undocumented is never ever kind of having a sense of security of permanent in place . . . and that never goes away. . . . If you are a citizen of the United States, some of that anxiety just doesn't exist because you have certain rights and protections." In HC7, a Latina participant gave perspective on the same condition: "I feel like this [Baltimore] is my home, but I still doubt it. . . . Every day I pray to God, because he said everything will be fine. . . . There is always insecurity. There's always an insecurity that one day we might be here or we might be there [deported]." Those exchanges about the vulnerability and anxiety associated with legal distinctions affecting immigrants indicated a nuanced and deep reflection among participants.

There were also critiques of the making and implementation of legal distinctions between immigrants and U.S.-born people. In terms of lawmaking, in HC1, for example, a White American man pointed out that "listening to your [immigrant participants] sharing, . . . I'm hearing and feeling that those people that 'make the laws' that immigrants have to face and somehow deal with are not very friendly laws. They are making it extremely difficult [for immigrants] to become part of society." In HC5, a Latina participant argued that "in this country, it has become clear that one race [White] has power for centuries, and they have created something that has sustained discrimination and injustice. . . . A group of people has the power to make laws . . . and as people of color, we are still suffering from all these laws." In HC6, a Latina participant stated that "other things that create obstacles for us is the lack of Latino people in the government because we are a minority and they do not legislate in our favor." Regarding the implementation of the law, White American, African American, and immigrant participants in HC1, HC2, HC3, HC4, and HC5 criticized racial profiling by law enforcement and the racial/ethnic disparities in mass incarceration. In HC1, for instance, an African American woman stated that although African Americans and Latinos are minority groups, they are the majority among the incarcerated population. In HC3, an African American woman discussed the profiling and the prison pipeline, arguing that it affects both African Americans and immigrants, with the caveat that immigrants can be deported after an arrest. This was yet another issue on which African American participants expressed solidarity with immigrants of color.

The flip side of this discussion of law-based differences between immigrants and U.S.-born people was a recognition, by both immigrant and U.S.-born participants, of the privileges of being born in the United States. For instance, in HC5, after Latino participants brought up the challenges of traveling without a nationally valid identification document, a White American man recalled being able to get on a domestic flight with his daughter after forgetting his wallet in the car. He wondered if that had happened "because of the way I look and if I speak English, and I'm a citizen?" In a similar realization of U.S.-born privilege, a White American woman in HC7 argued that "being born here is an automatic security of use, like inherited understanding of knowing. When I go to the restaurant, I go to the host, I walk up to the host desk. Just like [knowledge of] little tiny things that make you feel like you know how things work." From an equity perspective, the acknowledgment by U.S.-born participants was especially significant and consistent with the theoretical expectations in Chapter 2 about dialogues that explicitly examine intergroup differences.

## Economic Problems

Conversations about similarities and differences between immigrants and U.S.-born people often touched on economic problems. Participants discussed this topic most frequently in HC1 and HC2 and least frequently in HC3 and HC4, which does not indicate a clear pattern of variation according to the demographic makeup of dialogues. For instance, HC1 and HC2 were held in Catholic congregations, but so was HC4. Most participants of HC3 and HC4 leaned liberal in political ideology, but so did most participants of HC1 (and most participants of HC2 leaned conservative). HC1 and HC2 had a proportion of immigrant participants below the average of all dialogues, but so did HC4. What about variation according to individual participant identity? The distribution of statements was proportional to the race/ethnicity of speakers in the dialogue segment on similarities and differences. Two exceptions were African participants, who spoke about economic problems much more than one would expect based on the proportion of African speakers in that dialogue segment (10% of statements on economic problems vs. 4% of speakers), and Asian participants, who spoke about economic problems much less than one would expect based on the proportion of Asian speakers in that dialogue segment (1% of statements vs. 3% of speakers). Since the number of African and Asian participants was very small, one should be cautious not to overinterpret those discrepancies. A qualitative review of the statements about economic problems made by African or Asian participants does not suggest a theme that could explain the overrepresentation of the first and the underrepresentation of the latter in exchanges about that topic.

When I asked why people move to the United States or move within the country, participants often mentioned economic problems. They largely agreed that the search for better economic standing is a key reason why people move. Some U.S.-born participants drew parallels between the experiences of contemporary immigrants to the United States, their own history of migration within the country, or the experiences of their immigrant ancestors. By way of illustration, in HC1, an African American woman corroborated the migration stories of previous participants, saying, "My parents were the same [in motivation for moving to another place]. They were all farmers, and there were twelve kids in my mom's family, but they all hated farming, and they said it was hard work. . . . So when they moved up this way [to Maryland], they could have their own money." Several African American participants in HC1 and HC3 drew parallels between the international migration of Latinos and the Great Migration of African Americans from the south to the north of the United States in the early and mid-twentieth century.

In HC1, HC4, and HC5, several participants—Latino, African American, White American, and African—saw poverty as a common problem for immigrants and U.S.-born people. Some of the participants even understood poverty as an issue around which they should act collectively. For example, in HC1, a White American man advocated for "organizing not just one people of color, but all people of color to work together and to say to their quite often White bosses, 'You gotta pay us a decent wage.'" In HC4, an African American woman argued that "how we can adjust poverty in our communities is very important." Yet, both U.S.-born and immigrant participants tended to see immigrants as facing additional economic challenges compared to U.S.-born people, from undocumented immigrants being more likely to receive unfair wages to high-skilled immigrants having trouble getting their professional credentials recognized in the United States. Regarding professional credentials, a Latino participant in HC6 argued that "the educational system here is very different in comparison to Peru's. I had come with this illusion of studying, getting involved in the church, and working. . . . I am moving forward little by little. Through the Methodist Church, there is support to have my previous studies accepted here. . . . Those are the obstacles that are in our way." A White American man took perspective from him, saying, "I have heard a lot of that here, from people from other places, that the education system is different but also professional licenses. . . . They are educated people, with experience, with skills to share, but they cannot easily or immediately work here in this country. That makes it very difficult for them to support their families and also for their identity because many times our identity is involved in our vocation." A Latina participant then gave perspective on her own experience as an undocumented immigrant who ventured into entrepreneurship: "I have a small cleaning business, and I always tell my clients that I may suffer an accident and break something, but I don't have [business] insurance, so I have to let them know in advance. . . . And, because of that, my services [have to be] much cheaper than the services of an established business."

Feelings of economic anxiety (economic insecurity and concern about one's economic prospects) were expressed only in HC2 and largely by White American participants. One of them argued that "a lot of people that are coming here [to the United States] don't realize that the upward mobility that existed in one time in this country . . . isn't there anymore. . . . The American dream is still attainable; it's just much more difficult than it was in the past." Another participant corroborated, saying that "the economic challenge challenges everyone equally. . . . What we used to call the middle class . . . now is probably in a museum because it doesn't really exist. . . . There are much less jobs because, frankly, technology has eliminated a lot of jobs." These participants tended to assume that immigrants shared this economic anxiety with them, but that was not the case. Across the dialogues, immigrant participants discussed economic problems but were generally thankful for the economic opportunities the United States offered them. They did not express pessimism about the economy. For example, the Latina participant of HC6 who talked about the challenges of running a small business while being undocumented claimed that her U.S.-born daughters "will have many opportunities; doors will open to them that have been closed to us." In HC7, a Latino participant said, "I am here, and I can't complain. We came to the land of the opportunities, as long as we appreciated them." For most immigrants in the United States, migration means upward mobility, which contrasts with the feelings of actual or potential downward mobility expressed by White Americans in HC2 (and might explain some of the anti-immigrant sentiment revealed by some of them in that dialogue).

Unfortunately, in HC2 there were not many immigrant participants, and two of them seemed keener to please the White American participants who had dominated that dialogue than to offer counterpoints to their mistaken assumptions about immigrant economic anxiety. A Latina participant of HC2 actually took perspective from the White American participants on economic anxiety and expressed solidarity with them by saying, "My coworkers will say every so often, 'I remember when one income was enough to support a family,' and I can relate to that, because, uh, it's really tough with one income. . . . You know, having two kids in private school . . . [I] pay eleven hundred [dollars] every two weeks for my health insurance, which is a lot of money." Had HC2 had a larger proportion of immigrant participants, one of them might have corrected the White American participants' assumption about a shared concern over the economy's future.

In addition to economic anxiety, a perception that immigrants compete with U.S.-born people for economic resources can generate anti-immigrant sentiment. Several immigrant participants—in HC1, HC4, and HC6—talked about the hostility immigrants face because of feelings of economic competition among natives. In HC1, for instance, a Latina participant told the story of when she participated in the auction of a vehicle and made the winning bid, which prompted a disgruntled White American man to say, "How come you're going to give this car to this immigrant?!" In that same dialogue, African American participants acknowledged the narrative of economic competition with immigrants that circulates in their community but saw that as a result of misconceptions and misinformation. An African American woman, for example, said that "sometimes we get the wrong so-called truth. . . . I had neighbors, and they said they hated immigrants because when they [immigrants] come over here they get . . . twice as much [welfare benefits] as poor people here, and they get some kind of allowance so they can get decent housing and they automatically are found jobs as well. . . . We know it's not true." In HC2, a White American woman reported that when her son tried to register his children in public preschool, a school official said they were going to be placed on a waitlist because the school was prioritizing low-income families and children with limited English proficiency. She thought that was unfair because her son and his wife were "both working and paying taxes." Hers was the only direct personal experience of economic competition with immigrants reported by a U.S.-born participant in that dialogue segment.

## Family

In many of the exchanges discussed so far in this chapter, participants told stories about their families. This happened to the largest extent in HC1 and HC2 and at a lower, but approximately even, frequency across the other dialogues. This distribution does not suggest a clear pattern of variation across dialogue demographic makeup. HC1 and HC2 differ in racial/ethnic composition, political-ideological composition, and other demographic variables. They shared the Catholic denomination, but so did HC4 and HC6. Regarding the race/ethnicity of individual participants, there was not a clear pattern of variation either. The distribution of statements about family corresponded closely to the proportion of speakers according to race/ethnicity in the dialogue segment on similarities and differences.

When participants referred to the family, it was more than a context in which their stories about marginalization, discrimination, language differences, legal boundaries, or economic problems unfolded. Participants often mentioned family reunification, the search for a better life for their children, or the provision of income for those left behind as primary reasons for people to move to the United States. In HC1, for example, a Latina participant said, "My sisters and I were separated when we were very young. Kids of three, four, and six. . . . And after ten years, my mom had the opportunity to find out where my sisters were because they were kidnapped. So . . . my mom went to the station to come [to the United States]. You know, a mom will do anything to find her children. So I didn't blame her for it. . . . After a year almost, my brother and I had to decide whether or not I wanted to come because I had a full ride for the university [in Mexico] . . . and my mom said, 'Well, you have to decide, right?!' . . . But for me, seeing basically my little brother, you know, leaving by himself . . . I told my mom, 'Okay, I'm leaving with him.' So that was the main reason that I came." Several U.S.-born participants mentioned family-related reasons to migrate while taking perspective from immigrants or while giving perspective based on their own family histories of migration to or within the United States. By way of illustration, in HC6, a White American woman said, "I know my dad, his family came because they were really poor in Italy, they were farmers . . . they believed that coming to the United States in the future would offer a better life for themselves, and more importantly, . . . for their children."

The exchanges about family migration stories in the dialogues suggest that the framing of migration as an act to protect the family has the potential to generate solidarity between immigrant and U.S.-born people. Most people can understand the migration decision of loving parents who fear for the safety or economic future of their children. By way of illustration, in HC4, an African American woman said, "A lot [of the reason to emigrate] has to do with wanting to be close to family. . . . I used to teach English as a second language . . . a lot of them [students] were immigrants . . . they really wanted to be close to family. . . . I learned a lot from them . . . respectful individuals who really put family first." Even politically conservative people, who tend to hold more negative attitudes toward immigration, might express solidarity toward them because of the importance they typically attribute to the nuclear family and traditional family values. In HC2, for instance, a conservative White American man argued that "we don't have in this country today, generally speaking, this traditional family . . . there's a breakdown of values that I think as Catholics we would be hard pressed to deny. . . . My experience of different immigrant groups, in their deep-seated faith, is that [they feel] this [coming to the United States] is like 'Welcome to Sodom and Gomorrah' compared to what they're used to." In that same conversation, a White American woman who had expressed conservative opinions pointed out that caring about children is common both for immigrants and for U.S.-born people: "Well, probably everybody wants their children to have a good education and a good life. Everybody wants that for kids, no matter who they are, where they come from." Her sentiment was echoed by an African woman in HC5, who said, "I believe that, well, everybody, no matter where you're living, whether you're in America or Nigeria or Brazil, we have the same, you know, aspirations. . . . You want to have your kids be educated." In HC6, a White American man also pointed out the education of children as a common interest of immigrants and U.S.-born people: "Our children . . . share the same schools, the same teachers. . . . We are all part of our schools here in the neighborhood, so I think there are opportunities to collaborate there, in the schools, or just with the children, between the churches, or in the entire community, and help children in their development." As I show in Chapter 5, participants often saw youth education as an area where they could collaborate after the dialogues.

When it came to recognizing the challenges that immigrants face in comparison to U.S.-born people in the area of family life, U.S.-born participants focused on the need to migrate abroad to offer a better standard of living for families or to be reunited with family. Several immigrant participants expanded this notion by discussing the challenge of educating children in a foreign cultural environment. This included teaching children how to respond to discrimination and the parents' native language and customs, all while integrating into U.S. society. Immigrant participants also gave perspective on problems that may never cross the mind of a U.S.-born person. In HC5, for example, a Latino participant discussed how undocumented immigrants cannot travel internationally (or domestically by plane) to visit family. In HC6, a Latina participant said, "If a Latino dies in the United States, to repatriate the body to Mexico costs a lot of money. If you want that your loved one arrived at their destination, it costs a lot of money." As in relation to language-related, legal, and economic challenges, this discussion led to a few U.S.-born participants recognizing their U.S.-born privilege. To illustrate, in HC7, a White American woman claimed that "whereas here [in the United States] it is kind of expected or normal to leave, maybe move twelve hours away at eighteen [years old] . . . it is one thing to leave your family . . . knowing you probably can go back, knowing how close [geographically] you are . . . and then here you have free access to go back and forth . . . and just, like, no one understands what it takes to do the opposite [move abroad without knowing whether you will be able to return to be with family]." This perspective-taking on family issues is another signal of an equitable pattern of communication with awareness of intergroup power imbalances.

In several of the stories that immigrant participants shared, a belief in divine providence seemed to have contributed to coping positively with life challenges. Earlier in this chapter, when discussing discrimination against immigrants, I referred to two participants who had invoked religious beliefs to cope with discrimination. I repeatedly observed this in participants' stories about situations other than discrimination. One was the case of an Asian participant of HC2, whose family was devoted to the Virgin Mary and saw the name Maryland as reinforcing their decision to settle in the state of Maryland. In HC3, a Latina participant thanked God for putting her in a job where she could advocate for other Latina women. In HC6, a Latino participant claimed that throughout his immigration challenges, "the hand of God was always there . . . and God started to open opportunities." There were many references like this, which might have demonstrated to U.S.-born participants the faith of immigrant participants, potentially contributing to a mutual connection based on shared religiosity.

Asking participants about similarities and differences between immigrants and U.S.-born people could have suggested that those are hermetic categories of people. However, the integration of immigrants into U.S. society (including processes like acculturation or naturalization) blurs those distinctions. When I asked participants what it means to be an American, they did engage in interactive critical thinking about those distinctions. Participants were evenly split between civic and ethnocultural definitions of American identity. Civic definitions were visible in references to birthright citizenship, the values enshrined in the Declaration of Independence and the Constitution, the naturalization process, and the Pledge of Allegiance. Ethnocultural definitions were varied, including statements that centered Native Americans as the "true" Americans, assumed the English language as a common denominator for Americans, and presented the United States as a diverse land of opportunity for immigrants. In the first example, everyone other than Native Americans would exist forever as a foreigner in the United States (a permanent situation of difference). In the second example, immigrants become American by learning English (an acquired similarity that defines the nation). In the third example, America is immigrant by definition, and inside-outside boundaries are always in flux.

Only two participants articulated Christian nationalist understandings of American identity. They were both White American participants of HC2. One of them, a woman, said, "My personal belief is that the Holy Spirit was in it [the founding of the nation] even though people didn't recognize it or won't acknowledge that. . . . As Catholic Christians, we believe that we were created with freedom. And I think that's at the core of what America should stand for." Her perspective was corroborated by the other participant: "Our founding fathers . . . were deists. Whether you like it or not, they generally believed in God. . . . You're endowed by your creator with certain unalienable rights. These rights are not the gift or privilege of the government to give or take. They're God-given rights." Both participants were thus giving religious meaning to a civic value: individual freedom. Their statements, however, prompted a critique from another White American participant of that dialogue: "We say those good things [about the founding of the nation], and you think the founding fathers promoted this equality when they didn't. They didn't promote equality for women. They didn't promote equality for Blacks." Critiques of different aspects of American national myths also appeared in other dialogues. In HC3, an African American woman said that "being an American would be to understand what being bipolar is, because from the very beginning of elementary school, I learned to pledge allegiance to a flag and sing the national anthem, and yet, so many things were denied to me. . . . The biggest lie that our nation has ever told . . . was that all people are created equal." Two Latino participants of that dialogue corroborated by pointing out that people sometimes assume that Whiteness is a typical American trait (an argument also voiced in HC4 by an African participant). Overall, there was no substantial evidence that participants of a certain race/ethnicity were more likely to embrace a specific understanding of American national identity.

Lastly, in the dialogue segment on similarities and differences, several participants (two in HC1, three in HC4, two in HC5, two in HC6, and two in HC7) discussed the diversity and, in some cases, tensions that exist within the immigrant population (even within the Latino population). For instance, in HC4, a White American woman pointed out that "when we did the survey [in our multicultural congregation], we put Latinx [as an option for respondents to identify themselves] [but we learned that] people identify with the country they're from, Mexico, or Guatemala, or El Salvador." In HC7, after a Latina participant born in El Salvador complained about being bullied at school by Latino students born in the United States, a Latino participant called attention to the difference between Latinos born abroad and U.S.-born Latinos (who have birthright citizenship): "I feel bad about . . . everything that she said, the difference between the ones that were born here and the ones that arrived as immigrants. . . . The ones that were born here have all the benefits. . . . I saw [it] when my daughter was born, she had everything." These statements suggest a nuanced discussion of similarities and differences that acknowledged differences that exist among immigrants.

## 4.3 Conclusion

Table 4.1 summarizes the main thematic and relational patterns found in the segment about similarities and differences between immigrants and U.S.-born people. The salience of agreement, perspective-giving, and perspective-taking indicates that those conversations were dialogical in the sense of being marked by mutual understanding between participants. The much lower pres-

**TABLE 4.1 THEMATIC AND RELATIONAL PATTERNS OF SEGMENT ON SIMILARITIES AND DIFFERENCES**

| Thematic Patterns | Relational Patterns | |
|---|---|---|
| Inclination to diversal cosmopolitanism, including in congregations | Agreement | Mostly through corroboration |
| Black-Brown awareness of shared marginality | | Between and within groups |
| Economic problems and family care as commonalities across groups | | Immigrants led most agreement with U.S.-born participants |
| | Perspective-giving | Mostly by immigrants |
| Recognition of immigrant disadvantages (especially of undocumented immigrants and immigrants of color) | Perspective-taking | Mostly by U.S.-born participants |
| | Domination by U.S.-born or immigrant participants (word count) | No |

ence of disagreement, however, is worrisome. Had the questions in that dialogue segment been only about similarities and common interests, the ample prevalence of agreement would have been expected, but the segment also had questions specifically about intergroup differences. This discrepancy may have been a result of a lack of diversity of opinions within some dialogues or of participants self-censoring potentially controversial opinions during the conversations. At least, the occurrences of agreement generally had strong dialogical qualities: they involved corroboration rather than mere acquiescence, happened between participants of different race/ethnicity, and were not marked by domination by members of high-power groups.

The dialogue questions about participants feeling like outsiders, their reasons for moving, and the problems they had experienced in the United States elicited much perspective-giving and perspective-taking, with both processes often happening in a single utterance. The relative concentration of perspective-giving among immigrant participants and of perspective-taking among U.S.-born participants indicates an equitable conversation centered on the experiences of immigrants, which is in line with theoretical expectations about diversity-focused dialogues. As stated in Chapter 2, diversity-oriented dialogues that offer opportunities for members of historically marginalized groups to voice their perspectives can lead members of high-power groups to acknowledge their privilege and engage in social justice work along with members of historically marginalized groups. This acknowledgment was present in the dialogue segment on similarities and differences. The consideration of similarities and differences, which makes the LRJC dialogues diversal rather than diversity-focused, could have amplified the potential of the dialogues to generate intergroup solidarity by developing awareness of shared interests on top of a realization of privileges. Yet, solidarity was far from being a salient relational process—and to the extent that it was present in that dialogue segment, it happened between Latino and African American participants.

Throughout the dialogue segment on similarities and differences, participants articulated ideas and reported observations aligned with cosmopolitanism, especially of the diversal variety. Universalist cosmopolitanism was primarily expressed by White American participants. As stated in Chapter 2, high-power members—White American participants, in this case—tend to identify as individuals rather than as group members and subscribe to colorblind ideologies (Nagda et al. 2012), which is consistent with universalist cosmopolitanism. Particularist cosmopolitanism was less prevalent in the conversations about similarities and differences, suggesting that most participants did not see immigrant groups and U.S.-born people as hermetic categories. In some exchanges, participants deconstructed those categories, pointing out the diversity within the immigrant population and exploring multiple ways of defining American nationhood.

Regarding similarities, several participants saw poverty as a common problem both for immigrants and for U.S.-born people. Many U.S.-born participants empathized with immigrants' economic and family reasons to move, drawing parallels with their family histories. Furthermore, most participants had experienced churches as cosmopolitan spaces of welcome, though not always with the promotion of intergroup relations (as in the case of ethnic churches). While the search for better economic opportunities and caring for the family could have been grounds for the emergence of broad intergroup solidarity during the dialogues, this relational process happened largely between African American participants and immigrant participants around their experiences of marginalization in U.S. society.

In terms of differences, there was a clear contrast between the outsider experiences of White American participants (which tended to be temporary and superficial) and those of African American and immigrant participants (which tended to be recurrent and deep). Questions about differences also opened the way for identifying disadvantages that immigrants experience in comparison not only to White Americans but to U.S.-born people in general. The main disadvantages were associated with the linguistic and legal barriers that unnaturalized immigrants face with regard to having access to resources and opportunities and to having protection under the law. As part of this discussion, many participants—including several U.S.-born participants—acknowledged the privilege that comes with being born in the United States. Although poverty was seen as a problem common both to immigrants and to U.S.-born people, participants also saw the economy as a dividing issue because of the competition for jobs and public resources. In line with theoretical expectations about intergroup dialogue on differences, the exchanges between participants surfaced inequalities that exist between immigrants and U.S.-born people, between different immigrant groups (immigrants of color vs. White immigrants, documented vs. undocumented immigrants), and between U.S.-born people (Black vs. White, poor Whites vs. rich Whites).

Interestingly, when participants discussed the problems that immigrants face, they often understood those problems in relational ways, that is, as problems integral to the relations between immigrants and U.S.-born people (such as the discrimination against immigrants, or U.S.-born people's perception of immigrants as their economic competitors). For the most part, participants did not explain the problems that immigrants face as a result of supposedly inherent attributes of immigrants. The one exception was the need for more English-language proficiency and greater knowledge of American culture and laws among immigrants, which participants generally understood as an attribute inherent to the immigrant condition. However, even in regard to language, immigrant participants were able to give perspective on being discriminated against because of their accents and not having time to take English classes because of burdensome work and family care responsibilities.

Altogether, this chapter's findings point to a process of diversal cosmopolitanization during the dialogues, through which people of different racial/ethnic groups developed mutual understanding, empathy, and, to a lesser extent, solidarity across differences while heeding the singularity of each group's experiences and power asymmetries that exist between them. Congregation dialogues on similarities and differences between immigrants and U.S.-born people seem to have the potential to unleash a diversal variety of Christian cosmopolitanism.

# 5

## Envisioning Collaboration with Immigrants

In national democracies and local communities experiencing growing diversity, tolerance between diverse people is insufficient to improve living conditions. Diverse people should be able to collaborate to solve collective problems and pursue common interests. One of the main goals of the Latino Racial Justice Circle (LRJC) dialogue program is to promote collaboration between immigrants and U.S.-born people. A set of dialogue questions guided participants in envisioning collaboration across national background differences. In the first session of the dialogues, I asked participants what helped (or could have helped) them feel more included in situations where they felt like outsiders. I also asked them to recall positive interactions between immigrants and U.S.-born people. In the last session, they returned to the topic of positive intergroup relations but with a forward-looking perspective. To help them conceive a vision for the future of immigrant-native relations, I asked what kinds of things we would see, hear, or feel in our communities if those relations were excellent. We followed up with a recollection of local efforts already underway that could contribute to making that vision a reality and the identification of one issue on which immigrants and U.S.-born participants could collaborate. In the end, participants discussed specific and concrete actions they would take together on that chosen issue after the dialogue. In this chapter, I analyze those conversations to understand how participants interacted while envisioning the future and to comprehend the substance of their visions. I also examine the collaborative actions they pursued in the aftermath.

## 5.1 Participant Interactions

From a relational perspective, participants engaged mainly in agreement, per-spective-giving across differences, and curiosity across differences in the seg-ment on envisioning collaboration. Agreement happened across all dialogues, which was expected because this dialogue segment focused on participants' collaborating. This relational process was especially pronounced in HC1, HC2, and HC4 and comparatively sparse in HC3, HC5, and HC7, which does not indicate a clear variation according to the demographic makeup of the dialogues. To illustrate, HC1, HC2, and HC4 were held in Catholic con-gregations, but so was HC7. Agreement happened between participants of different racial/ethnic identities and between participants of the same racial/ethnic identity, but more often between participants of different racial/eth-nic identities (about two-thirds of the instances of agreement), which indi-cates mutual understanding across differences. Of the thirty-eight instances of agreement, seventeen (45%) were between immigrant and U.S.-born par-ticipants, as they developed shared understandings about specific topics. De-spite being only 43% of the speakers, immigrants led most of the instances of agreement with U.S.-born participants (65%) by making original state-ments that U.S.-born participants followed or elaborated on.

Of the thirty-eight dialogue passages coded as occurrences of agreement, twenty-three (60%) were cases of corroboration, in which a participant added logical reasoning or evidence to support what another participant had pre-viously said. This suggests that most participants were not simply acquiescing to what others were saying. Only two of the thirty-eight instances of agree-ment were likely instances of domination, in which a participant belonging to a historically marginalized group expressed agreement with a participant belonging to a historically dominant group without articulating a corrobo-rating logic or evidence. In these two passages, an immigrant participant sim-ply acquiesced to what a U.S.-born participant had said.

In HC2, an interesting exchange between two Latinas and a White Amer-ican man did not consist of a participant from a marginalized group acquiesc-ing to something a participant from a dominant group said but could be an instance of implicit domination. In Chapter 4, I discussed a previous instance of possible implicit domination that involved one of those two Latina par-ticipants. The new exchange happened after a White American man had ex-pressed several conservative positions, including arguing that the rule of law is central to American identity. The exchange started with one of the Latina participants saying, "When you go to [another person's] house, you try to adapt to the people living in there. If [we] are immigrants to another country, we try in many ways to adapt to the culture, the rule, and many things." The other Latina participant agreed: "I think that, as an immigrant, we should respect the rules that America has. This way, the other people are going to respect us. . . . For example, with my husband, . . . we are trying to follow all the rules that America requires. This is how the other Americans are going to accept us." Shortly after, the White American man praised them for such attitude: "I'm listening to these lovely women speak, and I'm very touched by their telling of what they see their responsibilities as. But natives also have the responsibility to accept, to be understanding and compassionate to people who are coming here." So even in what could have been an instance of implicit domination, the exchange was not quite asymmetric as the man concluded by saying that not only immigrants but also U.S.-born people have a responsibility over immigrant integration.

Perspective-giving across differences was also a very common relational process, especially in response to the question about positive interactions between immigrants and U.S.-born people, which elicited personal stories. Perspective-giving happened in all dialogues, but mostly in HC3, HC5, and HC7, and the least in the other dialogues, which does not indicate a clear pattern in terms of the demographic makeup of the dialogues. HC3, HC5, and HC7 have very different demographic profiles. What about variation according to individual participant identity? Immigrants were largely overrepresented in occurrences of perspective-giving. Of the thirty-five instances of perspective-giving in segments on envisioning collaboration, 74% were by immigrant participants (Latino, African, and Asian). While immigrants tended to give perspective on integration into U.S. society (acculturation, navigation of cultural differences), U.S.-born participants tended to share stories of positive experiences of contact with people of another national background, in or outside of the United States.

Curiosity across differences was much less frequent than agreement or perspective-giving, but it passed the threshold set in this study to be considered a top relational process. Neither was it as widespread as those two relational processes, happening only in HC1, HC2, and HC3. All examples of curiosity across differences consisted of U.S.-born participants (African Americans and White Americans) wanting to better understand immigrants. As an illustration, in HC1 an African American woman asked a Latina participant to elaborate on why she said she did not feel like she belonged in her current neighborhood. In HC2, a White American man asked the Latino participants if "people from Latin American countries [are] concerned to be a separate race." This finding suggests not only a dialogical pattern of communication focused on mutual learning but also an equitable pattern of communication in which dominant participants (in terms of nationality) made room for immigrant participants.

In a conversation where participants discuss alternative proposals for future collaboration, one could expect interactive critical thinking to be a salient relational process. Although it did not turn out to be a top relational process in this segment of the dialogues, it was common. Interactive critical thinking happened across all dialogues as participants spent a lot of time discussing the pros and cons of proposals for collaborative action, refining them along the way. This process was most prominent in HC1, HC5, and HC6 and, to the same extent, least prevalent in the remaining dialogues, which does not indicate a clear pattern regarding the demographic makeup of the dialogues. There is a wide variation in demographic features across HC1, HC5, and HC6. Almost all occurrences of interactive critical thinking were among participants of different racial/ethnic identities, with various combinations.

Disagreement was rare but happened in HC1, HC2, HC4, and HC5. The total number of exchanges was so low (six) that it would be unwise to try to draw any patterns from their distribution across the dialogues. In HC1, an African American man disagreed with an African American woman over whether the people or political leaders had more responsibility for improving political representation. In HC2, a White American man said that Mexican people "have a bad reputation for being . . . not highly motivated, not highly educated, whereas people from Central America are the opposite." A Latina participant, one of the women who earlier had seemed to try to please that man by stating support for the rule of law and American customs, agreed with the statement about Mexicans: "The attitude, right, the attitude [of Mexicans]." She was Central American but could have been offended by such a generalization about a whole Latin American nationality. It was two other White American men who then pushed back against the generalization: "We need to be very careful not to broad-brush," one said. "I was stationed at a parish . . . 90% of them were Mexican . . . they were working their asses off to send money back to their moms," said the other. The White American man who had called Mexicans lazy finally admitted his mistake, saying, "I could not agree with you more." As the exchange shifted, so did the opinion of the Latina participant, who then said, "I think there are bad people everywhere. . . . Every country has bad people and good people."

In HC4, an African woman proposed organizing a new program for youth of the congregation outside of religious settings, but a White American woman disagreed, stating a preference for taking advantage of "an opportunity right here in what we are [already] doing [in the congregation]." In HC5, two Latino participants who had spoken from a racial justice perspective disagreed a couple of times with an African participant who had expressed conservative positions on racism. In one instance, a Latino said that White Americans are "concerned about losing their privilege" and spoke of "White supremacy," which the African man challenged by claiming that immigrants often show off their material gains, provoking jealousy, and that long-standing residents' concern with demographic change in a neighborhood is a "natural human emotion." Later, a Latina said that White Americans in her community claim to be "all social justice" but do not show up to talk about immigrants' "really difficult situations," to which the African man responded by shifting the blame onto immigrants: "immigrants of all communities do not reach out enough" and isolate in ethnic churches. Although disagreement was infrequent, the fact that it happened in various dialogues, among various types of participants, and over various topics suggests that this segment of the dialogues allowed for argument between participants (but never of the vitriolic kind). In the next section, I analyze the key themes of this segment of the dialogue and point out how the aforementioned relational processes were associated with them.

## 5.2 Conversation Themes

While talking about positive immigrant-native relations and future collaboration, participants often shared stories, feelings, or ideas consistent with cosmopolitanism. This happened in all dialogues, but to the most extent in HC1, HC4, and HC5, and to the least extent in HC3 (where it happened only once). This distribution does not suggest a pattern in terms of the demographic makeup of the dialogues. For instance, no demographic feature is unique to HC3, except for the combination of all of its demographic features, which, however, I have no theoretical reason to connect with the salience of cosmopolitan thinking. There was no significant variation in the articulation of cosmopolitan stories, feelings, or ideas according to individual participant race/ethnicity, except for African participants, who accounted for only 4% of speakers in this dialogue segment but made 22% of the statements categorized as aligned with cosmopolitanism. However, given the very small absolute number of African participants (only three in this dialogue segment), we cannot make plausible claims connecting their overrepresentation in cosmopolitan statements with their race/ethnicity.

In most dialogues (HC1, HC2, HC3, HC5, and HC7), various participants mentioned schools as sites where positive intergroup experiences had taken place, including intergroup friendships, events that featured immigrants and their culture, and student clubs that represented minority students. In HC1, HC2, HC3, and HC4, participants of various racial/ethnic identities centered youth in visions of future positive intergroup relations, and some stressed the need to prepare youth for that future through youth-focused initiatives for understanding and collaboration across differences. Statements on preparing youth for the future often involved suggestions of working with schools (including religiously affiliated schools) or revising church youth programs (such as youth preparation for sacraments, youth choir, or youth Bible study) to make them more intercultural. Various participants in HC1, HC2, HC3,

HC5, and HC6 discussed neighborhoods as sites of positive intergroup experiences. Most of these participants were Latino (who accounted for only 34% of speakers in this dialogue segment but made 56% of the statements about neighborhoods as spaces of intergroup contact). Most of the positive intergroup experiences they reported were intergroup contact during cultural celebrations open to the community. A few participants, however, did mention people's negative reactions to demographic changes in neighborhoods, including segregation laws, redlining practices, and "people start[ing] to be angry" after "you have a community that is always peaceful and suddenly people start moving into that community" (African participant in HC5).

Stories, feelings, and ideas with a cosmopolitan orientation were also common in statements about faith communities. Talk about faith communities happened in all dialogues in the segment on envisioning collaboration, probably because the dialogues were held in congregations and these were obvious sites for future collaboration. Several participants of various racial/ethnic identities and across the dialogues saw faith communities performing a cosmopolitan role—for instance, through supporting missions in other parts of the world; by providing a religious common ground between diverse people; through service with immigrants; or by connecting newcomers to long-standing residents in worship, service, or friendships. However, several participants across the dialogues also discussed limitations to the cosmopolitan role of faith communities or ways in which faith communities have played an anticosmopolitan role. Two participants of HC4, three participants of HC5, and one participant of HC6 shared stories of racial/ethnic discrimination in faith communities. Most of them were immigrants, except for one African American woman and one White American man. An African American woman in HC1 criticized top religious leaders for establishing separate Black and Hispanic ministries that, in her view, further segregate minority people. Another African American woman in HC1 wondered why some congregations were so successful in bringing together diverse people while others were not. An African woman in HC4 said occasional resentment existed between ethnic groups in her congregation over control of sacramental processes and church operations. An African man in HC5 argued that his congregation did not care much for immigration because there were not many immigrants in that community, where most people were working-class going about their daily lives. It seems that members of historically marginalized groups (immigrants and people of color) were the most aware of anticosmopolitan events taking place in faith communities.

In terms of varieties of cosmopolitanism, it was not always possible to categorize cosmopolitan statements as universalist, particularist, or diversal because participants often did not articulate fully fleshed-out arguments. Some statements actually contained elements of more than one variety. For instance, in HC2, a woman said that the future should not be just about "accepting [other] people" but "actually supporting them and understanding them." She said we should incorporate the beliefs of other groups into our own thinking for "better changing our environment, our intervention in the economy and society." These statements suggest the participant was critical of particularist cosmopolitanism and in line with diversal cosmopolitanism, but then she said, "which creates the melting pot theory—if we're all as one, we'll work as one," a universalist statement referring to cultural assimilation and oneness.

Among the statements that did lean toward a specific variety of cosmopolitanism, most reflected particularist or diversal cosmopolitanism. Rarely in the segment on envisioning collaboration did universalist cosmopolitanism emerge. Participants leaning toward this approach usually thought that consideration of differences limited collaboration between diverse people. In HC5, an African participant said, "What I have personally found out is when people approach one another as basic human beings, barriers fall off. . . . In many churches around Baltimore . . . you can easily say 'This is a Hispanic church, this is a Nigerian church, this is a Black American church.' . . . We all claim that we belong to Christ, but we single [out] the [ethnic] name tag." In HC2, two White American participants pushed back against a suggestion for their pastorate to start a ministry of service to new Latino congregants. One said, "I don't think we should just limit it to just a specific group. I think just any newcomer [should be the beneficiary of this ministry]. . . . I think that will foster a sense of community." This was one of the few examples of cosmopolitan ideas being shared in a context of disagreement between participants.

Particularist cosmopolitanism was usually present when participants talked about past or future multicultural events where ethnic or national groups could express their cultures and celebrate cultural diversity. Some of these events happened in faith communities, being instances of particularist religious cosmopolitanism. Examples of activities carried out in these events were reading scripture or singing songs in different languages during worship services. In HC4, however, participants discussed the limits of particularist religious cosmopolitanism, such as misunderstandings between groups and the lack of a cohesive community. In the words of an African participant of that dialogue, "They [another ethnic group] seem to have their own church within our church. . . . It's as if a different church entirely."

The limits of particularist cosmopolitanism also appeared in conversations about food. Participants talked about food in HC1, HC2, HC4, HC6, and HC7. The topic was prominent in HC2, HC4, and HC7, which indicates no pattern in terms of the demographic makeup of the dialogues (for instance, those dialogues share the Catholic denomination, but so does HC1). Exchanges about food involved mainly corroboration and interactive critical thinking between participants. In HC1, HC2, HC4, HC6, and HC7, many participants expressed enthusiasm for sharing food as a multicultural collaborative activity, sometimes based on past experiences like a multicultural potluck at the workplace or a Hispanic heritage celebration at school. As a White American woman in HC2 said, "Food always brings people together," or, as another White American woman in HC4 commented, "Breaking bread together" gives a "feeling you're a part of the family." Interestingly, of the fourteen participants of those dialogues who appreciated food as a possible facilitator of intergroup relations, 44% were White Americans and only 36% were immigrants but immigrants made up 43% of speakers. This apparent asymmetry in interest may result from immigrant participants thinking that their food is just the food they eat, while for U.S.-born participants, immigrant food is "ethnic" or "exotic" and, therefore, interesting. Also, while immigrants might appreciate an opportunity to share their food culture (and a few statements from different dialogues did suggest that), they might be more appreciative of U.S.-born people listening to them give perspective on other things. In HC6, a Latina participant said it eloquently: "I know that we want to celebrate our culture and share it with everyone, but we also need space for honest conversations. So [the collaboration between participants] could be a dinner . . . and you give a conversation topic that is personal to people . . . so the topic is not just of my culture, but of everyone . . . and we will try to understand each other. . . . It would be a neutral space in the sense that there would not be pressure on someone [an immigrant] to come teach something, neither of someone [a U.S.-born person] that would receive something in a fetishized way. There is a way to present your culture in a way that is not fetishized."

Participants who articulated diversal cosmopolitanism went beyond an appreciation of cultural diversity to advocate for intercultural connections. They emphasized interaction, mutual influence, and giving and receiving between groups. For example, a Latino man in HC6 complimented a local celebration of *Día de los Muertos* for bringing together the "people who have those traditions and the people who were open to learning about them, that are sharing and appreciating. They are people trying to unite people, and they do it well." A White American participant of HC7 said that the collaborative action they were planning should "be something mutual. . . . We, the Americans, have some to offer, but we also need a lot to receive. . . . It has to be back and forth." These two participants were pointing out the importance of cultural diffusion, of elements of one culture migrating into another.

In diversal cosmopolitan statements, group identities were seen not as mutually exclusive but as permeable and overlapping. In HC6, a Latina participant said she tries to instill a binational identity in her U.S.-born daughters: "Love your country but also love mine. Speak English among yourselves, but with me, speak in Spanish." In the same dialogue, a White American participant referred to a parade that used to happen decades past in the neighborhood. The annual event was called "I am an American" and would have immigrant communities marching on a central avenue to celebrate "their American identity but also . . . their own identity as immigrants." In a similar vein, a White American participant of HC7 described a simultaneous experience of difference and sameness while traveling to Puerto Rico: "They wanted to know more—in my case, Irish-Catholic born in America—about different traditions that we had, so it was a nice sharing of traditions and culture . . . but I felt very embraced also, I think, because of the religious aspect, being Catholic and the group [that I was interacting with] was part of the Catholic community in Puerto Rico."

Preference for religious diversal cosmopolitanism appeared prominently in HC4 as participants discussed how ethnically siloed their church had been and how their church programs could be more intentional in promoting cross-cultural relationships. For several years, the congregation had celebrated Diversity Day, when congregants of different ethnic and national identities shared their culture through food and dance in a large picnic area adjacent to the main church building. Dialogue participants liked the event but thought it reproduced ethnic silos in the congregation. As one of them remarked, "In terms of Diversity Day, I think . . . we do a lot of good things in that [event], but I do think . . . we need to look at diversity and how to make it more intercultural versus being multicultural, and I think we could be more intentional about that in the event itself."

Three other themes were salient in these conversations but did not fit neatly into any variety of cosmopolitanism: language; exploitation, abuse, or discrimination of historically marginalized people; and political action (from the most salient to the least salient). Language was a prominent topic in the segment on envisioning collaboration in five of the seven dialogues (HC1, HC3, HC4, HC6, HC7). The topic was most prevalent in HC1, HC3, and HC7 and least prevalent in HC2 and HC5, which does not point to a clear pattern regarding the demographic makeup of the dialogues. To illustrate, HC2 and HC5 share a predominance of conservative-leaning participants, but so does HC7, which showed one of the highest incidences of statements on language. What about variation according to individual participant identity? The Latino proportion of statements on language was very close to their proportion among speakers in this dialogue segment (33% vs. 34%). In contrast, White Americans were underrepresented in conversations about language (20% vs. 37%), African Americans were overrepresented (36% vs. 18%), and Africans were also overrepresented (11% vs. 4%). It is not clear why. It does not seem to be a matter of nationality, because Latino participants (who, like Africans, were immigrants) spoke about language in proportion to their numbers among speakers, and White Americans (who, like African Americans, were U.S. nationals) spoke less about language than their numbers about speakers would suggest. The statements about language by African American and African participants were usually about language in the context of their congregations, such as the need to translate church bulletins to languages other than English, a church choir's habit of singing in different languages, and the idea of having Hispanic and U.S.-born congregants teach Spanish and English to each other.

In response to the question about positive interactions between immigrants and U.S.-born people in the past, some participants—of various racial/ethnic identities—gave perspective with stories of positive encounters with language differences. For instance, in HC6, a Latina said, "When I arrived [in this neighborhood] years ago, almost no one would speak in Spanish. . . . I always tell my clients, 'I am sorry for my bad English,' and some of them have replied to me, 'Forgive me for not learning Spanish,' so that makes me feel like we are on the same level." In HC4, an African American man recalled visiting friends in Puerto Rico: "They would take the time to actually speak to me in English, and they would tell me what it meant in Spanish."

In four dialogues (HC2, HC3, HC4, HC7), various participants mentioned the successful navigation of language differences as part of cosmopolitan experiences in faith communities. For instance, in HC7, a Latina and a White American woman talked about language learning groups that had emerged in congregations they had belonged to. In HC4, an African woman mentioned scripture reading in different languages at worship service, and another African woman said the children in the church choir liked to sing in different languages. In that same dialogue, however, the first woman complimented the existence of bilingual (English-Spanish) service but acknowledged that many congregants were confused by the switching between languages, and a White American woman then pointed out that the bilingual service had the lowest attendance. While thinking critically in deliberations about future collaboration, participants of a majority of dialogues (HC1, HC3, HC4, HC7) explicitly considered how language differences could be navigated, for instance, through the translation of informational materials to foreign languages (HC1) and the inclusion of language learning in a proposed intercultural cooking workshop (HC7).

Exploitation, abuse, or discrimination of historically marginalized groups appeared in five of the seven dialogues (HC1, HC2, HC5, HC6, HC7). This topic was especially covered in HC1 and HC5. In HC1, most statements about exploitation, abuse, or discrimination referred to marginalized groups generically or to racism against African Americans. In HC5, most of those statements referred specifically to the marginalization of immigrants. This is consistent with the large proportion of African American participants in HC1 and the large proportion of immigrant participants in HC5. However, HC3—like HC1—had many African American participants, but racism was not a prominent topic in the segment on envisioning collaboration. Regarding individual participant identity, Latino and African participants were likelier to speak about the topic than White American and African American participants. Latino participants were 34% of speakers in the dialogue segment on envisioning collaboration but made 44% of statements about exploitation, discrimination, or abuse of historically marginalized groups. African participants accounted for only 4% of speakers but made 19% of statements about the topic. Immigrant participants (Latino and African) accounted for 63% of statements about exploitation, discrimination, or abuse of historically marginalized groups while being only 43% of speakers. In contrast, White Americans were 37% of participants but made only 22% of statements about the topic. African Americans' participation in exchanges about exploitation, discrimination, or abuse of historically marginalized groups was proportional to their numbers among speakers (15% of statements vs. 18% of participants). An examination of the corresponding transcripts shows that African and Latino participants often gave perspective to others based on personal experiences of discrimination in neighborhoods, churches, schools, and other spaces. Such statements were usually followed by corroboration by other participants. In HC5, an African participant shared the story of representing as a realtor a Latino person who wanted to purchase a home "in a particular area" but faced discrimination from a home seller. This led to a Latina participant talking about how Latino immigrants are mistreated by landlords who, now and then, say, "If you don't do 'this,' then I will call ICE [U.S. Immigration and Customs Enforcement] on you." One Latino participant in HC5 and two Latina participants in HC7 explicitly framed the discrimination against Latino immigrants as a matter of racism. As one of them said, "When I was going to the hospital for my [cancer] treatments . . . there was a White guy. He was a racist. . . . [He said] 'What are you doing here? Go back to your country!'" (Latina participant in HC7).

Interestingly, in HC2, it was White American participants who talked about the exploitation of immigrants. A White American male said that Latino immigrants often work in physically demanding jobs and are abused by employers who pay them "under the table." A White American woman agreed, saying that when workers are paid under the table, they are usually paid below "what they should be getting paid," to which another White American male said, "The people that hire them take advantage of them." Yet another White American woman in the same dialogue corroborated those ideas by talking about hiring Hispanic moving workers who were the "most polite, efficient and friendly." Three of these four White American participants had expressed conservative leanings throughout the dialogue but recognized the exploitation suffered by Latino immigrants who, they stressed, were hardworking people. In the words of one of them, "We [and the Hispanics] share a work ethic. And this sort of ties in somewhat to what you're saying about individual responsibility. . . . I can identify with them because we both know what it is to go out and earn a living, as opposed to other options of finding income. . . . [You] always hear that 'Oh, you know, . . . they're going to take our jobs' or that, you know, it's okay to have illegal immigration because they're just going to pick the vegetables and [do] stuff that we don't want to do. . . . The bottom line is I find that there's something in the Hispanic spirit that's very hardworking, and I can identify with that." This participant's statement illustrates an interesting (yet politically overlooked) common ground between conservative values (work ethic, individual responsibility) and the Latinos' reputation for being hardworking, to the point that the participant was willing to set aside concerns about illegal immigration and immigrants taking jobs from others.

While envisioning collaboration between immigrants and U.S.-born people, participants discussed political action in four of the seven dialogues (HC1, where such discussions were largely concentrated, and HC2, HC4, and HC5), which does not indicate a clear pattern regarding dialogue demographic makeup. One feature of HC1 that could explain a high incidence of talk on political action is the combination of mostly African American and Latino participants with a high predominance of liberal-leaning participants. African American and Latino participants tended to connect their experiences of marginalization in U.S. society throughout the dialogues and even to express solidarity toward each other. In the HC1 segment on envisioning collaboration, for instance, an African American woman subsumed the discrimination that African Americans and Latinos experience in neighborhoods under the frame of White supremacy: "The White man has always felt superior to anyone—not just African Americans, but anyone of any other nationality other than 100% White." Add the commonality of a liberal orientation among participants to that intergroup awareness of shared marginalization and you might have a strong potential for joint political action. However, that demographic profile was also present in HC3, where there was no talk of political action.

African American participants talked relatively the most about political action (accounting for 35% of those statements while being only 18% of speakers). White Americans talked in close proportion to their numbers among dialogue participants (accounting for 42% of those statements while being 37% of speakers). Latinos were slightly underrepresented in conversations about political action (accounting for 23% of those statements while being 34% of speakers). Examining the transcripts, it is not clear that the overparticipation of African Americans in the talk about political action is meaningful rather than random. It is largely due to extended exchanges on this topic in HC1 (which I discuss briefly in Section 5.3, Collaborative Actions). African American participants in other dialogues (such as HC3, which included a historically African American congregation) did not discuss political action. Participants of other racial/ethnic identities varied widely in how they approached the topic. In HC2, two White American men who had expressed conservative ideas throughout the dialogue criticized a regional immigrant advocacy organization for engaging in public demonstrations and identity politics, which they considered "counterproductive," and for making other people feel that the organization was a threat. That same organization was praised by a Latina participant in HC1 and by a White American man in HC4 for bringing immigrants and U.S.-born people together in public demonstrations, canvassing for electoral campaigns, and immigration court hearings. In HC5, a Latina participant called for U.S.-born people to stand in solidarity with immigrants because "immigrants don't have . . . power to change laws, but the people we want to do things with here, to collaborate with, many of them might have power . . . for example, to go and vote." In HC1, five participants (African American and Latino) emphasized collaborative political action, including action from within congregations, but, as I discuss in Section 5.3, Collaborative Actions, neither that dialogue nor others resulted in real political collaboration between participants.

## 5.3 Collaborative Actions

To study whether and how participants engaged in collaboration after the dialogues, I participated in those follow-up activities, kept track of the participating congregations on social media, or contacted participants afterward. For each dialogue, I discuss participants' collaboration plans and the collaborative projects they undertook.

In HC1, participants proposed two follow-up actions: (1) an "Immigration 101" talk by a cochair of LRJC at the host congregation to educate parishioners about the U.S. immigration system; and (2) the cross-marketing of events by LRJC and the congregation, such as the LRJC annual community fun day and the annual health and wellness fair of the congregation. Unfortunately, only the cross-marketing of events took place and not in a sustained manner.

In HC2, participants proposed hosting a multicultural potluck in the hall of one of their churches in the month after the dialogue. The pastor of the participating congregations liked the idea because it would give congregants who had not participated in the dialogue an opportunity to connect across cultural differences. Attendees would bring traditional food of their culture and whatever informational materials they would like to place next to it at the buffet, such as a flag or photograph of the home country. Since the pastor had coincidently served previously as pastor of the congregation that participated in HC1, members of that congregation were also invited to the potluck.

When HC2 participants were still discussing the plan for the potluck, they were hesitant to volunteer to help organize the event, which illustrates the difficulties in moving from conversation to action. In addition, there was the risk that those attending the event would engage with each other only at a superficial level, talking about how delicious the different dishes tasted but not really expanding the understanding of each other or building rapport on a deeper level. To minimize this risk, I brought to the potluck (in addition to some Brazilian food) an immigration trivia quiz that contained questions on politically controversial (and often misunderstood) topics, such as "What is the number of undocumented immigrants in the United States?" or "Who was the last president to give an amnesty to undocumented immigrants?" This was an instance in which my positionality (my interest in participants having exchanges that could expand their knowledge and cultural horizons) made a difference in the course of events.

The potluck happened as planned. We started the potluck with a prayer led by the hosting congregation's pastor. A few members of the congregation of HC1 attended the event, demonstrating that at least some participants of that dialogue were genuinely interested in follow-up collaboration. However, none of the most conservative participants of the second dialogue (all White Americans) attended the event. Still, in a city as racially segregated as Baltimore, an event bringing together a Latino congregation, two suburban White American congregations, and an African American congregation was quite a unique accomplishment.

HC3 happened online, at the height of the COVID-19 pandemic, before vaccines were available, which limited the kind of follow-up collaboration participants could consider. The pastor of one of the participating congregations (a historically African American Methodist church) had expressed appreciation for the dialogue with the other congregation (a Latino Methodist church). She said this kind of intercongregational work "has been one of my prayers" and that she had not "been successful getting with a White congregation which is within a two-mile radius . . . nothing ever happened, so this [dialogue] is great." During the deliberation about collaborative projects, participants gravitated toward the goal of bringing African American and Latino congregants together through three initiatives: (1) a joint program for youth of both congregations, (2) an exchange program through which members of each congregation would attend worship service at the other congregation and participate through scripture reading or other liturgical tasks, and (3) a joint Bible study group. Participants then formed committees to undertake each of the projects. Almost three months after the dialogue, I met with one of the leading participants and asked him about the status of the relationship between the two congregations. He said the two communities had held a joint prayer service after the January 6, 2021, insurrection by supporters of former president Donald Trump in Washington, DC. More than a year later, on Good Friday of 2022, they hosted a joint bilingual worship service on Holy Friday at the African American congregation, which suggests that the dialogue program had sowed seeds for a long-term relationship.

HC4 also happened online during the COVID-19 pandemic, but after vaccines became widely available, so participants were able to propose in-person follow-up actions. In the last dialogue session, they decided to focus on their youth programs. Their follow-up action would be to work with leaders of the youth programs to include cross-cultural relationship-building activities in those programs. However, they ended up working on a different program. In the "Diversity Day" that followed the dialogue, they added two activities for intentional intercultural relationship-building. In one activity, congregants were encouraged to meet a new friend from another nationality or ethnicity. They were given a form on which to write the friend's name, place of birth, time in the United States, and a few other ice-breaking questions. After having the conversation and completing the form, congregants could deposit it in a box to get a free raffle ticket. Another version of the same activity was organized for children, with questions adapted to that age group. The forms were available in English and in Spanish and will be available for future Diversity Days.

In HC5, thanks to a grant received to support the dialogue program, LRJC offered a total of $300 for participants to spend on a collaborative action of their choice. None of the previous dialogues had had this opportunity. In the last session of HC5, only three participants were present. The geographical distance between both congregations (ten miles) and the COVID-19 pandemic might have discouraged participation in the program, but those three participants reasoned that the disengagement was because of a lack of interest in immigration. Realizing that most of their cocongregants had not come to the dialogue, they decided to take the dialogue to them. In a sign of commitment to the program's mission, they proposed a series of testimonials by immigrants from the participating predominantly Latino congregation to be given at a worship service of the partner and predominantly White American congregation. Their goal was to have members of both congregations experience the kind of deep intergroup contact they had enjoyed in the dialogues and to educate members of the White American congregation on immigration.

The predominantly White American church had a substantial missionary program abroad, sending workers to care for the sick and to evangelize among impoverished people. Several of their missions were in Latin American countries from which congregants of the Latino congregation had come. The committee organizing the testimonials suggested that the pastor of the White American congregation showcase the church's missions in Latin America during the service in which the testimonials would be given. This would show the congregants how the reality of the countries where they have missions is connected to people who live in Baltimore. One of the leaders of the Latino congregation invited four Latin American members from the congregation to give testimonials at the other church. They would split the $300 from the LRJC grant in compensation for their time.

The worship service with immigrant testimonials happened about a month after the last session of HC5. The predominantly White American church had its normal attendance on that day. The pastor started by showing a video featuring the work of their missionaries in three different countries. The video had been produced by the headquarters of his denomination. The countries were in Africa and Asia. The missionary work consisted primarily of converting people from other religions to Christianity. There was no mention of community service in the video, except for the case of one missionary who had taken medicines and other supplies to a remote town. The videos suggested a lot of "othering" of non-Christian people abroad on the part of church missionaries. The faith traditions of the communities they entered (some of them Muslim) were not considered valid. They were framed as people who lived "in the darkness," "unreached" by the Christian "truth." There was no acknowledgment that, in their cultures, there could already be some element of the truth. The missionaries seemed to have genuinely good intentions, willing to go through significant hardship to live in places where they could evangelize. Yet, their approach was consistent with a universalist Christian cosmopolitanism that saw the encounter between Christians and non-Christians as an opportunity for the assimilation of non-Christians into an ever-expanding Christian faith.

At the end of the worship service, the pastor talked to the congregation about the dialogue program we had experienced and presented some information about the work of their denomination in Latin America. He then invited me to open the testimonial series. In my brief opening remarks, I connected the video to the testimonials, saying that the stories of the missionaries were also stories of migration, that just like the missionaries had moved from place to place, facing obstacles and relying on God to overcome those obstacles, so had the immigrants they were about to hear from. The three immigrant testimonials were very moving, including stories of persecution by the police, violence, search for better economic opportunities, and suffering because of living away from loved ones. They also expressed gratitude to God, acceptance of God's plans for them, and gratitude for living in the United States.

Unexpectedly, one of the organizers of the testimonial series invited the African man from the predominantly White American congregation who had participated in the dialogue to give a testimonial too. He started by saying that he would share things he probably had not shared with his congregation before but he thought now was the right moment to open up. He talked about experiencing violence in his home country and about moving to the United States but facing challenges raising one of his children here. Although he appreciated the opportunities the United States had offered him, he stated that discrimination also exists in this country. He said that beneath the skin we are all the same, all human beings when we get to our "bare bones."

During the testimonials, I could tell from facial expressions that people in the audience were moved, some with tears in their eyes, applauding the testimonials or saying "Wow." As studies of the 1980s immigrant sanctuary movement have shown, immigrant narratives and testimonials have been effective mobilization tools in the repertoire of immigrant advocacy movements (Chinchilla, Hamilton, and Loucky 2009:120; Freeland 2010, 504–5). After the testimonials, we all shared in communion, and the pastor said he was happy with the activity because it illustrated how he understands the Kingdom of God: people of different languages and cultures united in Christ. Right before I departed, the leader of the Latino congregation who had recruited the immigrants to give the testimonials told me that it was good for them to share their stories at the event, that it was "like therapy." As Bruneau and Saxe (2012) found, members of oppressed groups tend to enjoy giving their perspective to members of dominant groups, which, as stated in section 5.1, they did disproportionately more than U.S.-born participants across the dialogues. I felt reinvigorated by the event, realizing that the dialogue with the least attendance thus far had led to such a powerful intergroup experience.

In the last session of HC6, participants came together on the proposal of an intercultural event involving food, which would allow people to express their cultural identity, feel appreciated, socialize, and learn from others. The pastor of the participating Latino congregation had argued that culture is important but should not be "fetishized." In the pastor's view, the event should make room for open and safe conversations about topics that matter to people, such as parenting or immigration. A few participants, including the pastor of the other congregation, also pointed out that the event should be recurrent and allow for relationship-building across the two congregations. Since this dialogue happened in late October and early November, the participants planned to hold this event around holiday celebrations that were coming up. Their first collaborative event actually took a little longer to happen. In early January of the following year, the two congregations got together to celebrate the festival of the Epiphany, including Bible study and worship. In February, they held a joint food event in which a Latina member of one of the congregations, who had participated in the dialogue, taught people how to cook tamales. In the Holy Week of the same year, they hosted a joint bilingual worship service on Holy Friday at the Latino Methodist congregation. The fact that the congregations were located within a few blocks of each other and were nested in a heavily Latino neighborhood probably facilitated this sustained collaboration. LRJC had offered them $300 from grant funds to support their collaboration, but they never asked for the money.

In HC7, participants agreed that their follow-up collaboration should involve food and language learning as a way to develop the intercultural relationships that the dialogue program had started. After some hesitancy to volunteer, five participants, including members of all congregations, formed an organizing committee to flesh out an event following those guidelines: a cooking workshop that included some language learning. They used the $300 offered by LRJC toward a pilot workshop, which happened about a month after the last dialogue session. Only seven people participated in the event (four from the Latino congregation and three from the predominantly White American pastorate). During the workshop's planning, members of the organizing committee took a long time to answer each other and did not publicize the event broadly to their respective communities. Their congregations have active social media channels, but nothing was posted about the workshop, which might explain the small number of participants.

In a follow-up telephone call, a member of the organizing committee described the event to me. According to her, participants started the evening preparing the dishes and talking over easy questions like "How many children do you have?" or "What kind of work do you do?" At dessert time, the members of the Latino congregation spontaneously started talking about more sensitive topics, such as the challenges their community faces with low income, food insecurity, depression, and fragile immigration status. Most conversations happened in Spanish. Two participants from the Latino congregation invited two participants from the predominantly White American congregations for a Father's Day event that was coming up in their congregation. The participants also decided to schedule a second meeting of the cooking workshop for the next month and to act as "ambassadors" of this program in their respective communities. All this evidence points to the building of relationships on a more personal level.

Overall, leadership and attendance of collaborative work were diverse, with no signs that a particular type of person (immigrant vs. U.S.-born, clergy vs. laypeople, etc.) dominated them. In HC2, two Latinas, a White American woman, a White American priest, and I organized the multicultural potluck. Diverse people from four different congregations attended the event. In HC3, a Latino and an African American woman pastor led the collaboration. In

HC4, a diverse team of lay members who had participated in the dialogue led the revised program of their congregation's Diversity Day. In HC5, a Latina leader of one congregation did most of the planning of the immigrant testimonials held at the other congregation. I helped with the communication between them to decide on the date of the event and made brief remarks during the event. Most of the attendees were members of the predominantly White congregation, which was already the expectation and the reason for immigrants to give testimonials. In HC6, the pastors of each congregation (a White man and a Latina) led their follow-up joint programs. HC7 was an exception in the sense that a White European immigrant from a predominantly White congregation led Latino members of the other congregation who were on the committee organizing their collaboration. In four of the seven cases, pastors co-led the follow-up collaborations but only in HC6 were they the only ones to take charge. Clergy participation in the follow-up collaborations was not overbearing on the participation of laypeople.

## 5.4 Conclusion

Table 5.1 summarizes the main thematic and relational patterns found in the dialogue segment about visions and actions. The questions guiding this segment of the dialogues focused on positive intergroup experiences, common interests, and visions for future collaboration. As one would expect from conversations on such topics, participants tended to agree. Most agreement happened across differences of race/ethnicity, which indicates mutual understanding across differences. Most agreement also occurred in the form of corroboration, which, together with the significant presence of interactive critical thinking, suggests a deliberative pattern of communication (careful discussion of different alternatives and courses of action). The fact that immigrant participants led most instances of agreement suggests an equitable conversation not marked by domination by members of historically dominant social groups. Immigrants having led most exchanges of agreement is puzzling because this segment of the dialogues resembles the model of unity-focused dialogues. According to critiques of unity-focused dialogues, we could expect participants in this segment—especially the U.S.-born ones—to have minimized differences and ignored inequities between immigrants and U.S.-born people, favoring the psychological comfort of U.S.-born participants to the detriment of immigrant participants. However, not only did immigrant participants lead most exchanges of agreement across differences but also they gave perspective much more often than U.S.-born participants. This deviation from the expectations about a unity-focused dialogue segment might have happened because most of the conversations on envisioning collaboration took place after participants had talked about tensions over immigra-

**TABLE 5.1 THEMATIC AND RELATIONAL PATTERNS OF SEGMENT ON VISIONS AND ACTIONS**

| Thematic Patterns | Relational Patterns | |
|---|---|---|
| Critiques to multicultural activities in congregations for lacking intercultural depth | Agreement | Mostly through corroboration |
| Opportunities for congregants of historically marginalized groups to shape congregation life and language access policy contribute to cosmopolitan congregations | | Mostly between groups |
| Schools, neighborhoods, and congregations as key sites for intergroup relations and collaboration | | Immigrants led most agreement with U.S.-born participants |
| | Perspective-giving | Mostly by immigrants |
| | Curiosity across differences | Mostly by U.S.-born participants |
| Black-Brown awareness of shared marginality | Domination by U.S.-born or immigrant participants (word count) | No |
| Collaborative Actions | | |
| Mostly religious and cultural, not civic or political | Geographic proximity between congregations, attachment to regular congregation activities, and participant initiative and leadership skills contribute to sustainability and depth of collaboration | |

tion (mainly in the first session) and similarities/differences between immigrants and U.S.-born people (in the second session). These prior exchanges might have primed participants for a more equitable communication pattern.

Regarding thematic patterns, most participants gravitated toward particularist or diversal forms of cosmopolitanism. However, particularist cosmopolitanism was criticized by several participants in different dialogues. Conservative participants (an African man, a White American woman, and a White American man) offered universalist rebuttals to particularist organizations of religious life (ethnic congregations, in the case of the African man; a proposal for a Latino church welcome ministry, in the case of the White American woman and man). Diversal critiques of particularist approaches to cultural difference covered issues such as the fetishization of minority cultures and the ethnic siloing within multicultural congregations.

While participants emphasized schools, neighborhoods, and congregations as sites of cosmopolitan behavior and interactions, they also discussed examples of discrimination in those spaces, especially neighborhoods and congregations. This is one more sign that participants were not ignoring inequality for the sake of collaboration. Congregants of historically marginalized groups, however, were the most aware of anticosmopolitan occurrences in faith communities. In efforts to make congregations more cosmopolitan, faith leaders should therefore create regular spaces where members of those groups can share their perspectives and effectively shape congregational life. The analysis of the dialogues also indicates that congregations seeking to become cosmopolitan should have a language policy articulating a strategy for navigating linguistic diversity among congregants. In addition, youth-focused initiatives and food-centered events seem to have been popular among a broad array of participants, suggesting that cosmopolitan-minded faith leaders might have better chances of success pursuing work in those areas (with the caveat that the food-centered events risk generating a superficial form of intercultural contact). I found no clear evidence of variations in relational or thematic patterns according to the demographic makeup of dialogues, such as Catholic versus Protestant dialogues or White-Latino versus Black-Latino dialogues.

In terms of follow-up collaborations, the success was varied. Collaboration from one dialogue (HC1) was very limited in depth and duration; collaboration from three dialogues (HC2, HC5, HC7) allowed for a deepening of intergroup contact but was not sustained over time; collaboration from three dialogues (HC3, HC4, HC6) was meaningful and sustained over time. With the exception of HC1 and HC4, the collaborative projects actually undertaken were very close in nature to what participants had agreed upon during the dialogues. Only in HC2 and HC7 was there hesitance among participants to volunteer to lead follow-up collaboration. Circumstances specific to each congregation also seem to have played a role in collaboration. The congregations of HC5 were 10 miles from each other, and their collaboration consisted of a single event. The congregations of HC6 were only 0.2 miles from each other, and their collaboration was more sustained. The three most successful collaborations in terms of depth and duration (HC3, HC4, HC6) have in common an attachment to recurring congregation activities, such as annual church events and religious festivals. Collaborative initiatives were about culture, religion, or both. All of them took place in church spaces. The only collaboration with a political dimension came from HC3 in the form of a prayer service after the insurrection in the U.S. Capitol on January 6, 2021. As Livezey (2000, 20) argued, congregations often respond to change not through action in the public sphere but through service to their members. Internal cultural and religious events exemplify those services. None of the above variations in follow-up collaborative efforts are explained by the demographic makeup of the dialogues.

Clergy members acted generally as facilitators who offered legitimacy, physical space in the church, and a day in the church calendar for the collaborations. With the exception of HC6, pastors were not leaders in the execution of those projects. Financial support for collaboration from LRJC (a modest $300) did not make a difference. Participants of HC6 never asked for the money, and significant cooperation emerged between participants of other dialogues to whom LRJC was not able to offer financial support. In line with the findings of Ammerman (1997) about congregations' response to changing environments, I found that participants' initiative, commitment to the program's mission, and leadership skills were decisive. Most of the dialogues (HC1, HC2, HC5, HC7) happened because LRJC took the initiative to reach out to congregations, not because congregation leaders or members had the idea of pursuing the program. When the proposition to have a dialogue emerges from within a congregation, the likelihood of significant and sustained follow-up collaboration seems higher, as was the case with HC3, HC4, and HC6. In contrast, for the collaboration of HC2 and HC5 to occur, my participation in the planning and execution of collaborative projects was probably necessary. Overall, the LRJC dialogues seemed to have planted a seed for cosmopolitan collaboration within and between Christian congregations, but congregation members have to water the seed for it to grow. Dialogue is a prolific tool capable of generating critical thinking, mutual understanding, and collaboration plans, but on its own it cannot guarantee the execution of transformative collaboration beyond the conversations.

# 6

## CONCLUSION

The broader question driving the research for this book is how religion might play a cosmopolitan role in society, leading organizations, groups, and individuals to act as if all human beings belong to a global community in relation to which we have rights and duties. The contemporary rise of violence fueled by religious nationalism (Juergensmeyer 2010) and, more specifically, the rise of Christian nationalism across the world (Vergara 2022) have led to a public portrayal of religion as a sectarian force that undermines not only the building of a cosmopolitan world order but also national liberal democracies. But could religion make a different contribution to the public sphere? I investigated this question in the context of Christianity, focusing on deliberative dialogues about immigration in Christian congregations. How someone treats the foreigner is a litmus test of their cosmopolitan inclinations. In twenty-first-century American Christianity, talk about immigration—through sermons, lectures, panels, or group conversations between people of faith—has been integral to how congregations respond to the arrival of foreigners. I set out to research if, how, and to what extent deliberative dialogues between immigrants and U.S.-born people can turn Christian congregations into spaces of cosmopolitanization.

Faith-based efforts at building bridges across differences of nationality, race, and ethnicity should be of interest even to organizations, groups, and individuals who are not religious. Immigration has been a highly contentious political issue in the United States and many other countries, leading government and civil society organizations to engage in bridge-building efforts. According to the International Organization for Migration, the "meaningful so-cial mixing of people of different backgrounds is an increasingly important tenet of mainstream programming and policies aimed at promoting migrant inclusion and broader social cohesion at the local, national and even global levels" (International Organization for Migration 2021, iv). Could Christian congregations be a prolific space and deliberative dialogues an effective tool for "meaningful social mixing" in communities undergoing immigration?

I did not approach this question from a purely intellectual standpoint. Following the tradition of community-based research, the question emerged organically from my volunteering with a faith-based nonprofit organization based in Baltimore, Maryland—the Latino Racial Justice Circle (LRJC). I still remember how puzzled I was by the prayers they recited at the closing of their meetings, which referenced LGBTQ people, immigrants, and multicultural families in a positive light. That cosmopolitan spirit sharply contrasted with the image of right-wing nationalist Christianity that has dominated the rep-resentation of Christians in U.S. media for many years. As an organization devoted to immigrant integration with a focus on the Latino community, LRJC wanted to establish a program of dialogues about immigration in con-gregations. I offered to lead the program's creation as a community-based research project in partnership with LRJC volunteers and faith leaders.

Informed by a pilot dialogue that took place in 2018, I facilitated seven three-session dialogues involving fourteen congregations and ninety-seven congregants in the Baltimore metropolitan area between 2019 and 2022. The congregations were varied in terms of denomination, location (urban vs. sub-urban), and demographic profile. I collected data through an entry survey to characterize participants demographically, audio recordings of the dialogue sessions, and observation notes I took during the dialogues and in the col-laborative projects that participants undertook after the dialogues. The bulk of the analysis consisted of a thematic-relational analysis of the dialogue tran-scripts, which I describe in detail in Appendix A. In the analysis, I maintained a critical reflective attitude to strike a balance between, on the one hand, car-rying out a qualitative analysis that was systematic and objective and, on the other hand, respecting the complexity and uniqueness of each dialogue.

I followed a semistructured and minimalist approach to dialogue facilita-tion, asking questions from the dialogue guide, occasionally asking one or several of the participants probing questions, and enforcing ground rules. Most interventions to enforce ground rules consisted of giving participants who had signaled an intent to speak the opportunity to do so and interrupting participants who had taken too much of the time allotted to a question or who digressed. A few times, I answered a question from the dialogue guide after posing it to participants in order to clarify the meaning of the question, "break the ice," or build rapport with participants by sharing something about me. My answers were personal stories—not opinionated statements, which I actively refrained from making. At the beginning of every dialogue, I told participants I would not act as the arbiter of who was right or wrong on specific issues. Many times, I heard them saying something about immigration that I knew was inaccurate or that I disagreed with, but I stayed silent. After analyzing the dialogue transcripts, I noticed I could have done a better job preventing serial monologues (when participant after participant answers a question without establishing an explicit connection with answers previously given by other participants). I should have done more to encourage participants to engage with each other's statements and to ask each other questions. I could have asked more often, "What do others in the room think about what Participant A said about X, Y, and Z?" or "Is there anything you would like to ask each other about this topic?"

I cannot claim that my facilitation was absolutely neutral. I have implicit biases, and so do the dialogue participants. Implicit biases might have influenced whom I asked probing questions and whose utterances I limited to give others a chance to speak. These are challenges typically faced by researchers who conduct focus groups or interviews, which could have affected the relational and thematic outcomes of the dialogues. Yet, the word count analysis presented in Chapter 2 and detailed in Appendix A indicated that neither immigrant nor U.S.-born participants systematically dominated the dialogues. Domination occasionally happened by both immigrant and U.S.-born participants, depending on the dialogue session. The word count analysis found the same about clergy versus nonclergy participants: no systematic domination. Furthermore, no participant questioned my work as a facilitator during or after the dialogues. While I cannot claim that my facilitation was constant and neutral across the dialogues to the point of not affecting the outcomes, the minimalist facilitation approach, the word count analysis, and the absence of negative participant feedback indicate that my facilitation was not capricious.

## 6.1 Dialogue and Diversal Cosmopolitanism in Christian Congregations

The broadest lesson I learned from this research is that deliberative dialogues on immigration in Christian congregations that focus not only on common goals and similarities but also on differences and tensions between immigrants and U.S.-born people can promote diversal cosmopolitanism in democratic and religious life. More specifically, the LRJC dialogues can be a tool for community building and organizing in congregations diversified by immigration. In Chapter 2, I defined diversal cosmopolitanism as a philosophy that promotes an expansion of people's bonds of identity and solidarity across racial, ethnic, and national boundaries without erasing those boundaries. Avoiding the choice between universalism and particularism, diversal cosmopolitanism centers on intercultural connections and exchanges. Altogether, the findings showed that participants of different racial/ethnic groups developed mutual understanding, empathy, and, less pronouncedly, solidarity across differences while heeding the singularity of each group's experiences and power asymmetries between them.

Throughout the dialogues, participants often shared ideas or described situations that aligned with cosmopolitanism's tenets. Yet, the participants often did not elaborate their ideas and stories enough for them to be classified under a specific variety of cosmopolitanism. When participants' statements did contain an element typical of a variety of cosmopolitanism, it was usually in the form of diversal cosmopolitanism. Particularist cosmopolitanism came in at a distant second, and universalist cosmopolitanism at a distant third. This ranking should not be read as a hierarchy of participants' preferences. Most participants did articulate ideas aligned with diversal cosmopolitanism, valuing the integration of diversity and unity. However, the lower ranking of universalist cosmopolitanism in relation to particularist cosmopolitanism happened because many participant statements coded under particularist cosmopolitanism were critiques of real-life situations that embodied this variety of cosmopolitanism.

Many participants expressed dissatisfaction with communities where multiple racial/ethnic groups coexist peacefully but rarely engage with each other meaningfully, including faith communities. Although most participants tended to see churches as welcoming cosmopolitan spaces, they were aware of and critical of the lack of intergroup connections observed in some congregations. An emblematic statement of this sentiment came from a participant of HC4 who argued that one of the ethnic groups of their multiethnic congregation had, in practice, "their own church" inside the church. Many participants also criticized parochialism in religious life, expressed, for instance, in the form of mono-ethnic congregations, or congregations where a long-standing ethnic majority resists demographic change. Participants from historically marginalized groups were especially aware of discrimination within church life. Overall, participants' visions for their congregations resembled the shared parish model discussed in Chapter 2, where two or more cultural communities share a parish that gives space for each of them to sustain their language and faith traditions while providing common experiences that build connections across cultures and help the communities feel and operate like one church (Hoover 2014).

Participant exchanges about intergroup relations in congregations suggest conditions favorable for the integration of diversity and unity at churches:

(1) faith leaders with intercultural competence, (2) long-standing congregants who acknowledge privilege and make space for newcomers to shape congregation life, (3) intentional cross-cultural community building, and (4) a language policy that facilitates communication among diverse members. However, one should not infer from these findings that Christians generally prefer congregation life aligned with diversal cosmopolitanism. The prevalence of this preference among LRJC dialogue participants might have resulted (1) from participants with stronger intercultural and bridge-building attitudes having self-selected into the program and (2) from participants' exchanges during the dialogues having made them converge toward diversal cosmopolitanism (which is hard to verify in the absence of an entry assessment of their understandings about group identity and intergroup relations).

## 6.2 Interactions and Themes among Participants

The main types of interaction between participants were agreement, interactive critical thinking, perspective-giving, and perspective-taking. Most instances of agreement (68%) happened through corroboration, indicating that participants were thinking through others' statements rather than just acquiescing to them. Agreement happened largely between participants of different racial/ethnic identities, indicating that the dialogues were not marked by racial/ethnic echo chambers. In the segment about similarities and differences between immigrants and U.S.-born people and the segment about visions and actions, immigrants led most of the instances of agreement by making original statements that other participants corroborated.

Immigrant participants gave perspective much more often than U.S.-born participants.[1] Perspective-taking was a mirror image of perspective-giving: U.S.-born participants took perspective much more often than immigrant participants.[2] The combination of agreement (predominantly through corroboration and across race/ethnicity), interactive critical thinking, perspective-giving, and perspective-taking indicates dialogical and deliberative communication across differences. Moreover, although the word count analysis of dialogue transcripts indicated that neither immigrant participants nor U.S.-born participants dominated the LRJC dialogues, the leadership of immigrant participants in many instances of agreement, the relative concentration of perspective-giving among immigrants, and the relative concentration of perspective-taking among U.S.-born participants point to an equitable pattern of communication centered on the voices of immigrant participants. These findings about the relational dimension of the dialogues are consistent with the diversal religious cosmopolitanism that inspired the LRJC dialogues, which asked participants to consider not only their similarities and common goals but also their differences and tensions.

The bridge-building function of the LRJC dialogues was visible in the segment about the cultural, economic, and legal tensions that immigration may bring to communities. On the one hand, participants acknowledged or expressed the discomfort or anxiety that many U.S.-born people feel about immigration. On the other hand, they recognized the discrimination, abuse, or exploitation that immigrants suffer in the cultural, economic, and legal realms (which were among the most recurring topics across the dialogues). Immigrant participants shared many stories that illustrated their problems in those areas. HC2 offered an emblematic example of bridging the two perspectives on immigration-related tensions. After the group disagreed on illegal immigration, a conservative White American participant synthesized a compromise, saying that we have an obligation toward bona fide asylum seekers under international law and that mass deportations are inhumane, but we cannot allow people to cross the border without criteria.

The dialogue segment about similarities and differences between immigrants and U.S.-born people also involved bridging between participants. They saw poverty as a common problem for both groups. Many U.S.-born participants drew parallels between their family histories of international or internal migration and those of immigrant participants. Yet, the participants did not overlook the challenges that immigrants specifically experience in the United States in the areas of law (especially immigration law), culture (especially language), and the economy. As part of those discussions, some U.S.-born participants even acknowledged the privileges of being born in the United States (birthright citizenship, English as the first language, etc.).

While the above indicators of mutual understanding across differences and equity between immigrant and U.S.-born participants during the conversations are positive results from the perspective of the philosophy of dialogue and diversal cosmopolitanism, the relative scarcity of exchanges marked by disagreement or solidarity raises questions about the dialogical and deliberative qualities of the LRJC dialogues. I discuss both issues in the next two sections, Disagreement and Solidarity.

## Disagreement

Disagreement is not undesirable in intergroup dialogue and deliberation. While vitriol is detrimental to intergroup communication, a reasonable amount of civil disagreement suggests that participants are having open discussions, seriously considering the pros and cons of different arguments. In contrast, a preponderance of agreement could mean that some participants were not carefully considering others' comments or were refraining from making comments they thought would be controversial. Although disagreement happened in all dialogues and on various topics, it was primarily concentrated in HC2 (driven mainly by statements of conservative White American participants about illegal immigration) and in HC5 (driven mainly by comments made by a conservative African participant who argued that individual immigrants rather than society have primary responsibility for immigrant integration). This suggests that if more conservative-leaning people had participated in the dialogues, there would have been a higher incidence of disagreement. Also, we probably would have seen a higher incidence of Christian nationalist statements, which are more common among conservatives. As shown in Table A.3 in Appendix A, only about 16% of the participants identified as conservative-leaning. The lack of diversity in political ideology among participants might, therefore, be an explanation for the lack of disagreement.

The predominance of liberal-leaning participants in the LRJC dialogues is in itself a finding. It suggests that politically liberal Christians might be the most likely to carry out the cosmopolitan mission of the Church. It could also indicate the existence of a ceiling in the cosmopolitanization that deliberative dialogues on immigration can generate in U.S. Christianity, materialized in the formation of a diverse coalition of liberal White Christians and Christians of color. If deliberative dialogues on immigration tend to attract liberal members of congregations, one may be inclined to directly invite conservative congregants (or conservative-leaning congregations) to a dialogue program as a means to increase the political diversity of participants. The pastor of HC2 used this recruiting technique, resulting in a larger proportion of conservative-leaning participants compared to the other dialogues. In the faith leaders' focus group, however, there was great concern about this approach. The White American leader of a Lutheran congregation agreed that liberal Christians tend to self-select into faith-based programs oriented to social justice but was cautious about actively encouraging the participation of more conservative congregants. According to him, political diversity should be balanced with protecting immigrant participants from offensive anti-immigrant comments that conservative participants could make. In his view, the Christian call for siding with those at the margins should lead one to err on the side of protecting the most vulnerable dialogue participants (undocumented immigrants) instead of erring on the side of promoting political diversity.

In the focus group, the Latina leader of a Methodist congregation also saw a dilemma between equity and political diversity among dialogue participants. According to her, if you increase the proportion of conservative interlocutors for the sake of political diversity, you will likely increase the social desirability bias of immigrant participants, reducing the honesty of the conversations. She argued that social pressures to align with the dominant culture often lead immigrants to reproduce the "deserving immigrant narrative," which discursively constructs immigrants as holders of attributes that conservative White Americans appreciate, such as a hard work ethic and strong family values. I did observe this in HC2, as pointed out in previous chapters. Therefore, self-censoring—or changing what one says in anticipation of potential negative reactions—was probably not happening among conservative participants only. The aforementioned Latina pastor also pointed out that immigrants who have experienced traumatic events in their migration journey might ponder "How much can they [White Americans] withstand to hear?" As stated by an Afro-Caribbean pastor of a Catholic congregation in the focus group, when asked to talk about challenging past experiences, people might react by turning passive and just "going along" with the conversation. This pastor and another faith leader also asked, "How honest will these conversations be if people are not joining them spontaneously?" For all the above reasons, the name given by LRJC to its dialogue program—Honest Conversations on Immigration—should be seen as more aspirational than descriptive. Yet, the faith leaders cautioned me not to underestimate the benefits of dialogues between liberal U.S.-born people and immigrants, pointing out (1) that White American liberals are not always supportive of people of color; they have biases of their own and may arrive at an intergroup dialogue with a White savior mentality; (2) that we need bridging work not only between conservatives and liberals but also between immigrants from different countries (including Latinos from different countries); and (3) that intergroup dialogues between people from historically marginalized groups and their U.S.-born allies can be conducive to collective action for social justice, which is less likely to happen with more conservative participants (who, by definition, are interested in preserving the status quo of social hierarchies).

The religious context and content of the LRJC dialogues could also explain the large discrepancy between the incidence of agreement and the incidence of disagreement. All dialogue sessions occurred in religious spaces, such as church halls or rectory rooms, and started with participants reciting a prayer. In the creation of ground rules, participants of HC3, HC4, HC5, HC6, and HC7 reflected on how each rule might be grounded in Christian values or traditions. In all dialogues, I asked participants what their faith tradition says about immigration. Clergy was present in five of the seven dialogues. The religious dimension of the dialogues might have limited the range of behaviors and opinions shared by participants. Participants may have held back behaviors or emotions usually not expressed in the religious spaces they attend, such as verbal aggression or anger. Also, they might have self-censored opinions that they thought would not align with Christian principles or the opinion of the clergy.

Indeed, regarding religious principles associated with ground rules, most participants emphasized love, kindness, and respect for others. Exceptionally, participants mentioned values that could have made more space for disagreement, such as "Be honest in what you say" (from a participant in HC4) or "We agree to disagree" (participant in HC5). When participants discussed what the Christian faith teaches about immigration, they referred only to the pro-immigrant teachings mentioned in Chapters 1 and 2, such as the calls to welcome the stranger and love one's neighbor. No participant ever invoked biblical calls for people to be law-abiding and respectful of authority, which Christian nationalists have quoted to justify restrictive immigration policies (Burton 2018). Occasionally, participants referred to God in gratitude, to make meaning out of challenging experiences, or to justify pro-immigrant policies. Regarding the presence of clergy in the dialogues, however, evidence from the dialogues suggests that such presence was not associated with less disagreement. Comparing the dialogues where clergy were present (HC2, HC3, HC5, HC6, and HC7) with those without clergy (HC1 and HC4), I found the same average incidence of disagreement. Moreover, the quantitative content analysis presented in Chapter 2 and detailed in Appendix A did not find that clergy tended to dominate the dialogues in which they participated compared to lay participants. Future research could further investigate the effect of religious spaces, values, practices, and leaders on dialogues (including their potential incentive for nondialogical patterns of communication). This research should involve comparisons with dialogues held in secular settings.

## Solidarity

Solidarity—expressed in words during the dialogues and in follow-up collaborative actions—was the most ambitious goal of the LRJC dialogues. Participants were expected to move beyond mutual understanding toward acknowledging and acting upon a sense of mutual commitment. Yet, solidarity was not a common relational process during the dialogues. It happened primarily between African American and Latino participants, who often drew connections between their experiences as historically marginalized groups in U.S. society. While the solidarity that White American participants expressed toward immigrants was based on values (such as compassion) or on relationships they had with immigrants as friends, neighbors, or coworkers, the solidarity that African American participants expressed was based on their having lived through problems similar to those of immigrants.

One of the most remarkable patterns of the dialogues was the Black-Brown awareness of shared marginalization, which relativizes the idea stated in Chapter 1 that "the marginalized economic position of blacks" (Brown and Brown 2017, 4) makes them vulnerable to the framing of immigrants as an economic threat and therefore less likely to support expansive immigration policies. While that may be the case for low-income or conservative-leaning

African Americans, the African Americans who participated in the LRJC dialogues (predominantly liberal and college-educated) expressed strong sympathy toward immigrants. I also noted a gender dimension to Black-Brown solidarity in the dialogues. Women were much more likely than men to speak in intersectional terms, making claims with reference to the intersection of race/ethnicity and gender. The majority of those women were African American or immigrants, who at times drew parallels between their experiences. If an LRJC dialogue were held only among women of diverse racial/ethnic backgrounds, I would expect intersectional feminist solidarities to emerge. In this case, not only could the cosmopolitan potential of Christianity be unleashed but also challenges to the patriarchy that characterizes many Christian denominations could emerge.

A possible explanation for the overall modest level of solidarity I found during the dialogues is that I looked for overt expressions of solidarity by participants while analyzing the dialogues. The high level of agreement between diverse participants could be seen as indicative of an underlying solidarity between them. As an African American woman in the faith leaders' focus group pointed out, "Our histories [African American and Latino] are so much alike that we didn't have to say it [i.e., state words of solidarity], we did it by sharing our stories. We didn't use that term [solidarity], but we did it with our emotions and shared stories." A Latina faith leader concurred. A similar process might have happened among White American participants, whose instances of agreement with immigrants might have sometimes carried implicit feelings of solidarity. Moreover, while African American participants might have also felt solidarity while giving perspective ("sharing our stories"), for White American participants that probably happened more often while taking perspective from immigrants (as their life stories tended to be more different). This suggests an underestimation of the level of solidarity generated through the dialogues.

Besides the shared marginality of Latino and African American participants, the dialogues pointed to a few other issues and framings that could be the basis for multiracial intergroup solidarity and collaboration. The first issue is language, which participants of all racial/ethnic identities recognized as a major challenge for immigrants. Conservative participants tended to value immigrants being able to speak English in the public sphere, whereas liberal participants tended to view language differences as a basis for others to discriminate against immigrants and as a barrier for immigrants to access resources and opportunities. Immigrants and U.S.-born people across the political spectrum, therefore, share an interest in immigrants learning how to speak English and could collaborate in teaching English as a foreign language. As participants of HC7 mentioned, immigrants could also teach U.S.-born people to speak their homeland languages, making this collaboration a possible two-way street (and not just about making immigrants "more desirable"). Although conservative U.S.-born participants seemed to resent immigrants continuing to speak non-English languages in public spaces, they appreciated bilingualism as a condition that enriches the country and gives a person an advantage in the job market.

Economic hardship is another issue on which a broad intergroup solidarity could emerge. African American and Latino participants often spoke about discrimination in the job market, the workplace, and housing. Conservative White American participants—despite their discomfort with non-English languages, their economic anxiety, and their concern with illegal immigration—expressed appreciation for the hard work ethic of Latino immigrants and were sensitive to their overexploitation in the economy. This suggests a potential for intergroup class-based solidarity and collaboration in areas such as workforce and business development. U.S.-born participants—conservative and liberal, White and African American—also expressed sensibility for the religiosity of immigrants, the conditions in homeland countries that force migration, and immigrants' commitment to family. Faith leaders could use those framings in dialogues and elsewhere to promote solidarity with immigrants in their congregations—but with caution, in order to avoid reproducing the "deserving immigrant narrative."

In the expressions of intergroup solidarity mentioned in this section, people of different racial, ethnic, and national identities do not shed their group identities in favor of an overarching identity, which would be aligned with universalistic cosmopolitanism. However, neither were those expressions of intergroup solidarity limited to the peaceful coexistence of essentialized groups in shared social spaces, which would be aligned with particularistic cosmopolitanism. Instead, they resemble what Garcia Agustín and Jørgensen (2021) called "transversal solidarity," which emerges from below as two groups engage in open dialogue and collectively forge commonalities without excluding differences or generating a third collective identity.

## Collaborative Actions

Like the conversations between participants, their follow-up collaboration did not display a strong sense of solidarity among diverse participants. While some dialogues resulted in sustained and deep collaboration between participants and their congregations (such as recurring joint religious services), others resulted in one-time events (such as multicultural potluck). By and large, collaborative action was religious or cultural in nature rather than civic or political, despite so much of the dialogues having revolved around civic or political issues like poverty, discrimination against people of color, and immigration policy. Dialogues that started from within a congregation (with leaders or congregation members reaching out to LRJC rather than the other way around) generally had the most sustained collaborative outcomes. In the faith leaders' focus group, two participants agreed on the significance of people taking the first step toward intergroup dialogue from within congregations. According to them, that initiative suggests readiness for intergroup work and that some "inner work" might have already taken place in the minds of those individuals, a certain cosmopolitan disposition "to desire something better not just for their communities but for others as well" (Latina pastor). Ideally, clergy or lay leaders of a congregation would not only propose the idea of a deliberative dialogue on immigration but also facilitate the conversations. Having the legitimacy of insiders, they could adopt a more active role in the deliberation about collaborative actions, helping participants focus on an issue that the facilitator knows to be important for the communities involved. While I do not advise facilitators who are not community members to take a leadership role in deliberations, insider facilitators could take up that role and help participants move from conversation to deep and sustained collaboration.

In the deliberations about collaborative actions, participants often talked about engaging youth, which indicates an opportunity for intergenerational cosmopolitan engagement programs that connect congregants not only across racial, ethnic, or national divides but also across generations. These programs could include intentional and structured opportunities for two-way dialogue, storytelling, learning, and collaboration between youth and elders of congregations. Because of research ethics protocols, congregants younger than eighteen years old were not allowed to participate in the LRJC program. Their inclusion could have resulted in more successful collaboration.

Time is another condition that shaped the dialogue and postdialogue collaboration. Had the dialogues been longer than three weeks, we would likely have seen more significant shifts in mutual understanding and collaboration between participants. As a Latina pastor argued in the faith leaders' focus group, in the three weeks of dialogue "We just scratched the surface." In her view, participants need more time to understand each other's backgrounds, situate their stories in the context of oppressive social structures, and envision collaboration. Instead of a three-week dialogue program, leaders and members of Christian congregations interested in cosmopolitan work could establish a conversation club as a standing congregation or intercongregation program. The LRJC three-week dialogue could serve as the springboard for the conversation club, which later could move to topics other than immigration, building on the mutual trust and communication skills developed in the first three weeks. Yet, as pointed out by another Latina faith leader in the focus group, time is scarce. Increasing the length of the program could lead to deeper mutual understanding and more sustained collaboration, but it could also make the program too onerous for some to participate. In fact, one of the pastors told me that several of his congregants had declined an invitation to participate in the program because three days over three weeks was too much of a time commitment. People of faith interested in intergroup deliberative dialogues for action should be mindful of this trade-off.

Timing is also important. The exploration of Christian congregation conversations on immigration presented in Chapter 1 identified a steep increase in the frequency of those events during the election and administration of president Donald Trump. His promise to crack down on immigration (both legal and illegal) probably galvanized those interested in immigration affairs to organize public engagements with this issue. Those interested in organizing faith community dialogues on immigration oriented to collaborative action will probably be more successful with congregation engagement in times when immigration is prominent on the news.

## 6.3 Transferability of Findings and Future Research

Despite the quantitative procedures used to assist the thematic-relational analysis and the comparisons made across the demographic composition of the dialogues and the racial/ethnic identity of participants, the research for this book was primarily qualitative, providing a rich and contextualized understanding of Christian people's engagement with immigration. As a whole, the participants of the LRJC dialogues were not meant to form a representative sample of Christians in the United States. Therefore, one should not take specific findings of this study as lawlike statements readily generalizable to a population but instead should use them as guiding ideas transferable to other contexts where further study might extend or reformulate them.

To the extent that an intergroup dialogue is influenced by its geographical surroundings, an immediate context to which the conclusions could be transferred is the U.S. Rust Belt, the postindustrial region of the United States that stretches from the Northeast to the Midwest of the country, emblematically represented in cities like Baltimore, Pittsburgh, Cleveland, Detroit, and St. Louis. These urban areas tend to be racially bifurcated (White American and African American) and politically liberal-leaning, and to have local governments that have actively promoted immigration as a means to reverse population decline and economic decline (Filomeno 2017). I would expect deliberative dialogues between immigrants and U.S.-born people in Christian congregations of Rust Belt metropolitan areas to have outcomes similar to those of the LRJC dialogues in Baltimore. In other areas, the process and outcomes may differ significantly. By way of illustration, a deliberative dialogue on immigration held in Christian congregations in the Midwest could attract more conservative-leaning participants, leading to higher levels of dis-agreement among participants.

Studying more instances of dialogues on immigration in Christian con-gregations in the United States would expand the empirical basis against which specific findings of the present study could be assessed. Several of the find-ings discussed so far resulted from comparative analyses of thematic and rela-tional outcomes across the demographic makeup of the dialogues and across the racial/ethnic identity of individual participants. While the number of in-dividual participants (ninety-seven) was large enough to make variations in themes and relational processes visible across participants' racial/ethnic iden-tities, the number of dialogues (seven) was often too small for the compari-sons across dialogue demographic makeup to reveal clear patterns of varia-tion. For instance, the study did not find variations in dialogues according to the denomination of participating congregations. White Evangelicals are known for embracing Christian nationalism more than other Christians, but there were only two Evangelical congregations in this study, and only one was predominantly White. Future research could verify the plausibility of the conclusions beyond the LRJC dialogues conducted in Baltimore and gener-ate new insights.

Given the earlier discussion about the lack of disagreement in the LRJC dialogues and its possible connection with the low proportion of conserva-tive participants, future studies could deepen our understanding of the role of participants' political identities in deliberative dialogues on immigration in Christian congregations. Historically, Christianity has intersected with various political ideologies in the public sphere, including traditions such as Christian social democracy, Catholic social teaching, the Social Gospel, Chris-tian nationalism, Christofascism, and liberation theology. Considering the intersections of Christianity with political ideologies and the strong correla-tion of partisanship with immigration attitudes (Person-Merkowitz, Filindra, and Dyck 2016), the effects of political-ideological diversity on congregation-based deliberative dialogues on immigration deserve further investigation (without neglecting the warning from faith leaders in the focus group against favoring political diversity over equity). Moreover, considering how patriar-chal Christianity has been historically and how gender shapes immigration attitudes (Ponce 2017), future studies should further investigate the role of gender in deliberative dialogues about immigration in Christian commu-nities.

Transferring findings to locations outside of the United States would require caution. Let's consider the European context. As pointed out by Wil-liams (2020, 88), race "is to the United States what religion is in Western Eu-rope—a mark of otherness that becomes a basis for discrimination. Thus,

England, France, and Germany struggle with recent immigration through disputes over religious practice and identity (overwhelmingly Muslim), whereas race is the crucial hierarchy in America, and immigrants are evaluated based on that, rather than on their religion—hence the hostility to Mexican immigrants, even though they are Christian." The prominence of race and the racialization of religion in the United States (as seen, for instance, in the distinctiveness of White Evangelical Christianity) can limit how much solidarity a shared Christianity can generate across differences of race, ethnicity, and nationality. In the LRJC dialogues, the pronounced solidarity between Latino and African American Christians attests to how race influences the type of cosmopolitanization that Christianity can engender in the United States. However, the differences between the United States and Europe should not be overstated. Religious differences matter in the United States. As I discussed in Chapter 1, previous research shows significant differences in immigration attitudes across Abrahamic religions in the country. Racial differences matter in Europe. As Garner and Selod (2014) showed, the racialization of Muslims is associated with the rise of Islamophobia in both the United States and Europe. Investigating how deliberative dialogues on immigration play out in interfaith contexts in Europe and the United States would enrich our understanding of faith-based cosmopolitanization. Will religious differences between immigrants and native-born participants make agreement and solidarity less likely than in Christian-only dialogues? Will particularist cosmopolitanism be more pronounced than diversal cosmopolitanism in dialogues between immigrants and native-born people with an interfaith dimension? Will discrimination based on race be a less prominent topic?

One could also explore transferring findings from the present study to secular civic talks: deliberative dialogues open to the public that happen in nonreligious spaces. In Chapter 2, I mention several civic organizations that have promoted dialogues about immigration. It would be interesting to investigate how findings from the present study might transfer to those dialogues, especially in the spaces that participants of the LRJC dialogues so often mentioned as critical for intergroup relations: schools, neighborhoods, and workplaces. This would allow for comparisons with faith-based dialogues on immigration to investigate the potential effects of religious spaces, leaders, practices, and beliefs on those conversations. Lastly, some insights from the study of LRJC dialogues could inform the study and practice of deliberative dialogues in Christian congregations about other presently contentious topics, such as same-sex relationships, climate change, and the role of women in the church.

In any of the extensions of this study, I would expect one broad finding to be well transferable: dialogues that consider not only collaboration/similarity but also conflict/difference are more productive and equitable than dialogues that downplay conflict and difference. For instance, in the concluding section of an edited volume on "congregations talking about homosexuality," Bossart makes a case for "constructive conflict" over "harmonious dishonesty" (Bossart 1998, 103). Other findings, such as regarding the probability that participants will transition from dialogue to collective action, are more likely to vary according to the space and topic of the conversation.

## 6.4 A Christian Call for Deliberative Dialogues on Immigration

This final chapter has discussed the cosmopolitan possibilities, outcomes, and limitations of deliberative dialogues on immigration in Christian congregations based on the LRJC experience. In several dialogues, various participants expressed appreciation for the opportunity to engage in small-group dialogue between immigrants and U.S.-born people. They saw those dialogues as a stepping stone toward social harmony, a rare opportunity for different groups to realize common interests, a means for building connections deeper than the ones achieved through casual encounters in the public sphere, and an opportunity to learn about other people's experiences. As a way of conclusion, I make a call for clergy and lay members of Christian congregations to engage in intentional conversations about immigration. This call includes practical advice on congregation engagement and a religious rationale for those interested in this kind of cosmopolitan enterprise.

### Congregation Engagement

In the LRJC experience, the most decisive factor in congregation engagement was the attitude and commitment of the pastors toward the mission of the dialogue program. Pastors give legitimacy to the program and are the best recruiters. Yet, they are often overwhelmed with responsibilities, and the LRJC dialogue program came on top of everything else they were already doing. Securing a meeting with the faith leaders of a congregation (lay or clerical) was easier when an LRJC member had personal connections with the congregation. Direct, unsolicited contact with congregations without any previous introduction was almost always ineffective. I tried this outreach technique with Evangelical congregations that, based on their social media or website, seemed predominantly White American. This reinforces the aforementioned finding that deliberative dialogues on immigration will be more successful when spearheaded by a congregation member. When personal connections to congregations are lacking, those interested in leading a dialogue on immigration among Christians could start by attending events of congregations or religious institutions to build relationships. Alternatively, one can ask clergy whom they know for introductions to the clergy of other congregations, a "snowballing" outreach technique. When proposing the dialogue program, it is important to communicate to congregation gatekeepers and potential participants that the program is not partisan and that it responds to biblical calls. In introductory meetings with congregation leaders, I often quoted St. Paul's letter to the Corinthians: "Just as a body, though one, has many parts, but all its many parts form one body, so it is with Christ" (1 Corinthians 12:12). I also clarified that the LRJC dialogues did not aim to get participants to agree on immigration nor to move U.S.-born participants to help immigrants; the primary goal was to build mutual understanding and, from there, collaboration on goals that mattered for both U.S.-born and immigrant participants.

The role of financial incentives in congregation engagement is not clear. In the LRJC dialogues, individual participants were never compensated financially. When grant funds allowed, LRJC or my university (depending on who housed the grant) paid the congregations for use of their facilities, a small stipend for a program liaison in each congregation, and/or a modest seed grant for follow-up collaborative projects. These were all congregations that the LJRC or I had actively recruited to the program. The three congregations that reached out to LRJC were not financially compensated. This could mean that financial incentives played a role; however, none of the congregations ever talked to me about program costs, commented on the payments, or spontaneously asked for payments due after the program's conclusion. On the contrary, grant administrators at my university often contacted faith leaders repeatedly to request invoices and the information needed to process payments.

## Dialogue and Spiritual Growth

Dialogue is a mode of communication that involves the practice of Christ-like qualities. At the core of Christianity is a call to decenter the egotistic self, to reorient one's heart and mind toward God and others. The egotistic self will tend to have knee-jerk reactions to ideas that challenge its assumptions. It yearns for the short-term feelings of excitement that arise when we debunk someone's argument and relish the feeling of self-righteousness. In dialogue, we are encouraged to go in the opposite direction: to suspend our assumptions (softening our attachments to groups and ideas) and to listen actively to others with attention to their strong points (charitably offering them our time and understanding). When this attitude is reciprocal, interlocutors create an opening for the changing of hearts and minds, which rarely occurs when the dominant mode of communication is debate.

In Appendix C, I present instructions for a group discussion on Christian principles and traditions for dialogue, which can precede a congregation dialogue on immigration or any other topic. In fact, from the perspective of Christian cosmopolitanism, people of faith should engage in deliberative dialogues on other issues that also require mutual understanding and collaboration across race, ethnicity, and nationality, such as climate change, world poverty, war, and global pandemics. The cosmopolitan potential and teachings of Christianity are not bound to immigration. Moreover, since dialogue and deliberation are democratic practices, deliberative dialogues about those topics will not only make the Church more cosmopolitan but also bring it closer to democracy. They can be tools for Christians to engage in public affairs in ways that are collaborative and faithful rather than hierarchical and fundamentalist.

Yet, we should not place all our bets on deliberative dialogues on global issues as a means for Christians and the Church to make a cosmopolitan contribution to democratic life. Deliberative dialogues are one tool along with other nonviolent means in the Christian repertoire of collective action for cosmopolitanism, such as peaceful demonstrations, petitions to the government, and the provision of sanctuary to immigrants. Besides, as faith leaders in the focus group stressed, the institutional church has a cosmopolitan duty and the clergy needs to speak from the pulpit on issues of racism and xenophobia. After five years of practice and research on deliberative dialogues on immigration in Christian congregations, I have learned to see them in light of Jesus's parable about the mustard seed: "The kingdom of heaven is like a mustard seed, which a man took and planted in his field. Though it is the smallest of all seeds, yet when it grows, it is the largest of garden plants and becomes a tree, so that the birds come and perch in its branches" (Matthew 13:31–32). In this teaching, the mustard—an ordinary garden bush—stands in implicit contrast with the cedar of Lebanon, whose grandiosity among other trees made it a symbol of the Kingdom of God for the Israelites of Jesus's time (Keating 2010, 6–7). Deliberative dialogues on immigration in Christian congregations might not be a cosmopolitan praxis as grandiose as they would be at the General Assembly of the United Nations or the Assembly of the World Council of Churches, but, like the mustard seed, they can humbly and incrementally bring us closer to the cosmopolitan ideals of Christianity.

# APPENDIX A

## *Methodological Strategy*

This book results from community-based research that included a participant survey, a content analysis of dialogue transcripts, and participant observation of follow-up collaborative projects undertaken by faith communities. In this appendix, I explain in detail each of these components of the methodological strategy.

### A.1. COMMUNITY-BASED RESEARCH

When leaders of the Latino Racial Justice Circle (LRJC) first thought about the program "Honest Conversations on Immigration," they envisioned it as promoting mutual understanding and collaboration between immigrants and U.S.-born people in faith communities. After reviewing academic and nonprofit literature on dialogue and the academic literature on religious cosmopolitanism, I designed the LRJC dialogue model and articulated it in the *LRJC Guide for Honest Conversations on Immigration.* I brought a draft of the guide to an LRJC meeting, and members of the group suggested a few modifications, such as changes in language to make questions more culturally appropriate from the perspective of immigrants and people of faith. I also held a focus group with LRJC members who had facilitated a pilot version of the program in an ecumenical workshop on immigration. They noted that personal testimonials by immigrants had been an especially compelling element of the event and that the dialogue should have been longer than forty-five minutes (Filomeno 2019). As we implemented the dialogues and learned from those experiences, I revised the guide to improve its capacity to promote mutual understanding and collaboration between participants. The final version of the guide is presented in Appendix B. It includes the Spanish translation of the conversation script.

Implementing the dialogues required building rapport with clergy and lay leaders of the congregations that hosted the program. I collaborated with LRJC in reaching out to potential congregations, often taking advantage of personal connections between LRJC members and the congregations. We were intentional about including congregations that would allow our set of dialogues to be diverse according to location (urban vs. suburban), denomination (Catholic, mainline Protestant, Evangelical), and racial/ethnic composition (predominantly Latino, predominantly African American, predominantly White American, or diverse). This would allow for analytical comparisons. LRJC outreach was unsuccessful in three instances: (1) a Catholic parish that combined a predominantly White American congregation and a predominantly Latino congregation (their pastor was afraid that conversations about immigration would jeopardize incipient relations between the two communities); (2) an Episcopalian Latino congregation (their pastor said the congregation had been overwhelmed by the COVID-19 pandemic and could not take on an additional program); and (3) several Evangelical congregations (most of which I had emailed with a meeting request, and two in which I had telephone conversations with the pastor). While the Catholic and Episcopalian pastors explained their concerns with the program, the Evangelical pastors were irresponsive, which makes it difficult to assess why Evangelical openness to the program was very limited. As mentioned in Chapter 1, Evangelicals tend to express more restrictive attitudes toward immigration than other religious groups, and Evangelical denominations have a more limited engagement with immigration than Catholic or mainline Protestant churches.

At the planning stages of each dialogue, I met with congregation leaders and, sometimes, other LRJC members to introduce the program, answer questions, discuss participant recruitment, and plan the logistics of the program. I also used those meetings to learn more about the congregations: the size and ethnic composition of their membership, the state of intergroup relations among members, and previous engagement with immigration affairs. In these initial conversations, I introduced myself as an LRJC volunteer, a professor, and a congregant of a local Catholic parish. I also connected the program to the religious goal of building unity in the diversity of the Body of Christ. Most congregations did not have enough diversity among their members for a dialogue to happen within a single congregation. Usually, I brought two congregations together in each edition of the program. I tried to ensure that the program would not imply any costs to congregations. With support from grants, I offered each congregation in HC1, HC2, HC5, HC6, and HC7 refreshments for dialogue sessions and $400 for the use of facilities. In HC5, HC6, and HC7, grants also allowed me to offer a $300 stipend for a program liaison in each congregation to help with participant recruitment and program logistics and $300 toward participant collaborative projects. HC3 and HC4 happened online because of the COVID-19 pandemic, so I did not need to cover any costs. Individual participants were never financially compensated for participation.

I had to be very flexible, patient, and resilient in the face of setbacks during the outreach, planning, and execution of the dialogue program with congregations. One pastor thought the first dialogue session would be on a Thursday instead of a Wednesday, so I had to call them from outside the church on a cold evening to get them to open the hall for participants. Another pastor had agreed to have the dialogue in person, but when I arrived at the church, they had set up equipment for a hybrid event so that some congregants could join from home. There were also many rescheduled meetings and emails that had to be followed up. I was always understanding and, ultimately, appreciative of their openness to the program and their courage to bring their flock together to talk across differences about a politically sensitive topic in very polarized times.

As usual in community-based research, I had to balance scientific research goals and the interests of my community partners (LRJC and participating congregations). After each faith leader agreed to let the program happen in their communities, we had to compromise on recruiting participants. From a research perspective, I would have preferred to recruit participants randomly from congregation rosters and create control groups for comparisons. To some faith leaders, that would be too cumbersome, and others had, from the start, another recruiting strategy in mind. For instance, I recruited participants for HC1 by introducing the program from the pulpit immediately after mass and standing at the church exit with a sign-up sheet. For HC2, the pastoral team that oversaw the three participating congregations wanted to invite members directly. Knowing that variations in participant recruitment would somewhat limit the comparability of the dialogues, I asked congregation leaders to at least make sure they sent invitations to a diversity of congregants in terms of nationality, race, ethnicity, gender, and political orientation, a request they honored. I also asked them to limit the total number of participants to fifteen.

The minor revisions I introduced to the LRJC dialogue guide as the program developed also limit the comparability of the dialogues. However, I had to honor the goals of my community partners: to build mutual understanding and collaboration between immigrants and U.S.-born people. How could I not introduce revisions I knew would contribute to that goal? For the same reason, I allowed participants who had missed the first or second session of the program to join in the second or third session. While most participants attended the three sessions of the program, there was some variation in the number of sessions attended by participants. The late entrance of some participants could create methodological problems, but it was a welcome occurrence from the perspective of faith leaders who wanted their congregations engaged in the program.

Furthermore, since I played the roles of both practitioner and scholar, there were methodological issues typical of action research. On the one hand, the combination of those roles gave me an insider's perspective on the design and implementation of the dialogue and access to what Dezerotes (2018) called practice-based evidence. In the practice-based evidence process, "the facilitator . . . directly observes group dynamics, to help her determine if the methods she is using are assisting participants in achieving group goals" (Dezerotes 2018, 42). On the other hand, that combination of roles implies that I was in charge of evaluating a program that I had developed. To mitigate the effects of this potential conflict of interest, I took the following measures:

- I conducted the qualitative content analysis on the software NVivo in a systematic way with documented procedures to make the analysis more objective (as described below).
- I conducted a quantitative content analysis to verify if certain kinds of participants had dominated the dialogues and to identify instances in which my facilitation might have allowed for domination to happen.
- I intentionally looked for participant interactions that deviated from the expected goals of the program. For instance, I adopted a skeptical attitude towards moments of agreement because they could actually be moments in which participants were self-censoring or simply conforming to the opinions of dominating participants. That is hard to discern from an audio recording or a transcript, but when participants agreed with one another by offering corroborating evidence (such as a personal story) or expanding on the logic of a previous argument, I could, with less risk, classify such an interaction as an instance of mutual understanding rather than domination. I also used a code to mark moments of nondialogical disagreement characterized by a vitriolic confrontation between participants.
- While writing observation notes after each dialogue session and while writing the book, I included critical reflections about the dialogue and my positionality in the program.

- I presented preliminary research findings at different scholarly meetings to receive peer feedback (the Latin American Studies Association in 2019, the American Political Science Association in 2021 and 2023, and the Louisville Institute Seminar in 2022). I also gave public talks and facilitated workshops to promote the program in public events, including the 2019 Baltimore Immigration Summit and the 2019 and 2020 Social Ministry Convocations of the Baltimore Archdiocese, where I answered questions from participants.
- In February 2023, after I completed the analysis of all dialogues, I conducted a focus group with faith leaders from participating congregations to share key findings and listen to their criticism of those conclusions. I invited the faith leaders from all participating congregations. Six faith leaders, representing four of the seven dialogues, participated in the focus group: a Catholic African American woman, a Catholic Afro-Caribbean man, a Latina Evangelical, a Latino Evangelical, a Lutheran White American man, and a Latina Methodist. The focus group was, therefore, diverse in terms of gender, race/ethnicity, and denomination. For one hour, we discussed findings about how participants interacted during the dialogues, the themes they articulated (about unity and diversity in society, intergroup tensions brought by immigration, and similarities and differences between immigrants and U.S.-born people), and how they collaborated after the dialogues. The faith leaders' responses to the findings helped me refine the conclusions.

## A.2. SURVEY

At the beginning of the first session of each dialogue, participants completed an anonymous entry survey to provide demographic data. In HC1, HC2, HC5, HC6, and HC7, participants completed the survey in person. In HC3 and HC4, participants completed the survey online. The surveys were available in English and Spanish. A summary of the results of this survey is presented in Chapter 1 as part of an overall characterization of the dialogues.

*Survey Instrument*
Questionnaire for Participants

1. National origin
   - ☐ My parents and I were born in the United States.
   - ☐ I was born in the United States, but at least one of my parents was born abroad.
   - ☐ I was born abroad.
2. Race/ethnicity
   - ☐ Hispanic or Latino
   - ☐ White (not Hispanic or Latino)
   - ☐ Black or African American (not Hispanic or Latino)
   - ☐ Native Hawaiian or Other Pacific Islander (not Hispanic or Latino)
   - ☐ Asian (not Hispanic or Latino)
   - ☐ American Indian or Alaska Native (not Hispanic or Latino)
   - ☐ Two or More Races (not Hispanic or Latino)
3. Gender
   - ☐ Male
   - ☐ Female
   - ☐ Other

4. Age
  - ☐ Less than 18
  - ☐ 18–24
  - ☐ 25–34
  - ☐ 35–44
  - ☐ 45–54
  - ☐ 55 and over
5. Education
  - ☐ Elementary/Middle
  - ☐ High School
  - ☐ College/University
  - ☐ Postgraduate
6. Religious affiliation
  - ☐ Catholic
  - ☐ Protestant (not Evangelical)
  - ☐ Evangelical
  - ☐ Jewish
  - ☐ Muslim
  - ☐ Other (including nonaffiliated)
7. Political orientation
  - ☐ Very conservative (1)
  - ☐ Moderate (4)
  - ☐ Very liberal (7)

## Demographic Profile of Participants

To identify participants' race/ethnicity, I relied on observation notes. Participants categorized as White Americans were Caucasian U.S.-born people. Those classified as African Americans were Black people born in the United States. Those classified as Latinos were people of Latin American background who lived in the United States. In this study, all Latino participants identified as an immigrant. I did not distinguish between Latinos of different races. Only one Latino participant self-identified as an Afro-Latino; he attended only one session of HC6 and was classified as Latino. Participants classified as African were born in Africa (two in Nigeria and a third in another African country). Participants classified as Asian were born in Asia (one in Vietnam and another in the Philippines). One participant did not fit into the above categories: a White German woman who attended only one session of HC7; she was classified as White European in this study. This classification has problems (African and Asian are two broad regions of origin; Latinos can identify as White, Black, or mixed), but it allowed me to categorize each participant in a single group and also to distinguish between immigrant participants (Latino, African, Asian, White European) and U.S.-born participants (White American, African American). Alternative classification schemes would have their own limitations. For instance, if I had chosen to use Black as a category, it would have lumped together groups with very different experiences and views on immigration (Afro-Latinos, Black Africans, and African Americans).

## TABLE A.1 DISTRIBUTION OF PARTICIPANTS BY RACE/ETHNICITY

| Dialogue | Session | White American | African American | Latino[a] | Asian[a] | African[a] | White European[a] | Total | Immigrant (%) |
|---|---|---|---|---|---|---|---|---|---|
| HC1 | 1 | 3 | 9 | 2 | 0 | 0 | 0 | 14 | 14.29 |
| | 2 | 3 | 7 | 2 | 0 | 0 | 0 | 12 | 16.67 |
| | 3 | 3 | 7 | 2 | 0 | 0 | 0 | 12 | 16.67 |
| HC2 | 1 | 11 | 0 | 3 | 0 | 0 | 1 | 15 | 26.67 |
| | 2 | 7 | 0 | 3 | 1 | 0 | 0 | 11 | 36.36 |
| | 3 | 8 | 0 | 3 | 1 | 0 | 0 | 12 | 33.33 |
| HC3 | 1 | 1 | 5 | 4 | 0 | 0 | 0 | 10 | 40.00 |
| | 2 | 1 | 5 | 6 | 0 | 0 | 0 | 12 | 50.00 |
| | 3 | 1 | 4 | 2 | 0 | 0 | 0 | 7 | 28.57 |
| HC4 | 1 | 4 | 2 | 0 | 0 | 2 | 0 | 8 | 25.00 |
| | 2 | 4 | 2 | 0 | 0 | 1 | 0 | 7 | 14.29 |
| | 3 | 4 | 1 | 0 | 0 | 2 | 0 | 7 | 28.57 |
| HC5 | 1 | 0 | 0 | 7 | 0 | 1 | 0 | 8 | 100.00 |
| | 2 | 1 | 0 | 3 | 1 | 1 | 0 | 6 | 83.33 |
| | 3 | 0 | 0 | 2 | 0 | 1 | 0 | 3 | 100.00 |
| HC6 | 1 | 3 | 0 | 1 | 0 | 0 | 0 | 4 | 25.00 |
| | 2 | 4 | 0 | 9 | 0 | 0 | 0 | 13 | 69.23 |
| | 3 | 4 | 0 | 6 | 0 | 0 | 0 | 10 | 60.00 |
| HC7 | 1 | 4 | 0 | 12 | 0 | 0 | 0 | 16 | 75.00 |
| | 2 | 4 | 0 | 11 | 0 | 0 | 0 | 15 | 73.33 |
| | 3 | 5 | 0 | 9 | 0 | 0 | 1 | 15 | 60.00 |
| | | | | | | | | Average | 46.49 |

[a] All were foreign-born, with the exception of one participant from Puerto Rico in HC3 and HC6, who, however, identified as an immigrant during the conversations.

## TABLE A.2 DISTRIBUTION OF PARTICIPANTS BY GENDER

| Dialogue | Females | Males | Others | Female (%) |
|---|---|---|---|---|
| HC1 | 10 | 1 | 0 | 91 |
| HC2 | 7 | 3 | 0 | 70 |
| HC3 | 3 | 2 | 0 | 60 |
| HC4 | 5 | 3 | 0 | 63 |
| HC5 | 1 | 3 | 0 | 25 |
| HC6 | 6 | 5 | 0 | 55 |
| HC7 | 8 | 8 | 0 | 50 |
| Total | 40 | 25 | 0 | 61 |

*Note:* Based on the entry survey, except for HC1 and HC2, in which only an exit survey was applied. Numbers could vary from one session to another due to participant drop-in and drop-out. Most but not all participants turned in completed surveys.

## TABLE A.3 DISTRIBUTION OF PARTICIPANTS BY POLITICAL IDEOLOGY

| Dialogue | Lean Liberal | Moderate | Lean Conservative | Lean Liberal (%) |
|----------|--------------|----------|-------------------|------------------|
| HC1 | 7 | 3 | 0 | 70 |
| HC2 | 2 | 2 | 5 | 22 |
| HC3 | 3 | 2 | 0 | 60 |
| HC4 | 5 | 3 | 0 | 63 |
| HC5 | 0 | 2 | 2 | 0 |
| HC6 | 6 | 2 | 0 | 75 |
| HC7 | 4 | 7 | 2 | 31 |
| Total | 27 | 21 | 9 | 47 |

*Note:* Based on the entry survey, except for HC1 and HC2, in which only an exit survey was applied. Numbers could vary from one session to another due to participant drop-in and drop-out. Most but not all participants turned in completed surveys.

## TABLE A.4 DISTRIBUTION OF PARTICIPANTS BY LEVEL OF EDUCATION

| Dialogue | Elementary/ Middle School | High School | College/ University | Postgraduate |
|----------|---------------------------|-------------|---------------------|--------------|
| HC1 | 0 | 0 | 6 | 5 |
| HC2 | 0 | 1 | 8 | 1 |
| HC3 | 0 | 0 | 3 | 2 |
| HC4 | 0 | 0 | 2 | 6 |
| HC5 | 0 | 0 | 3 | 1 |
| HC6 | 0 | 2 | 5 | 4 |
| HC7 | 4 | 6 | 2 | 2 |
| Total | 4 | 9 | 29 | 21 |

*Note:* Based on the entry survey, except for HC1 and HC2, in which only an exit survey was applied. Numbers could vary from one session to another due to participant drop-in and drop-out. Most but not all participants turned in completed surveys.

## TABLE A.5 DISTRIBUTION OF PARTICIPANTS BY AGE

| Dialogue | 18–24 | 25–34 | 35–44 | 45–54 | 55 and Over |
|----------|-------|-------|-------|-------|-------------|
| HC1 | 0 | 1 | 1 | 0 | 9 |
| HC2 | 0 | 1 | 1 | 2 | 6 |
| HC3 | 0 | 0 | 0 | 1 | 4 |
| HC4 | 0 | 0 | 0 | 0 | 8 |
| HC5 | 0 | 1 | 0 | 0 | 3 |
| HC6 | 2 | 1 | 2 | 4 | 2 |
| HC7 | 2 | 2 | 3 | 1 | 3 |
| Total | 4 | 6 | 7 | 8 | 35 |

*Note:* Based on the entry survey, except for HC1 and HC2, in which only an exit survey was applied. Numbers could vary from one session to another due to participant drop-in and drop-out. Most but not all participants turned in completed surveys.

## A.3. CONTENT ANALYSIS

*Quantitative Content Analysis*

I used quantitative content analysis to verify the existence of patterns of domination in the dialogues. The conclusions of this analysis are presented in Chapter 2. I started by considering domination by U.S.-born participants, who can be considered relatively high-power in terms of nationality and immigration status. Following Hammack and Pilecki (2015), I used the number of words uttered by a participant to indicate how much time that participant took in a dialogue and, thus, as an approximate indicator of how much influence that participant exercised over the dialogue. I used that indicator as a descriptive statistic, not for inferential purposes. The transcripts of every dialogue session had notations indicating the nationality of participants (those marked as Latino, African, or Asian were immigrants).[1] For every dialogue session, a research assistant calculated how many of the words uttered had come from immigrant participants. The research assistant then compared that proportion of words to the proportion of immigrants in that dialogue session (presented in Table A.1). For instance, if 60% of the participants in a dialogue session were immigrants, but immigrant participants spoke only 30% of the words in that session, it is likely that U.S.-born participants were dominating that conversation.[2] I considered the immigrant proportion of words to be proportional to the immigrant proportion of participants whenever the difference between both was within 20%. This allowed me to flag instances in which under- or overparticipation was salient. The results of this analysis are shown below. Among the nineteen dialogue sessions in which both immigrant participants and U.S.-born participants were present, six had an overparticipation of immigrants, five had an underparticipation of immigrants, and eight had proportional participation of immigrants. When data from all sessions are lumped together, the immigrant proportion of words (49%) is quite close to the immigrant proportion of participants (46%). This suggests no systematic difference either in favor of immigrants or against immigrants.

### TABLE A.6 IMMIGRANT PARTICIPATION IN DIALOGUES

| Dialogue | Session | Immigrant Proportion of Participants (%) | Immigrant Proportion of Words (%) | Difference (%) | Conclusion |
|---|---|---|---|---|---|
| HC1 | 1 | 14 | 34 | 143 | Overparticipation |
| | 2 | 17 | 36 | 112 | Overparticipation |
| | 3 | 17 | 27 | 59 | Overparticipation |
| HC2 | 1 | 27 | 12 | −56 | Underparticipation |
| | 2 | 36 | 26 | −28 | Underparticipation |
| | 3 | 33 | 20 | −39 | Underparticipation |
| HC3 | 1 | 40 | 39 | −3 | Proportional participation |
| | 2 | 50 | 54 | 8 | Proportional participation |
| | 3 | 29 | 3 | −90 | Underparticipation |
| HC4 | 1 | 25 | 40 | 60 | Overparticipation |
| | 2 | 14 | 40 | 186 | Overparticipation |
| | 3 | 29 | 47 | 62 | Overparticipation |

| Dialogue | Session | Immigrant Proportion of Participants (%) | Immigrant Proportion of Words (%) | Difference (%) | Conclusion |
|---|---|---|---|---|---|
| HC5 | 1 | 100 | 100 | 0 | n/a[a] |
| | 2 | 83 | 68 | −18 | Proportional participation |
| | 3 | 100 | 100 | 0 | n/a[a] |
| HC6 | 1 | 25 | 18 | −28 | Underparticipation |
| | 2 | 69 | 74 | 7 | Proportional participation |
| | 3 | 60 | 72 | 20 | Proportional participation |
| HC7 | 1 | 75 | 86 | 15 | Proportional participation |
| | 2 | 73 | 70 | −4 | Proportional participation |
| | 3 | 60 | 57 | −5 | Proportional participation |
| Total | | 46 | 49 | 7 | Proportional participation |

**TABLE A.6 IMMIGRANT PARTICIPATION IN DIALOGUES** (*continued*)

[a] n/a = not applicable

Since studies reviewed in Chapter 2 argue that participants of relatively low-power groups tend to engage more in discussions of inequality and differences than in discussions of commonalities with other groups, we broke down the quantitative analysis in order to consider, on the one hand, responses to questions on collaboration and commonalities between immigrants and U.S.-born people and, on the other hand, responses to questions on tensions and differences between immigrants and U.S.-born people. For every dialogue session, the research assistant identified the questions in each category (collaboration/commonality vs. tension/differences) and calculated the proportion of immigrant-uttered words to be compared with the proportion of immigrant participants in each session. Again, there was no systematic difference between those values.

These results were helpful, however, in singling out individual sessions in which immigrants participated too much or too little. In every session of HC2, for instance, there was underparticipation of immigrants. Upon further scrutiny of the transcripts and a critical self-reflection, I concluded that I had let older White American males talk for too long in that dialogue. This, however, does not mean that dialogue domination happens necessarily across the expected lines of social stratification (U.S.-born participants dominating immigrants, men dominating women, etc.). In every session of HC1, there was overparticipation of immigrants. Upon further examination of the transcripts, I noticed that two Latina participants had talked a lot in those sessions. They were both community leaders who had worked in immigrant advocacy and, therefore, were comfortably outspoken in the dialogue.

I used the same kind of procedure to verify domination by clergy, who can be considered high-power actors in the context of their faith communities. I noted which participant identification codes in the transcripts corresponded to clergy participants. The results are given in Table A.7. Among the fourteen dialogue sessions in which clergy was present, three show an overparticipation of the clergy, seven show an underparticipation of the clergy, and four show proportional participation, which does not indicate a clear pattern in favor of clergy or against clergy.

| | | Clergy Proportion of Participants (%) | Clergy Proportion of Words (%) | Difference (%) | |
|---|---|---|---|---|---|
| **TABLE A.7 CLERGY PARTICIPATION IN DIALOGUES** | | | | | |
| Dialogue | Session | Clergy Proportion of Participants (%) | Clergy Proportion of Words (%) | Difference (%) | Conclusion |
| HC1 | No clergy present | | | | |
| HC2 | 1 | 7.14 | 0 | −100 | Underparticipation |
| | 2 | 8.33 | 2.76 | −67 | Underparticipation |
| | 3 | 8.33 | 3.8 | −54 | Underparticipation |
| HC3 | 1 | 20 | 25.73 | 29 | Overparticipation |
| | 2 | 16.67 | 28.28 | 70 | Overparticipation |
| | 3 | 14.28 | 16.69 | 17 | Proportional participation |
| HC4 | No clergy present | | | | |
| HC5 | 1 | 25 | 31.07 | 24 | Overparticipation |
| | 2 | 50 | 50.02 | 0 | Proportional participation |
| | 3 | 66.67 | 44.37 | −33 | Underparticipation |
| HC6 | 1 | 50 | 28.27 | −43 | Underparticipation |
| | 2 | 23 | 22.51 | −2 | Proportional participation |
| | 3 | 30 | 32.28 | 8 | Proportional participation |
| HC7 | 1 | 6.25 | 3.47 | −44 | Underparticipation |
| | 2 | No clergy present | | | |
| | 3 | 6.67 | 3.67 | −45 | Underparticipation |

*Qualitative Content Analysis*

I audio-recorded all the dialogue sessions, with the exception of the pilot dialogue that was part of the ecumenical workshop on immigration. After the research assistants transcribed the recordings, I divided the transcripts into equivalent segments for analysis. These segments correspond to the main themes of the LRJC dialogue model, which the LRJC dialogue guide covers sequentially: (1) tensions over immigration (first dialogue session), (2) similarities and differences between immigrants and U.S.-born people (second dialogue session), and (3) visions for collaboration between immigrants and U.S.-born people (third dialogue session). These segments correspond, respectively, to Chapters 3, 4, and 5 of the book. The discussion of ground rules and the question about faith traditions and immigration resulted in two other equivalent segments that were analyzed individually (with findings presented in Chapter 2). A few dialogue questions, however, did not fit this pattern, and the conversations about them had to be shifted for analytical purposes:

1. In HC1 and HC2, the question on tensions over unauthorized immigration appeared in the third session, so the resulting exchanges had to be shifted and analyzed together with the segment on cultural and economic tensions, which had appeared in the first session. For all other dialogues, the questions on legal, cultural, and economic tensions all appeared in the first session.

2. In all dialogues, the question about whether participants had ever felt like an outsider in a given social situation appeared in the first session. Since this question was about how participants established differences between themselves and others, I shifted the corresponding exchanges and analyzed them together with the segment on similarities and differences (which was in the second session).

3. In all dialogues, the question about what helped (or could have helped) participants feel included in a situation where they were outsiders and the question about positive interactions between immigrants and U.S.-born people were discussed in the first session. Since these two questions encouraged participants to recollect stories of relationship-building between immigrants and U.S.-born people that could inform visions for collaboration between the two groups, I shifted their discussions and analyzed them together with the segment on visions for collaboration (which was in the third session).

To analyze the conversations, I employed a thematic-relational analysis. In thematic analysis, the researcher systematically examines qualitative data to identify recurrent ideas and patterns of information, which are called themes. Coding is a central process of thematic analysis where the researcher assigns "a word or short phrase that symbolically assigns a summative, salient, essence-capturing, and/or evocative attribute for a portion of language-based or visual data" (Saldaña 2009, 3). In conventional thematic analysis, codes usually refer to the substance of the data. For instance, I applied the code "religious beliefs and values" when reading the statements "Our faith tells us to welcome the stranger" or "Love thy neighbor." For the purposes of this research, however, conventional thematic analysis was insufficient. Because the goal of the dialogues was to promote mutual understanding and collaboration between diverse participants, I also had to examine how they interacted with each other (the relational dimension of the data). Thus, in addition to using codes that referred to the substance of what participants said (thematic codes), I used codes that referred to their discursive interactions (relational codes). For instance, I applied the code "solidarity across differences" to segments of the dialogue in which participants of different identities expressed a feeling of mutuality upon acknowledging shared interests or values.

I created a preliminary thematic coding scheme based on the literature on religion and cosmopolitanism (especially works on religion and immigration). I created a preliminary relational coding scheme based on the literature on dialogue. I then conducted a pilot coding of the entire transcripts of HC1 and HC2 and of the segments on tensions over immigration of HC1, HC2, and HC3. This set of dialogues covered different Christian denominations (Catholic and Methodist), different locations (urban and suburban), and different demographic makeups (Latino and African American, Latino and White American; predominantly liberal, predominantly conservative). In this pilot coding, I adopted an open coding approach, creating new codes as needed. After the pilot coding, I revised the preliminary coding scheme (dropping, adding, relocating, or redefining codes), resulting in the coding scheme presented in Table A.8. The final coding scheme included thematic and relational codes. Some thematic codes were about topics (such as economic problems or language), others were theoretical concepts (such as universalist or particularist cosmopolitanism), and some were about spaces (such as neighborhoods or churches). I often applied more than one thematic code to the same utterance, which made it possible for me to look at the same piece of data from different thematic angles.

## TABLE A.8 CODING SCHEME

| Thematic Codes—A | Relational Codes—B[a] |
|---|---|
| A.1. Cosmopolitanism | B.1. Agreement |
| A.1.1. Universalist cosmopolitanism | B.1.1. Corroboration |
| A.1.1.1. Religious universalist cosmopolitanism | B.1.2. Possible domination |
| A.1.2. Particularist cosmopolitanism | B.2. Disagreement |
| A.1.2.1. Religious particularist cosmopolitanism | B.2.1. Confrontation |
| A.1.3. Diversal cosmopolitanism | B.2.2. Opposition |
| A.1.3.1. Religious diversal cosmopolitanism | B.3. Disagreement to agreement |
| A.2. Economic problems | B.4. Interactive critical thinking |
| A.2.1. Poverty | B.5. Curiosity across differences |
| A.2.2. Economic anxiety | B.6. Perspective-giving across differences |
| A.2.3. Economic competition | B.7. Perspective-taking across differences |
| A.3. Exploitation, abuse, or discrimination | B.8. Solidarity across differences |
| A.3.1. Exploitation, abuse, or discrimination of immigrants | B.9. Suspension of assumptions |
| A.4. Youth | |
| A.5. Food | |
| A.6. Ground rules | |
| A.7. Language | |
| A.8. Law | |
| A.8.1. Citizenship | |
| A.9. Migrant-sending countries | |
| A.10. Nationalism | |
| A.11. Out-group perceptions | |
| A.11.1. Anti-immigrant sentiment | |
| A.11.2. Hard-working immigrants | |
| A.11.3. Stereotypes | |
| A.12. Police | |
| A.13. Political action | |
| A.14. Race | |
| A.15. Religion | |
| A.15.1. Religion and dialogue | |
| A.15.2. Religion and immigration | |
| A.15.3. Religion and race | |
| A.15.4. Religious communities | |
| A.15.5. Religious institutions | |
| A.15.6. Religious parochialism | |
| A.15.7. Religious values and beliefs | |
| A.16. Social identity and belonging | |
| A.16.1. American identity | |
| A.17. Spaces of intergroup contact | |
| A.17.1. Church | |
| A.17.2. Neighborhood | |
| A.17.3. School | |
| A.17.4. Workplace | |

[a] Agreement, curiosity across differences, perspective-taking, solidarity, and suspension of assumptions are all indicators that mutual understanding is happening. Even disagreement can include mutual understanding, especially if participants say things like "I see what you're saying" or "I understand" but end up still in disagreement. Interactive critical thinking, agreement, disagreement, and suspension of assumptions are indicators of deliberation.

I always coded first for thematic codes and second for relational codes. While thematic codes were applied to single utterances, relational codes were applied to single or multiple utterances. The relational codes agreement, disagreement, and interactive critical thinking were typically applied to exchanges between participants covering multiple utterances. The relational codes curiosity across differences, perspective-giving across differences, perspective-taking across differences, solidarity across differences, and suspension of assumptions were typically applied to single utterances in which a participant performed one of those actions discursively. In order to write Chapter 5, I applied the final coding scheme to all segments on envisioning collaboration between immigrants and U.S.-born people and analyzed the resulting data. I did the same thing for all the segments on ground rules and faith traditions in order to write Chapter 2, for all segments on tensions over immigration to write Chapter 3, and for all segments on similarities and differences between immigrants and U.S.-born people to write Chapter 4.

I also applied codes to identify participants. On NVivo, these codes are called cases, where each participant is a case to which demographic attributes can be assigned. I set race/ethnicity and gender as attributes of cases and assigned them to each case according to the notation identifying each participant in the transcripts. So every utterance by a participant was coded under the corresponding case.

The following three procedures then allowed me to examine each of the dialogue segments from multiple angles in search of multiple patterns (thematic or relational) and puzzling absences (themes or interactions that, based on the literature, I expected to be salient in a certain dialogue segment but were not). These procedures involved some quantification of the transcripts to assist the qualitative analysis by indicating where patterns might exist in the data. The quantification was descriptive and instrumental to the qualitative analysis rather than inferential.

(1) **Most salient themes:** Using hierarchy charts on NVivo, I identified the most recurrent thematic parental codes.[3] I reviewed all the excerpts coded under each of the most recurrent thematic parental codes and took notes along the way. Using matrix coding on NVivo, I also considered how each of those codes varied on the level of dialogues and their demographic makeup.[4] For instance, did discussions about language happen more often in dialogues between Latinos and African Americans than in dialogues between Latinos and White Americans? Was there any patterned variation in the substance of those discussions? Using the same tool, I also considered how each of the most recurring thematic codes varied on the level of individual participant race/ethnicity (which is the most important axis of social stratification for this study and encompasses the immigrant-native divide). For instance, did Latino and White American interlocutors talk about language to different extents? Was there any patterned variation in the substance of what they said? I then combined my notes from these analyses into analytical memos summarizing the thematic patterns.[5]

In the analysis of thematic codes according to participant race/ethnicity, for each major dialogue segment (tensions over immigration, similarities/differences between immigrants and U.S.-born people, envisioning collaboration), I calculated the total number of speakers and their breakout according to race/ethnicity. For example, in the segment about envisioning collaboration, across all dialogues, there were sixty-two active speakers, of whom 40.32% were White American, 17.74% were African American, 35.48% were Latino, 1.61% were Asian, and 4.84% were African. These values served as a baseline for comparisons about that dialogue segment. For each top thematic code, I calculated how many of the coded utterances came from White American, African American, Latino, Asian, and African participants. I then compared the resulting values with the baseline values to verify over-, proportional, or underrepresentation of participants of different racial/ethnic identities. For instance, in the segment on envisioning collaboration, immigrants (Latino, Asian, and African) accounted for only 41.94% of active speakers but accounted for 77.78% of utterances about exploitation, abuse, and discrimination of immigrants (therefore being largely overrepresented in conversations about this topic).

(2) **Most salient relational processes:** Using hierarchy charts on NVivo, I identified the most recurrent relational parental codes. Using the same procedures as with thematic codes, I identified the most recurrent relational parental codes, reviewed all the excerpts coded under them, and took notes along the way to develop analytical memos. The only difference is that I analyzed the relational codes typically applied to single utterances separately from those typically applied to multiple utterances. Putting them together to identify the most recurrent codes would have given an advantage to the codes applied to single utterances. Using matrix coding on NVivo, I also considered how each of the most recurrent relational codes might have varied on the level of dialogues. For instance, was agreement more common in dialogues between Latinos and African Americans than in dialogues between Latinos and White Americans? Using the same tool, I also considered how each of the most recurring relational codes varied based on individual participants' race/ethnicity. For instance, did most instances of perspective-giving come from Latino, Asian, and African interlocutors rather than U.S.-born interlocutors? I then combined my notes from these analyses into analytical memos summarizing the relational patterns.

In analyzing relational codes according to participant race/ethnicity, for each major dialogue segment, I used the number of speakers and their race/ethnicity breakout as a baseline for comparison. When a top relational code was applied to single utterances, I proceeded as in the thematic analysis. "Perspective-giving" was one such relational code, applied whenever a participant shared with others how they experienced the world (so each excerpt coded under perspective-giving corresponded to a single participant). This allowed me to find, for instance, that in the segment on similarities and differences, immigrants accounted for only 48% of speakers but accounted for 77% of the instances of perspective-giving (therefore being largely overrepresented in this relational process).

Other top relational codes, however, were typically applied to several utterances by multiple participants. For instance, the code agreement would be applied to an excerpt in which a Latino participant made a claim and an African American participant followed with a corroboration. I could not, therefore, mark each excerpt of agreement as referring to a single participant's race/ethnicity and then make comparisons with the baseline values. Instead, I calculated manually on the coded transcript passages how much of that relational process took place between participants of the same racial/ethnic identity (for instance, a White American speaker agreeing with another White American speaker) or between participants of different racial/ethnic identities (for instance, a Latino participant agreeing with an African American participant). I looked at these values in light of the baseline values to verify outstanding discrepancies. For instance, if half of the speakers in a dialogue segment were U.S.-born and half were immigrants, but data showed that three-fourths of instances of agreement happened between U.S.-born participants, I would flag that finding and look into the transcripts to understand what transpired in that segment. That finding could indicate, for instance, an "echo chamber" of U.S.-born participants.

(3) **Variation of relational codes across thematic codes:** Using matrix coding on NVivo, I examined how relational codes varied across thematic codes to consider questions like "Was disagreement more common in discussions of language than in discussions of other topics?"

I also examined data under nonsalient codes in certain situations: when a code was not empirically significant but had theoretical importance (for instance, the code cosmopolitanism in the dialogue segment on similarities and differences), to refine the analysis of passages coded under the most salient codes, or to look into puzzling absences (for example, in the segment on tensions over immigration, one could reasonably expect a significant amount of disagreement between participants, so I had theoretical reasons to look into instances of disagreement even if disagreement turned out not to be one of the most recurrent parental relational codes in that segment).

While interpreting the data from the dialogue transcripts, I also relied on observation notes that I took shortly after meetings with the pastoral teams of host congregations, during dialogue sessions, and after dialogue sessions. My analysis of follow-up collaborative projects is also based on observation notes, which I took shortly after participating in those projects. Because of scheduling conflicts, I did not participate in the collaborative projects from HC3 and HC7. I checked in with participants of those dialogues through email or telephone afterward to collect information about the follow-up projects.

I combined the analytical memos resulting from the procedures described in this section into chapter drafts. The next and near-final step of the analysis consisted of a comprehensive thematic-relational analysis of all segments of all dialogues together (instead of each of the three main segments being analyzed separately: tensions over immigration, similarities/differences, and visions for collaboration). I limited this analysis to hierarchy charts and matrix coding in order to identify the most salient thematic codes, the most salient relational processes, their most salient intersections, and their variation across participant race/ethnicity. At this stage, I did not analyze variations across dialogues, nor did I review the actual transcript passages classified under salient codes, because the goal of this step was to provide a bird's-eye view of the data against which findings from specific dialogue segments could be juxtaposed. The only exceptions were the passages classified under the codes disagreement and solidarity, whose coded passages I reviewed because of their unexpectedly low incidence. After juxtaposing the specific findings from individual chapters with the big picture of the data, I arrived at the key findings of the study and shared them for discussion in the focus group with faith leaders (which I described previously in this appendix). The focus group allowed me to refine the key findings and generate a final conclusion.

Tables A.9 through A.26 show the data generated and used in the analytical steps just described, according to each dialogue segment and for the comprehensive thematic-relational analysis. For all tables, WA = White American, AA = African American, L = Latino, As = Asian, Af = African, WE = White European, and U = Unassigned.

Segment on Tensions over Immigration (Chapter 3)

TABLE A.9 RACE/ETHNICITY OF SPEAKERS IN SEGMENT ON TENSIONS OVER IMMIGRATION—ABSOLUTE NUMBERS PER DIALOGUE AND OVERALL PERCENTAGES

| Race/Ethnicity | HC1 | HC2 | HC3 | HC4 | HC5 | HC6 | HC7 | Total | % |
|---|---|---|---|---|---|---|---|---|---|
| WA | 3 | 7 | 0 | 4 | 0 | 4 | 3 | 22 | 32 |
| AA | 6 | 0 | 5 | 2 | 0 | 0 | 0 | 13 | 19 |
| L | 2 | 3 | 3 | 0 | 4 | 6 | 10 | 28 | 41 |
| As | 0 | 0 | 0 | 0 | 0 | 0 | 0 | 0 | 0 |
| Af | 0 | 0 | 0 | 2 | 1 | 0 | 0 | 3 | 5 |
| WE | 0 | 1 | 0 | 0 | 0 | 0 | 1 | 2 | 3 |
| U | 0 | 0 | 0 | 0 | 0 | 0 | 0 | 0 | 0 |
| Total | 11 | 12 | 8 | 8 | 5 | 10 | 14 | 68 | 100 |

TABLE A.10 TOP THEMATIC CODES IN SEGMENT ON TENSIONS OVER IMMIGRATION—TOTAL NUMBER OF UTTERANCES AND PERCENTAGE DISTRIBUTION OF UTTERANCES PER DIALOGUE

| Thematic Code | Total | HC1 | HC2 | HC3 | HC4 | HC5 | HC6 | HC7 |
|---|---|---|---|---|---|---|---|---|
| Youth | 29 | 28 | 18 | 21 | 0 | 4 | 4 | 25 |
| Cosmopolitanism | 31 | 17 | 14 | 0 | 45 | 17 | 7 | 0 |
| Economic problems | 50 | 14 | 29 | 9 | 4 | 2 | 9 | 33 |
| Exploitation, abuse, or discrimination | 68 | 12 | 5 | 17 | 6 | 8 | 19 | 33 |
| Language | 40 | 8 | 3 | 25 | 17 | 0 | 6 | 41 |
| Law | 60 | 25 | 13 | 0 | 4 | 2 | 16 | 40 |
| Religion | 52 | 15 | 2 | 9 | 50 | 2 | 20 | 2 |
| Social identity and belonging | 24 | 4 | 42 | 42 | 4 | 0 | 8 | 0 |
| Spaces of intergroup contact | 60 | 24 | 5 | 11 | 19 | 9 | 16 | 16 |

TABLE A.11 TOP THEMATIC CODES IN SEGMENT ON TENSIONS OVER IMMIGRATION—TOTAL NUMBER OF UTTERANCES AND PERCENTAGE DISTRIBUTION OF UTTERANCES PER SPEAKER RACE/ETHNICITY

| Thematic Code | Total | WA | AA | L | As | Af | WE | U |
|---|---|---|---|---|---|---|---|---|
| Youth | 29 | 21 | 41 | 38 | 0 | 0 | 0 | 0 |
| Cosmopolitanism | 31 | 65 | 10 | 19 | 0 | 6 | 0 | 0 |
| Economic problems | 50 | 34 | 12 | 50 | 0 | 4 | 0 | 0 |
| Exploitation, abuse, or discrimination | 68 | 19 | 22 | 54 | 0 | 5 | 0 | 0 |
| Language | 40 | 20 | 22 | 55 | 0 | 3 | 0 | 0 |
| Law | 60 | 36 | 7 | 55 | 0 | 2 | 0 | 0 |
| Religion | 52 | 73 | 4 | 21 | 0 | 2 | 0 | 0 |
| Social identity and belonging | 24 | 38 | 33 | 21 | 0 | 0 | 0 | 8 |
| Spaces of intergroup contact | 60 | 40 | 25 | 32 | 0 | 3 | 0 | 0 |

## TABLE A.12 TOP RELATIONAL CODES IN SEGMENT ON TENSIONS OVER IMMIGRATION—TOTAL NUMBER AND PERCENTAGE DISTRIBUTION PER DIALOGUE

| Relational Code | Total | HC1 | HC2 | HC3 | HC4 | HC5 | HC6 | HC7 |
|---|---|---|---|---|---|---|---|---|
| Agreement | 19 | 16 | 26 | 5 | 16 | 0 | 11 | 26 |
| Perspective-giving across differences | 74 | 17 | 10 | 26 | 6 | 0 | 15 | 26 |
| Perspective-taking across differences | 13 | 23 | 8 | 8 | 0 | 0 | 15 | 46 |

*Note:* For agreement, the number of exchanges; for perspective-giving and perspective-taking, the number of utterances.

## TABLE A.13 TOP RELATIONAL CODES IN SEGMENT ON TENSIONS OVER IMMIGRATION—TOTAL NUMBER OF UTTERANCES AND PERCENTAGE DISTRIBUTION OF UTTERANCES PER PARTICIPANT RACE/ETHNICITY

| Relational Code | Total | WA | AA | L | As | Af | WE | U |
|---|---|---|---|---|---|---|---|---|
| Perspective-giving across differences | 74 | 15 | 21 | 58 | 0 | 3 | 3 | 0 |
| Perspective-taking across differences | 13 | 69 | 31 | 0 | 0 | 0 | 0 | 0 |

*Note:* Only top relational codes applied to single utterances.

### Segment on Similarities and Differences between Immigrants and U.S.-born People (Chapter 4)

## TABLE A.14 RACE/ETHNICITY OF SPEAKERS IN SEGMENT ON SIMILARITIES AND DIFFERENCES—ABSOLUTE NUMBER OF SPEAKERS PER DIALOGUE AND OVERALL PERCENTAGES

| Race/Ethnicity | HC1 | HC2 | HC3 | HC4 | HC5 | HC6 | HC7 | Total | % |
|---|---|---|---|---|---|---|---|---|---|
| WA | 3 | 9 | 1 | 4 | 1 | 3 | 4 | 25 | 34 |
| AA | 6 | 0 | 4 | 2 | 0 | 0 | 0 | 12 | 17 |
| L | 2 | 3 | 4 | 0 | 5 | 6 | 10 | 30 | 41 |
| As | 0 | 1 | 0 | 0 | 1 | 0 | 0 | 2 | 3 |
| Af | 0 | 0 | 0 | 2 | 1 | 0 | 0 | 3 | 4 |
| U | 1 | 0 | 0 | 0 | 0 | 0 | 0 | 1 | 1 |
| Total | 12 | 13 | 9 | 8 | 8 | 9 | 14 | 73 | 100 |

## TABLE A.15 TOP THEMATIC CODES IN SEGMENT ON SIMILARITIES AND DIFFERENCES—TOTAL NUMBER OF UTTERANCES AND PERCENTAGE DISTRIBUTION OF UTTERANCES PER DIALOGUE

| Thematic Code | Total | HC1 | HC2 | HC3 | HC4 | HC5 | HC6 | HC7 |
|---|---|---|---|---|---|---|---|---|
| Exploitation, abuse, or discrimination | 109 | 29 | 7 | 19 | 22 | 16 | 1 | 6 |
| Language | 101 | 13 | 30 | 11 | 12 | 9 | 7 | 18 |
| Economic problems | 93 | 27 | 24 | 4 | 6 | 15 | 13 | 11 |
| Youth | 88 | 18 | 19 | 15 | 15 | 16 | 7 | 10 |
| Social identity and belonging | 82 | 15 | 18 | 18 | 23 | 12 | 5 | 9 |
| Law | 79 | 34 | 6 | 3 | 5 | 32 | 10 | 10 |
| Religion | 76 | 5 | 24 | 6 | 17 | 24 | 3 | 21 |
| Spaces of intergroup contact | 66 | 36 | 6 | 11 | 24 | 8 | 3 | 12 |

## TABLE A.16 TOP THEMATIC CODES IN SEGMENT ON SIMILARITIES AND DIFFERENCES—TOTAL NUMBER OF UTTERANCES AND PERCENTAGE DISTRIBUTION OF UTTERANCES PER SPEAKER RACE/ETHNICITY

| Thematic Code | Total | WA | AA | L | As | Af | U |
|---|---|---|---|---|---|---|---|
| Exploitation, abuse, or discrimination | 109 | 17 | 29 | 38 | 1 | 15 | 0 |
| Language | 101 | 41 | 11 | 41 | 3 | 3 | 1 |
| Economic problems | 93 | 30 | 15 | 44 | 1 | 10 | 0 |
| Youth | 88 | 24 | 17 | 39 | 2 | 18 | 0 |
| Social identity and belonging | 82 | 29 | 11 | 39 | 3 | 18 | 0 |
| Law | 79 | 24 | 11 | 61 | 0 | 4 | 0 |
| Religion | 76 | 29 | 6 | 42 | 3 | 20 | 0 |
| Spaces of intergroup contact | 66 | 15 | 32 | 41 | 1 | 11 | 0 |

## TABLE A.17 TOP RELATIONAL CODES IN SEGMENT ON SIMILARITIES AND DIFFERENCES—TOTAL NUMBER AND PERCENTAGE DISTRIBUTION PER DIALOGUE

| Relational Code | Total | HC1 | HC2 | HC3 | HC4 | HC5 | HC6 | HC7 |
|---|---|---|---|---|---|---|---|---|
| Agreement | 41 | 12 | 35 | 12 | 7 | 22 | 7 | 5 |
| Perspective-giving | 152 | 13 | 15 | 13 | 15 | 14 | 6 | 24 |
| Perspective-taking | 62 | 24 | 24 | 11 | 15 | 10 | 6 | 10 |

*Note:* For agreement, the number of exchanges; for perspective-giving and perspective-taking, the number of utterances.

## TABLE A.18 TOP RELATIONAL CODES IN SEGMENT ON SIMILARITIES AND DIFFERENCES—TOTAL NUMBER OF UTTERANCES AND PERCENTAGE DISTRIBUTION OF UTTERANCES PER PARTICIPANT RACE/ETHNICITY

| Relational Code | Total | WA | AA | L | As | Af |
|---|---|---|---|---|---|---|
| Perspective-giving | 152 | 14 | 9 | 60 | 4 | 13 |
| Perspective-taking | 62 | 66 | 29 | 5 | 0 | 0 |

*Note:* Only top relational codes applied to single utterances.

Segment on Envisioning Collaboration (Chapter 5)

## TABLE A.19 RACE/ETHNICITY OF SPEAKERS IN SEGMENT ON ENVISIONING COLLABORATION—ABSOLUTE NUMBER OF SPEAKERS PER DIALOGUE AND OVERALL PERCENTAGES

| Race/Ethnicity | HC1 | HC2 | HC3 | HC4 | HC5 | HC6 | HC7 | Total | % |
|---|---|---|---|---|---|---|---|---|---|
| WA | 3 | 9 | 2 | 2 | 0 | 4 | 4 | 24 | 37 |
| AA | 6 | 0 | 5 | 1 | 0 | 0 | 0 | 12 | 18 |
| L | 2 | 2 | 3 | 0 | 3 | 5 | 7 | 22 | 34 |
| As | 0 | 0 | 0 | 0 | 1 | 0 | 0 | 1 | 2 |
| Af | 0 | 0 | 0 | 2 | 1 | 0 | 0 | 3 | 4 |
| WE | 0 | 1 | 0 | 0 | 0 | 0 | 1 | 2 | 3 |
| U | 0 | 1 | 0 | 0 | 0 | 0 | 0 | 1 | 2 |
| Total | 11 | 13 | 10 | 5 | 5 | 9 | 12 | 65 | 100 |

**TABLE A.20 TOP THEMATIC CODES IN SEGMENT ON ENVISIONING COLLABORATION—TOTAL NUMBER OF UTTERANCES AND PERCENTAGE DISTRIBUTION OF UTTERANCES PER DIALOGUE**

| Thematic Code | Total | HC1 | HC2 | HC3 | HC4 | HC5 | HC6 | HC7 |
|---|---|---|---|---|---|---|---|---|
| Youth | 38 | 19 | 3 | 38 | 30 | 5 | 5 | 0 |
| Cosmopolitanism | 92 | 20 | 13 | 2 | 30 | 19 | 7 | 9 |
| Exploitation, abuse, or discrimination | 27 | 41 | 11 | 0 | 0 | 30 | 7 | 11 |
| Food | 26 | 12 | 19 | 0 | 19 | 0 | 12 | 38 |
| Language | 36 | 31 | 0 | 22 | 17 | 0 | 8 | 22 |
| Out-group perceptions | 16 | 0 | 69 | 0 | 6 | 6 | 0 | 19 |
| Political action | 26 | 80 | 8 | 0 | 4 | 8 | 0 | 0 |
| Race | 21 | 38 | 9 | 0 | 9 | 24 | 0 | 20 |
| Religion | 108 | 16 | 10 | 11 | 22 | 25 | 7 | 9 |
| Social identity and belonging | 15 | 27 | 27 | 0 | 0 | 0 | 46 | 0 |
| Spaces of intergroup contact | 82 | 46 | 14 | 6 | 3 | 17 | 10 | 4 |

**TABLE A.21 TOP THEMATIC CODES IN SEGMENT ON ENVISIONING COLLABORATION—TOTAL NUMBER OF UTTERANCES AND PERCENTAGE DISTRIBUTION OF UTTERANCES PER SPEAKER RACE/ ETHNICITY**

| Thematic Code | Total | WA | AA | L | As | Af | WE | U |
|---|---|---|---|---|---|---|---|---|
| Youth | 38 | 31 | 42 | 11 | 0 | 16 | 0 | 0 |
| Cosmopolitanism | 92 | 33 | 14 | 30 | 0 | 22 | 1 | 1 |
| Exploitation, abuse, or discrimination | 27 | 22 | 15 | 44 | 0 | 19 | 0 | 0 |
| Food | 26 | 69 | 0 | 23 | 0 | 4 | 4 | 0 |
| Language | 36 | 20 | 36 | 33 | 0 | 11 | 0 | 0 |
| Out-group perceptions | 16 | 69 | 0 | 19 | 0 | 12 | 0 | 0 |
| Political action | 26 | 42 | 35 | 23 | 0 | 0 | 0 | 0 |
| Race | 21 | 14 | 34 | 38 | 0 | 14 | 0 | 0 |
| Religion | 108 | 26 | 24 | 25 | 4 | 21 | 0 | 0 |
| Social identity and belonging | 15 | 13 | 7 | 80 | 0 | 0 | 0 | 0 |
| Spaces of intergroup contact | 82 | 29 | 20 | 43 | 2 | 6 | 0 | 0 |

**TABLE A.22 TOP RELATIONAL CODES IN SEGMENT ON ENVISIONING COLLABORATION—TOTAL NUMBER AND PERCENTAGE DISTRIBUTION PER DIALOGUE**

| Relational Code | Total | HC1 | HC2 | HC3 | HC4 | HC5 | HC6 | HC7 |
|---|---|---|---|---|---|---|---|---|
| Agreement | 38 | 24 | 24 | 3 | 26 | 5 | 15 | 3 |
| Perspective-giving across differences | 35 | 9 | 9 | 19 | 7 | 19 | 9 | 28 |
| Curiosity across differences | 5 | 60 | 20 | 20 | 0 | 0 | 0 | 0 |

*Note:* For agreement, the number of exchanges; for perspective-giving and curiosity, the number of utterances.

**TABLE A.23 TOP RELATIONAL CODES IN SEGMENT ON ENVISIONING COLLABORATION—TOTAL NUMBER OF UTTERANCES AND PERCENTAGE DISTRIBUTION PER PARTICIPANT RACE/ETHNICITY**

| Relational Code | Total | WA | AA | L | As | Af | WE | U |
|---|---|---|---|---|---|---|---|---|
| Perspective-giving across differences | 35 | 12 | 14 | 51 | 6 | 17 | 0 | 0 |
| Curiosity across differences | 5 | 20 | 80 | 0 | 0 | 0 | 0 | 0 |

*Note:* Only top relational codes applied to single utterances.

Comprehensive Analysis

**TABLE A.24 RACE/ETHNICITY OF SPEAKERS**

| Race/Ethnicity | Speakers | % |
|---|---|---|
| WA | 30 | 31 |
| AA | 15 | 16 |
| L | 43 | 44 |
| As | 2 | 2 |
| Af | 3 | 3 |
| WE | 2 | 2 |
| U | 2 | 2 |
| Total | 97 | 100 |

**TABLE A.25 TOP THEMATIC CODES—TOTAL NUMBER OF UTTERANCES AND PERCENTAGE DISTRIBUTION OF UTTERANCES PER SPEAKER RACE/ETHNICITY**

| Thematic Code | Total | WA | AA | L | As | Af | WE | U |
|---|---|---|---|---|---|---|---|---|
| Cosmopolitanism | 181 | 40 | 11 | 29 | 0 | 19 | 1 | 0 |
| Economic problems | 154 | 34 | 14 | 43 | 1 | 8 | 0 | 0 |
| Exploitation, abuse, or discrimination | 204 | 19 | 25 | 44 | 0 | 12 | 0 | 0 |
| Language | 179 | 32 | 18 | 43 | 2 | 5 | 0 | 1 |
| Law | 150 | 29 | 10 | 58 | 0 | 3 | 0 | 0 |
| Youth | 155 | 25 | 28 | 32 | 1 | 14 | 0 | 0 |
| Religion | 308 | 37 | 15 | 31 | 2 | 15 | 0 | 0 |
| Spaces of intergroup contact | 215 | 29 | 26 | 38 | 1 | 6 | 0 | 0 |

**TABLE A.26 TOP RELATIONAL CODES—TOTAL NUMBER OF UTTERANCES AND PERCENTAGE DISTRIBUTION PER PARTICIPANT RACE/ETHNICITY**

| Relational Code | Total | WA | AA | L | As | Af | WE | U |
|---|---|---|---|---|---|---|---|---|
| Agreement | 111 | n/a[a] | | | | | | |
| Interactive critical thinking | 57 | n/a[a] | | | | | | |
| Perspective-giving across differences | 264 | 14 | 13 | 59 | 3 | 10 | 1 | 0 |
| Perspective-taking across differences | 80 | 67 | 29 | 4 | 0 | 0 | 0 | 0 |

*Note:* Percentage distribution per participant race/ethnicity only for top relational codes applied to single utterances.
[a] n/a = not applicable

# Appendix B

*The Latino Racial Justice Circle Guide for Honest
Conversations on Immigration*

## B.1. BACKGROUND AND GOALS

One of the biggest challenges for society today is to ensure that diverse people can peacefully coexist and, if possible, work together for the common good. Immigration is one of the main sources of diversity in society. According to the Pew Research Center, immigrants accounted for 13.6% of the United States population in 2017. Immigration influences the economy, politics, and culture in multiple ways, making it a topic of significant controversy. In response to this context, the Latino Racial Justice Circle (LJRC) was created in 2015 as a faith-based group of volunteers that seeks to create opportunities throughout Maryland for meaningful, authentic conversations about immigration among people of different cultures, forming cross-cultural, faith-based communities focused on spiritual growth and improving social relationships.

In 2018, LRJC established the program "Honest Conversations on Immigration," which brings together diverse people of faith to share personal stories, feelings, and thoughts about immigration; to reflect on differences and commonalities between immigrants and those born in the United States; and to deliberate on collaborative action to advance common interests and shared values. From summer 2018 to summer 2019, Dr. Felipe Filomeno—an LRJC volunteer and professor of political science at the University of Maryland Baltimore County (UMBC)—led the design, implementation, assessment, and analysis of pilot "Honest Conversations on Immigration." The design of the conversations was informed by a review of the academic literature about the intersection of religion, race, and immigration and a review of existing models for intergroup community dialogue.

Based on this year-long community-based research project, Dr. Filomeno—in deep and extensive collaboration with LRJC members—wrote the *LRJC Guide for Honest Conversations on Immigration*. The guide describes, step by step, how to implement the program. LRJC hopes it will enable faith communities everywhere to use conversation for mutual understanding and collaboration between immigrants and people born in the

United States. The guide includes organization procedures, recommendations for facilitators, ground rules and prayer, and questions for conversation. Although the guide was based on the experience of conversations among mostly Catholic participants, it is adaptable to other faith traditions and interfaith contexts.

## B.2. ORGANIZATION

At least two people should be in charge of organizing Honest Conversations on Immigration. One should be the facilitator; the other should be the logistics coordinator, who will lead the scheduling of conversation sessions, the recruitment of participants, the communication with faith leaders and staff, the securing of a room for the conversation sessions, the purchase supplies, the setup and cleanup of the room. Two organizers, however, is the minimum. Ideally, a committee would be in charge of the organization. This committee should include representatives of the faith communities involved. This will facilitate the implementation of the conversation and increase the trust of participants in the process. The Honest Conversations on Immigration should have between ten and fifteen participants. Participants sit in a circle and are given name tags, pens, paper, and refreshments. To recruit participants, organizers may circulate flyers and sign-up sheets after worship events, in faith community bulletins, or through other means. A fruitful conversation depends on a diversity of identities and perspectives among participants. If a faith community is already diverse regarding race, ethnicity, nationality, or another form of social stratification, organizers can easily recruit a diverse sample of participants. If a faith community is nearly homogeneous, organizers might want to include members of a different faith community in the conversation. The conversation should have a balanced representation of members of different groups so that members of one group do not feel overpowered by others in the conversation.

When diversity implies the inclusion of participants who are not fluent in English, organizers can translate the materials to other languages and have facilitators fluent in those languages. In this guide, the essential materials are presented in English and Spanish (in italics, following the passages in English).

When more than fifteen people are interested in the conversation, participants can be split into small groups as long as each group is diverse and has a facilitator. The small groups can reconvene at the end of the activities and share their conclusions.

The Honest Conversations on Immigration happen in three meetings, with one meeting per week over three consecutive weeks. The first meeting lasts for about two hours; the second and third last for about one hour and thirty minutes. The program is divided into three parts: introduction, conversation, and conclusion. In the introduction, the facilitator welcomes participants, states the goals of the conversation and the role of the facilitator, and leads participants' agreement on ground rules for conversation and the Prayer of Saint Francis of Assisi. Organizers may choose another prayer, depending on the faith traditions of participants. It is important that the prayer invoke the spirit of mutual understanding.

The conversation is the core of the program. It is divided into three sections: (1) personal stories, feelings, and thoughts about immigration; (2) perceptions of differences and commonalities between immigrants and people born in the United States; and (3) visions of how participants' communities should approach immigration and deliberation on collaborative action to achieve that vision. The Honest Conversations on Immigration are, therefore, deliberative conversations in which communication for mutual understanding is followed by communication for a collective decision. Moreover, it strives for a critical exploration of what unites people and what differentiates them without assuming that participants should focus on either.

## B.3. RECOMMENDATIONS FOR FACILITATORS

Read the *LRJC Guide for Honest Conversations on Immigration* carefully, with special attention to the role assigned to facilitators.

- Your main task is to keep the discussion focused, stay neutral, and enforce the ground rules. Do not act as a teacher or expert. You should not become the "go-to" person to answer questions.
- Rehearse the dialogues with at least one other person before the actual dialogues using the *LRJC Guide*.
- At the beginning of the first conversation session, welcome and thank all participants. At the end of the last conversation session, thank all participants.
- Value people and their ideas, promoting critical thinking on those ideas without being judgmental. Ask questions about the pros and cons of ideas or facts and about assumptions and concerns underlying ideas.
- If a participant says something that is controversial or upsetting for others, do not censor it. Instead, use one or more of the following tactics:
  - Ask the participant to clarify the controversial statement and explain how the participant reached that conclusion. This will allow other participants to "work through" the controversial statement. For instance, if the statement is based on an individual experience or anecdote, another participant might share a contrasting experience or anecdote, showing the problems with overgeneralizing from specific situations.
  - Invite the group to reflect on the controversial statement and share thoughts, including why they think it is problematic.
  - Help participants identify common ground but do not force consensus (McCoy, Flavin, and Reaven 1999, 9). In times of political polarization, people tend to overlook common ground. For instance, those who support mass deportations and those who support giving amnesty to undocumented immigrants might think they are total opposites, but they agree that having millions of immigrants living in the shadow of the law is a problem. However, the first think the solution is to strictly enforce existing laws, and the others think existing laws should be improved. To direct attention to emerging points of agreement, you can say, "From what I am hearing, it seems that several of you agree that . . ."
  - Remind people that disagreement is normal and should not be personalized. Sometimes people can just agree to disagree.
- Not all disagreements are bad, and not all agreements are good. Share counterpoints as needed to help remove false consensus (Sustained Dialogue Campus Network 2017, 2) or to promote critical thinking. If necessary, you may share factual information as long as it comes from widely accepted sources. However, as much as possible, participants should be the ones offering counterpoints, not you.
- Prevent outspoken participants from monopolizing the conversation (You may say, "Rob, could you please wrap up your thoughts in one sentence?"). Don't single out individuals who are not participating ("Jen, what do you think?") but in-

stead ask for new voices or perspectives ("I'd like to hear from someone who feels differently" or "I'd like to hear from those who haven't spoken yet") (Sustained Dialogue Campus Network 2017, 2).

- Mutual understanding and genuine collaboration require honest speaking and active listening. The conversation should not be a serial monologue in which participants do not ask each other questions and do not follow up on each other's points. You may ask a participant, "And how would you relate what you just said to John's idea about . . . ?"
- Don't be afraid to directly refocus the group. You may close tangents or set them aside in a "parking lot" for consideration later (Sustained Dialogue Campus Network 2017, 2). If someone starts digressing, you may say, "I'm having trouble connecting what you're saying to this question about . . . Can you make the connection?" (Herzig 2011, 23).
- Do not fear silence. Participants will need time to reflect before addressing a question. If silence follows a question on a "touchy" subject, remind participants that this is a safe space to share opinions without fear of judgment and that we are not required to agree. The dialogue should not be confined to easy topics and superficial conversations.
- Do not be shy in intervening to enforce ground rules, especially at the beginning of the conversation, to set the tone for the process.

## B.4. CONVERSATION SCRIPT

*First Session*
**Introduction**
    FACILITATOR: Welcome, everyone! My name is _____. I will work as the facilitator of this Honest Conversation on Immigration. Although this is a conversation on immigration, the goal is not to make people who were born here help immigrants or to have everyone agree on immigration matters; the goal is to allow immigrants and those who were born here to understand each other, build relationships and work together on something that matters for both groups. We will meet today and in the next two weeks as well. My role will be to keep our conversation focused and to enforce the ground rules we will create. I will not share my own opinions or judge who is right or wrong. *¡Bienvenidos a todos! Me llamo _____. Trabajaré como facilitador de este diálogo de comunidad de fe sobre inmigración. Aunque este es una conversación sobre inmigración, el objetivo no es hacer que las personas que nacieron aquí ayuden a los inmigrantes o que todos estén de acuerdo en asuntos de inmigración; el objetivo es permitir que los inmigrantes y los que nacieron aquí se entiendan, construyan relaciones y trabajen juntos en algo que sea importante para ambos grupos. Nos reuniremos hoy y también en las próximas dos semanas. Mi papel es mantener nuestra conversación enfocada y hacer cumplir las reglas básicas que crearemos. No compartiré mis propias opiniones ni juzgaré quién tiene razón o no.*

    Now, let's go around the circle with introductions. My name is _____ and my family is originally from _____. Please say your name and the country where your family originally came from. *Ahora, recorramos el círculo con presentaciones. Mi nombre es _____ y mi familia es originaria de _____. Por favor diga su nombre y el país de donde su familia es originaria.*

FACILITATOR: Our next step is to establish ground rules for the conversation. You have in front of you a list of suggested rules [distribute handout], which we can edit as we wish. Let's start by reading each of the rules together out loud and stop to reflect on each of them for a minute. *Nuestro paso siguiente es establecer reglas básicas para el diálogo. Tiene frente a usted una lista de reglas sugeridas, que podemos editar como lo deseemos. Comencemos leyendo cada una de las reglas en voz alta y detengámonos para reflexionar sobre cada una de ellas por un minuto.*

FACILITATOR AND PARTICIPANTS: We agree to talk in good faith. We will listen to others carefully, speak honestly, and be open to thinking together. *Estamos de acuerdo en dialogar de buena fe. Escucharemos a los demás con atención, hablaremos con sinceridad, y estaremos abiertos a cambiar de opinión y a trabajar juntos.*

FACILITATOR: What do you think of this rule? *¿Qué opina de esta regla?*

[If the participants agree with the rule, the facilitator might want to explain the following to participants.] We tend to identify with our views and defend them almost automatically. Here, we will try to suspend our automatic judgment and give each other a chance, thereby creating a space to think together about immigration. *Nosotros tendemos a identificarnos con nuestros puntos de vista y defenderlos casi automáticamente. Aquí, intentaremos suspender nuestro juicio automático y darle una oportunidad al otro, creando así un espacio para pensarnos juntos sobre la inmigración.*

FACILITATOR AND PARTICIPANTS: We will raise our hands to the facilitator every time we want to speak. We will talk one person at a time and keep our comments brief. *Levantaremos nuestras manos al facilitador cada vez que queramos hablar. Hablaremos una persona a la vez y mantendremos nuestros comentarios breves.*

FACILITATOR: What do you think of this rule? *¿Qué opina de esta regla?*

FACILITATOR AND PARTICIPANTS: We will face and work through disagreements respectfully. Disagreements will be about ideas and not personalized. It is okay to disagree. *Abordaremos los desacuerdos con respeto. Los desacuerdos serán sobre ideas y no personalizados. Está bien no estar de acuerdo.*

FACILITATOR: What do you think of this rule? *¿Qué opina de esta regla?*

FACILITATOR AND PARTICIPANTS: We understand that conversations on immigration can be difficult and unlikely to have closure within a single meeting. We will stay open to talking about these issues in the same spirit as today. *Entendemos que conversaciones sobre inmigración pueden ser difíciles y es poco probable que se concluyan en una sola reunión. Estaremos abiertos a hablar sobre estos temas con el mismo espíritu que hoy.*

FACILITATOR: What do you think of this rule? *¿Qué opina de esta regla?*

FACILITATOR AND PARTICIPANTS: We allow the facilitator to remind us of these rules during the conversation. *Permitimos que el facilitador nos recuerde estas reglas durante la conversación.*

Would anyone like to suggest changes to the ground rules? *¿A alguien le gustaría sugerir cambios a las reglas básicas?* [Participants might suggest changes and have to agree on them. The facilitator should write the rules on a board.]

FACILITATOR: Now I will give you pieces of paper for you to write down one to three religious values, beliefs, or practices that connect to those rules. You will have a few of minutes to do this and we will then share our responses. It's important to make our conversation rules meaningful to our faith. [Give people time and ask them to share their answers]. *Ahora les daré pedazos de papel para que escriban de uno a tres valores, creencias, o prácticas religiosas que se conectan con esas reglas. Tendrá unos minutos para hacer esto y luego compartiremos nuestras respuestas. Es importante que nuestras reglas de conversación estén relacionadas con nuestra fe.*

FACILITATOR: Before we move on, would you like to say the prayer of Saint Francis? *Antes de continuar, ¿les gustaría decir la oración de San Francisco?* [Show and distribute handout with prayer.]

FACILITATOR AND PARTICIPANTS:

*Lord, make me an instrument of your peace.*
*Where there is hatred, let me sow love;*
*Where there is injury, pardon;*
*Where there is doubt, faith;*
*Where there is despair, hope;*
*Where there is darkness, light;*
*And where there is sadness, joy.*
*O divine master, grant that I may not so much seek to be consoled as to console;*
*to be understood, as to understand;*
*to be loved, as to love.*
*For it is in giving that we receive,*
*it is in pardoning that we are pardoned,*
*and it's in dying that we are born to eternal life.*
*Amen*

*Oh, Señor, hazme un instrumento de Tu paz.*
*Donde hay odio, que lleve yo el amor.*
*Donde haya ofensa, que lleve yo el perdón.*
*Donde haya discordia, que lleve yo la unión.*
*Donde haya duda, que lleve yo la fe.*
*Donde haya error, que lleve yo la verdad.*
*Donde haya desesperación, que lleve yo la alegría.*
*Donde haya tinieblas, que lleve yo la luz.*
*Oh, Maestro, haced que yo no busque tanto ser consolado, sino consolar;*
*ser comprendido, sino comprender;*
*ser amado, como amar.*
*Porque es dando, que se recibe;*
*Perdonando, que se es perdonado;*
*Muriendo, que se resucita a la vida eterna.*
*Amen*

FACILITATOR: We will say this prayer at the beginning of each conversation session. Do you have any questions? *Diremos esta oración al comienzo de cada sesión de diálogo. ¿Tiene usted alguna pregunta?*

### Part I: Personal Stories, Feelings, and Thoughts about Immigration

FACILITATOR: What does your faith tradition say about foreigners and immigrants? *¿Qué dice tu tradición de fe sobre los extranjeros y inmigrantes?*

FACILITATOR: Have you ever been an outsider, a minority, or invisible in a social context? You can answer this through a story about yourself or others. *¿Alguna* *vez ha sido un extraño, una minoría o invisible en un contexto social? Puede responder esto en forma de una historia sobre usted u otros.*

FACILITATOR: What helped you or could have helped you be more included? *¿Qué te ayudó o podría haberte ayudado a ser más incluido?*

FACILITATOR: Have you seen or experienced in your community tensions between immigrants and those born in the United States around cultural issues such as language, religion, or ways of life? *¿Ha visto o vivido en su comunidad tensiones entre inmigrantes y personas nacidas aquí en temas culturales como el idioma, la religión, o los estilos de vida?*

FACILITATOR: Have you seen or experienced in your community tensions between immigrants and those born in the United States around economic issues such as jobs, taxes, or social services? *¿Ha visto o vivido en su comunidad tensiones entre inmigrantes y personas nacidas aquí en torno a problemas económicos como empleos, impuestos, o servicios sociales?*

FACILITATOR: Have you seen or experienced tensions in your community around unauthorized immigration? *¿Ha visto o experimentado tensiones en su comunidad en torno a la inmigración no autorizada?*

FACILITATOR: Instead of tensions between immigrants and people born in the United States, have you seen or experienced positive interactions between immigrants and people born here? *En lugar de tensiones entre inmigrantes y personas nacidas en los Estados Unidos, ¿ha visto o vivido interacciones positivas entre inmigrantes y personas nacidas aquí?*

## Second Session
### Part II: Perceptions of Differences and Commonalities between Immigrants and People Born in the United States

FACILITATOR: Welcome, everyone, to our second conversation session. Today we will talk about differences and commonalities between immigrants and people born in the United States. Let's start by saying again the prayer of Saint Francis, which is in the handout. *Bienvenidos a todos a nuestra segunda reunión de diálogo. Hoy hablaremos sobre las diferencias y puntos en común entre los inmigrantes y las personas nacidas en los Estados Unidos. Comencemos diciendo nuevamente la oración de San Francisco, que se encuentra en el folleto.*

FACILITATOR: Why do people come to the United States? *¿Por qué la gente viene a los Estados Unidos?*

FACILITATOR: Is there any similarity between those reasons and why you or your family came to settle in Maryland? You can answer this through a story about yourself or others. *¿Existe alguna similitud entre esas razones y las razones por las que usted o su familia llegaron a Maryland? Puede responder esto en forma de una historia sobre usted u otros.*

FACILITATOR: Is there any difference between those reasons and the reasons you or your family came to settle in Maryland? You can answer this through a story about yourself or others. *¿Existe alguna diferencia entre esas razones y las razones por las que usted o su familia llegaron a Maryland? Puede responder esto en forma de una historia sobre usted u otros.*

FACILITATOR: What problems do immigrants face in the United States? *¿Qué problemas enfrentan los inmigrantes en los Estados Unidos?*

FACILITATOR: Is there any similarity between those problems and the ones you face? You can answer this through a story about yourself or others. *¿Hay alguna similitud entre esos problemas y los que usted enfrenta? Puede responder esto en forma de una historia sobre usted u otros.*

FACILITATOR: Is there any difference between those problems and those you face? You can answer this through a story about yourself or others. *¿Hay alguna diferencia entre esos problemas y los que usted enfrenta? Puede responder esto en forma de una historia sobre usted u otros.*

FACILITATOR: Based on our conversations, what might be some issues on which immigrants and people born here could work together? *Según nuestras conversaciónes, ¿cuáles podrían ser algunos problemas en torno de que inmigrantes y personas nacidas acá podrían trabajar en conjunto?*

*Third Session*
**Part III: Visions of How Participants' Communities Should Deal with Immigration and Actions that Participants Should Take to Achieve That Vision**

FACILITATOR: Welcome, everyone, to our third conversation session. Today we will talk about how our communities should deal with immigration in the future and actions that we could take to achieve this vision. Let's start by saying again the prayer of Saint Francis, which is in the handout. *Bienvenidos a todos a nuestra tercera sesión de conversación. Hoy hablaremos sobre cómo nuestras comunidades deberían lidiar con la inmigración en el futuro y las acciones que podríamos tomar para lograr esta visión. Comencemos repitiendo la oración de San Francisco, que está en el folleto.*

FACILITATOR: If we had excellent relations between immigrants and people born in the United States, what kinds of things would we see, hear, or feel in the communities? You can imagine a story that exemplifies excellent relations between immigrants and people born here. *Si tuviéramos excelentes relaciones entre inmigrantes y personas nacidas en los Estados Unidos, ¿qué tipo de cosas veríamos, escucharíamos, o sentiríamos en las comunidades? Puedes imaginar una historia que ejemplifique excelentes relaciones entre inmigrantes y personas nacidas aquí.*

FACILITATOR: What efforts are underway in our communities to make this vision a reality? *¿Qué esfuerzos se están realizando en nuestras comunidades para hacer realidad esta visión?*

FACILITATOR: Now let's choose one of the issues discussed so far and think of a concrete, specific action that we could take as a group to help solve that issue. In our last session, we arrived at a list of issues on which immigrants and people born here could work together. [Show list to participants.] Whatever issue we choose, we can either engage with an existing effort to solve that problem or start a new effort. *Ahora escojamos un de los problemas discutidos hasta ahora y pensemos en una acción concreta y específica que podríamos tomar como grupo para ayudar a resolver ese problema. En nuestra última sesión, llegamos a una lista de problemas en torno de que los inmigrantes y las personas nacidas aquí podrían trabajar conjuntamente. Cualquiera sea el problema que escojamos, podemos trabajar en un esfuerzo ya existente para resolver ese problema o comenzar un nuevo esfuerzo.*

FACILITATOR: Which issue should we focus on? *¿En cuál problema debemos centrarnos?* [Participants agree on a problem, discuss possible actions, and plan follow-up collaboration.]

## Conclusion

If the Honest Conversations on Immigration were conducted in small groups, the organizers would reconvene the groups and ask each group to share the collaborative action that each will pursue. If the program was conducted in a single group, jump to the next paragraph.

> FACILITATOR: As we approach the end of our conversation, I'd like to thank you for your participation. I am also giving you a handout with sources of information on immigration. Remember to stick to your action commitment, and please share what you have learned today with your family and friends. Thank you! [Distribute handout—to be created.] *A medida que nos acercamos al final de nuestra conversación, me gustaría agradecerles su participación. También les doy un folleto con fuentes de información sobre inmigración. Recuerde cumplir con su compromiso de acción, y comparta lo que ha aprendido hoy con su familia y amigos. ¡Gracias!*

Organizers might want to create and apply their own questionnaires to receive participant feedback. Organizers might also take this moment to share reliable information sources about immigration, such as the U.S. Citizenship and Immigration Services, the American Immigration Council, Welcoming America, and the Center for Migration Studies.

# Appendix C

## Group Discussion of Christian Principles and Traditions for Dialogue

This exercise can be applied before a Christian group engages in dialogue in order to help participants understand the concept of dialogue and ground it in their faith tradition. The exercise is not specific to dialogues about immigration. If the group is large, split participants into small groups (three to five people) and reconvene as needed for representatives of each group to share ideas with the broader group.

Dialogue is a mode of communication oriented to mutual understanding. For each of the following religious principles or scriptural passages, participants will collectively (1) explain the principle or passage with their own words and (2) discuss how it connects to the concept or practice of dialogue.[1]

- Saint Ignatius's Presupposition: "Let it be presupposed that every good Christian is to be more ready to save his neighbor's proposition than to condemn it. If he cannot save it, let him inquire how he means it; and if he means it badly, let him correct him with charity" (Ignatius of Loyola 1987; Spiritual Exercises no. 22).
- Communion: "The fact that there is only one loaf means that, though there are many of us, we form a single body because we all have a share in this one loaf" (1 Corinthians 10:17).
- Compassion: "For we do not have a high priest who is unable to empathize with our weaknesses, but we have one who has been tempted in every way, just as we are—yet he did not sin" (Hebrews 4:15).
- Humility: "Nor are you to be called instructors, for you have one Instructor, the Messiah. The greatest among you will be your servant. For those who exalt themselves will be humbled, and those who humble themselves will be exalted" (Matthew 23:10–12).
- Generosity: "You received without pay, give without pay" (Matthew 10:8).

- Temperance: One of the cardinal virtues. "Be sober-minded; be watchful. Your adversary the devil prowls around like a roaring lion, seeking someone to devour" (1 Peter 5:8). "Know this, my beloved brothers: let every person be quick to hear, slow to speak, slow to anger; for the anger of man does not produce the righteousness of God. Therefore put away all filthiness and rampant wickedness and receive with meekness the implanted word, which is able to save your souls" (James 1:19–21).
- Diversity: "Now there are a variety of gifts, but the same Spirit. . . . To each is given a manifestation of the Spirit for the common good. . . . For just as the body is one and has many members, and all the members of the body, though many, are one body, so it is with Christ" (1 Corinthians 12:4, 7, 12).
- Seeing God in others: "No one has ever seen God. Yet, if we love one another, God remains in us, and His love is brought to perfection in us" (1 John 4:12).

After participants have had enough time to complete the tasks, they should propose three to five ground rules that Christians should follow when engaging in dialogue. They could also write a prayer for dialogue grounded in those principles. Both the ground rules and prayer can be recited before a dialogue. Below is a prayer for dialogue written by this book's author:

### A PRAYER FOR DIALOGUE

*Dear God,*
*As I have received Your love,*
*may I be loving to those I disagree with.*
*May I be a generous listener,*
*offering them my time and attention.*
*May I be more ready to save their propositions than to condemn them.*
*And, if I cannot save their propositions,*
*may I correct them with charity and temperance.*
*Lord,*
*You have called on us to be humble.*
*May I recognize that I do not know what I do not know.*
*For just like the eyes need the ears to hear,*
*and the ears need the eyes to see,*
*I need others to understand the nuances of your creation,*
*and to have compassion for those whose situations I cannot fully understand.*
*But most of all,*
*May I love my neighbors.*
*For You dwell in all of us,*
*And all of us are one in You.*
*Amen.*

Inspired by the words of Saint Paul (1 Corinthians 12:4, 7, 12) and Saint Augustine (1885) on unity in diversity in the Body of Christ and by the words of Saint Ignatius of Loyola (1987) on presupposition.

# Notes

## CHAPTER 1

1. In this book, I use the term *Latino* to refer to people of Latin American background who live in the United States, many of whom are immigrants. While I recognize the importance of gender-neutral language (and have myself used the term *Latinx* in day-to-day conversations), *Latino* is the term used in the immigrant communities I worked with for this study.

2. Intersectionality refers to the interconnected nature of systems of social stratification, such as race, class, and gender. Every person or group is positioned at an intersection of multiple systems of social stratification, which imply qualitatively different social experiences. For instance, the life of an African American Catholic woman is not merely the addition of the experiences of an African American person, a Catholic person, and a woman, because those categories interact to produce a specific life experience.

3. I conducted a search on Google in October 2021 using the following terms: conversation OR dialogue OR discussion, immigration, church OR congregation. I limited the search to the first one hundred fifty results on Google. From the website of each organization or event, I collected data about the title of the program, denomination, year, location, rationale and goals, and format.

4. The web search was not exhaustive, and some congregation conversations on immigration were likely not published on the Internet.

5. For additional preparation, in the beginning of the project, I studied numerous dialogue facilitation manuals, watched online instructional talks, and attended two facilitator training workshops (one on peace circles and another on difficult political conversations).

6. This pilot experience informed the design of the subsequent dialogues. An evaluation based on participant exit questionnaires and a focus group with facilitators was peer-reviewed and published in 2019 (Filomeno 2019).

7. In Appendix A, I present the survey data.

8. Throughout the chapters, I refer to individual participants by their race/ethnicity as well as by their gender (because this is an aspect of participant identity that was easy to document in observation notes and transcripts). More information on the scheme of demographic categorization adopted in this study can be found in Section A.2 of Appendix A.

## CHAPTER 2

1. Agonism is a political theory that emphasizes the positive role that radical clashes of ideas can play in a society as long as such conflicts are nonviolent and respect the norms of democracy.

## CHAPTER 3

1. Expressions of racism by dialogue participants were very rare and usually veiled. For instance, in HC2, a White American woman complained indirectly about the lack of personal responsibility among African Americans, with references to fashion and behavioral stereotypes often associated with African Americans: "I'm not talking about immigrants, I'm talking about Americans here . . . at the neighborhood tavern. People would come up dressed to the nines, the earrings, the Coach bags, the fancy shoes, roll up in a Mercedes. And they have a cover charge into the bar, and they're complaining about the cover charge. And when they open their wallet, they all got an independence [credit] card. . . . They know how to work the system."

## CHAPTER 4

1. I removed this question from subsequent dialogues because it did not seem to have engaged participants of HC1, HC2 and HC3 as much as other questions.

## CHAPTER 6

1. Latino speakers accounted for 59% of perspective-giving instances but only 44% of speakers, African speakers accounted for 10% of the instances, but only 3% of speakers, and Asian speakers accounted for 3% of the instances, but only 2% of speakers. In contrast, White American speakers accounted for only 14% of perspective-giving instances, but 31% of speakers, and African American participants accounted for only 13% of instances, but 15% of speakers.

2. White American speakers accounted for 67% of the instances of perspective-taking but only 31% of speakers, and African American speakers accounted for 29% of the instances but only 15% of speakers. Latino speakers accounted for only 4% of perspective-taking instances but 44% of speakers, and African and Asian speakers accounted for 0% of the instances but 3% and 2%, respectively, of speakers.

## APPENDIX A

1. For instance, Participant1MAA meant participant number one who is a man and African American, and Participant3WL meant participant number three who is a Latina. To identify the race, ethnicity, or gender of an individual participant, I relied on mem-

ory, observation notes, and participant statements. At times, I or a participant mentioned names ("Susan, were you trying to say something?") or stated their social identities ("As an African American woman, I think . . ."). Because the dialogues were held in small groups and were spaced in time, I was able to assign social identities to participants using the procedures stated above. HC3 and HC4 were also video-recorded, which made the classification more straightforward.

2. Word-counting can provide only approximate indicators of domination in a dialogue. For instance, if Participant A corroborates what Participant B said, the words of Participant A are not necessarily words of domination. Participant A is actually taking the lead of Participant B. However, an extensive corroboration could indicate that Participant A is trying to take control of the conversation, even if substantively in agreement with what Participant B said. Another example is if Participant A asks Participant B to elaborate on a thought. The words of Participant A in that question are not words of domination; on the contrary, they indicate active listening on the part of Participant A. When comparing the relative number of words spoken by each type of participant (immigrant vs. U.S.-born; clergy vs. layperson) to offer a big picture of the dialogues, I assumed that domination false positives (utterances of agreement, corroboration, or probing questions) are present to the same degree in the statements by each type of participant. Since that assumption might not always hold, I explored participant interactions in more depth in Chapters 3, 4, and 5.

3. A parental code is one that may have child codes under it. In the coding scheme of this study, not every parental code has child codes, but no child code is a parental code. The number of passages associated with a parental code includes the passages associated with the child codes it may have. A hierarchy chart shows the number of passages in the transcripts that each code was applied to. I calculated the 0.66 percentile of the number of passages to identify a cutoff number above which the top third most recurrent codes would be found. For instance, for the segments on tensions over immigration, the 0.66 percentile was twenty-two passages, so every parent code that was applied to at least twenty-two passages was considered a potential bearer of salient themes.

4. A matrix coding query produces a table showing a certain parameter on the lines (for instance, thematic codes) and another parameter on the columns (for instance, dialogues), allowing us to see the number of passages coded at the intersection of the parameters (for instance, the thematic code "exploitation, abuse, or discrimination of immigrants" was applied to seven statements in HC1, five statements in HC2, etc.).

5. Analytical memos are mini-analyses that summarize partial findings, "examine data at a greater level of abstraction," and "explore hypotheses, relationships and explanations contained within the data" (Birks, Chapman, and Francis 2008, 73).

## APPENDIX C

1. It is not necessary to assign all principles or passages presented here. Given time constraints, the facilitator might want to select only a few principles.

# REFERENCES

Abu-Nimer, M. 2018. "Interfaith Dialogue and Religious Leaders in the Israeli-Palestinian Context Needs and Limitations." In *Religion, Conflict, and Peacemaking: An Interdisciplinary Conversation*, edited by M. Schmidt, 9–28. Salt Lake City: University of Utah Press.

Adami, R. 2013. "Intersectional Dialogue—A Cosmopolitical Dialogue of Ethics." *Cosmopolitan Civil Societies Journal* 5, no. 2: 45–62.

Alcoff, L. 2007. "Mignolo's Epistemology of Coloniality." *CR: The New Centennial Review* 7, no. 3: 79–101.

Allport, G. 1954. *The Nature of Prejudice*. Garden City, NJ: Doubleday.

AlSheddi, M. 2020. "Humility and Bridging Differences: A Systematic Literature Review of Humility in Relation to Diversity." *International Journal of Intercultural Relations* 79:36–45.

Ammerman, N. T. 1997. *Congregation and Community*. New Brunswick, NJ: Rutgers University Press.

Andrews, R. 2011. "Religious Communities, Immigration, and Social Cohesion in Rural Areas: Evidence from England." *Rural Sociology* 76, no. 4: 535–61.

Appadurai, A. 2017. "The Risks of Dialogue." *Mecila: Working Paper Series*, Working Paper no. 5. Maria Sibylla Merian International Centre for Advanced Studies in the Humanities and Social Sciences Conviviality-Inequality in Latin America, São Paulo, Brazil.

Appiah, K. 2019. "The Importance of Elsewhere: In Defense of Cosmopolitanism." *Foreign Affairs*, March/April: 20–26.

ARISE and the Labor Council for Latin American Advancement (LCLAA). 2011. "Let's Talk Immigration: An Interactive Workshop Promoting Public Dialogue on Immigration." Curriculum Guide. Accessed October 5, 2023. https://www.albany.edu/cpr/jones/Jones_LTI_Curric_Version_4.1.pdf.

Augustine, Saint. 1885. *Expositions on the Book of Psalms*. Oxford: J. H. and J. Parker.

Bakhtin, M. 1981. *The Dialogic Imagination: Four Essays*. Austin: University of Texas Press.

Baltimore Museum of Immigration. 2020. "Home." Accessed October 11, 2020. http://www.immigrationbaltimore.org.

Bauman, S., and J. Yang. 2013. "An Evangelical Perspective on Immigration." *Tikkun* Magazine 28, no. 3: 49–50.

Beck, U. 2008. "Reframing Power in the Globalized World." *Organization Studies* 29, no. 5: 793–804.

Berg, J. 2015. "Explaining Attitudes toward Immigrants and Immigration Policy: A Review of the Theoretical Literature." *Sociology Compass* 9, no. 1: 23–34.

Berger, R. M. 2008. *Strangers in the Land: A Six-Week Devotional Guide on Immigration, the Church, and the Bible*. Sojourners Magazine. e-Book available at https://www.amazon.com/Strangers-Land-Six-Week-Devotional-Immigration-ebook/dp/B00FL2VH40.

Birks, M., Chapman, Y., and Francis, K. 2008. "Memoing in Qualitative Research: Probing Data and Processes." *Journal of Research in Nursing* 13, no. 1: 68–75.

Blakenhorn, D. 2018. "My Debate with 'Dialogue.'" *The American Interest*, January 10, 2018. Accessed April 12, 2021. https://www.the-american-interest.com/2018/01/10/my-debate-with-dialogue/.

Bloom, P., G. Arikan, and M. Courtemanche. 2015. "Religious Social Identity, Religious Belief, and Anti-Immigration Sentiment." *American Political Science Review* 109, no. 2: 203–21.

Bohm, D. 2002. *On Dialogue*. London and New York: Routledge.

Boryczka, J. M., D. Gudelunas, and G. Gil-Egui. 2015. "Strangers as Neighbors: How Religious Dialogue Can Help Re-Frame the Issue of Immigration." *Strangers as Neighbors—Research Publications* 4. https://digitalcommons.fairfield.edu/strangersasneighbors-pubs/4.

Bossart, D. 1998. "Constructive Conflict or Harmonious Dishonesty." In *Congregations Talking about Homosexuality: Dialogue on a Difficult Issue*, edited by Beth Ann Gaede, 103–14. Bethesda, MD: Alban Institute.

Bower, S. 2016. "Review of *Cosmopolitanism, Religion and the Public Sphere*, by M. Rovisco and S. Kim (eds)." *SITES: New Series* 13, no. 1: 238–40.

Breitkreutz, C. 2011. "Religious Affiliation and Attendance as Predictors of Immigration Attitudes in Nebraska." Master's thesis, University of Nebraska.

Brenneman, R. 2005. "Faith and the Foreigner: Exploring the Impact of Religion on Immigration Attitudes." Master's thesis, The Graduate School at the University of Notre Dame.

Brown, L. 2019. "Racism and Segregation in Baltimore." Transcript of a talk given as part of an academic panel discussion sponsored by The Center for the Study of Religion and the City at Morgan State University, Baltimore.

Brown, R. K., and R. E. Brown. 2017. "Race, Religion, and Immigration Policy Attitudes." *Race and Social Problems* 9, no. 1: 4–18.

Bruneau, E., and R. Saxe. 2012. "The Power of Being Heard: The Benefits of 'Perspective-Giving' in the Context of Intergroup Conflict." *Journal of Experimental Social Psychology* 48, no. 4: 855–66.

Brunett, A. 2001. "What Dialogue Means for Catholics and Muslims: An Address by Archbishop Alexander J. Brunett." *Origins: CNS Documentary Service* 30, no. 41, March 29, 2001. Accessed April 13, 2021. https://www.usccb.org/committees/ecumenical-interreligious-affairs/what-dialogue-means-catholics-and-muslims.

Budiman, A. 2020. "Key Findings about U.S. Immigrants." Accessed March 29, 2022. https://www.pewresearch.org/fact-tank/2020/08/20/key-findings-about-u-s-immigrants/.

Burity, J. 2013. "Latin American Pentecostalism and Ecumenical Alterglobalism as Cases of Agonistic Cosmopolitanism." In *Cosmopolitanism, Religion and the Public Sphere*, edited by M. Rovisco and S. Kim, 68–84. Abingdon, UK: Routledge.

Burton, T. I. 2018. "The Bible Says to Welcome Immigrants. So Why Don't White Evangelicals?" *Vox*, October 30, 2018. Accessed March 2, 2023. https://www.vox.com/2018/10/30/18035336/white-evangelicals-immigration-nationalism-christianity-refugee-honduras-migrant.

Carbaugh, D. 2013. "On Dialogue Studies." *Journal of Dialogue Studies* 1, no. 1: 9–28.

Catholic Review. 2012. "Maryland Catholics Urged to Engage in Immigration Dialogue." Accessed December 31, 2022. https://www.archbalt.org/maryland-catholics-urged-to-engage-in-immigration-dialogue/.

Chinchilla, N. S., N. Hamilton, and J. Loucky. 2009. "The Sanctuary Movement and Central American Activism in Los Angeles." *Latin American Perspectives* 36, no. 6: 101–26.

Coco, A. 2015. "Roman Catholicism: A Communication Quandary." Paper presented at the Women in Education Forum, Independent Education Union, Ballina, Australia, August 5.

Cornille, C. 2013. "Conditions for Inter-Religious Dialogue." In *The Wiley-Blackwell Companion to Inter-Religious Dialogue*, edited by Catherine Cornille, 20–33. Hoboken, NJ: Wiley-Blackwell.

Cortland, C., J. Shapiro, R. Neel, M. Craig, J. Richeson, and N. Goldstein. 2017. "Solidarity Through Shared Disadvantage: Highlighting Shared Experiences of Discrimination Improves Relations Between Stigmatized Groups." *Journal of Personality and Social Psychology* 113, no. 4, 547–67. https://doi.org/10.1037/pspi0000100.

Cramer Walsh, K. C. 2007. *Talking about Race: Community Dialogues and the Politics of Difference*. Chicago: University of Chicago Press.

Deitz, S. 2014. "Religiosity and Attitudes toward Immigrants and Immigration." Research Paper 514. Southern Illinois University Carbondale Graduate School. http://opensiuc.lib.siu.edu/gs_rp/514.

Delanty, G. 2011. "Cultural Diversity, Democracy and the Prospects of Cosmopolitanism: A Theory of Cultural Encounters." *British Journal of Sociology* 62, no. 4: 633–56.

Dessel, A. 2011. "Dialogue and Social Change: An Interdisciplinary and Transformative History." *Smith College Studies in Social Work* 81, no. 2–3: 167–83.

Dezerotes, D. 2018. "The Use of Dialogue in Transforming Religious Conflict." In *Religion, Conflict, & Peacemaking: An Interdisciplinary Conversation*, edited by M. Schmid, 29–44. Salt Lake City: University of Utah Press.

Diaz, A., and R. Perrault. 2010. "Sustained Dialogue and Civic Life: Post-College Impacts." *Michigan Journal of Community Service Learning*, Fall: 32–43.

Dictionary.com. 2021. "Cosmopolitan." Accessed April 8, 2021. https://www.dictionary.com/browse/cosmopolitan.

Discipleship Ministries of the United Methodist Church. 2016. "Courageous Conversations About Immigration." Accessed February 9, 2022. https://www.umcdiscipleship.org/resources/courageous-conversations-about-immigration.

Dougherty, K. D., M. Chaves, and M. O. Emerson. 2020. "Racial Diversity in US Congregations, 1998–2019." *Journal for the Scientific Study of Religion* 59, no. 4: 651–62.

Edwards, S. 2017. "Intergroup Dialogue and Religious Identity: Attempting to Raise Awareness of Christian Privilege and Religious Oppression." *Multicultural Education*, Winter: 18–24.

Evangelical Immigration Table. 2022. "A Guide to Engaging in Respectful Conversations about Immigration." Accessed February 9, 2022. https://evangelicalimmigrationtable .com/take-action/conversation-guide/.

Falwell, J. 1981. *The Fundamentalist Phenomenon*. New York: Doubleday Galilee Books.

Filomeno, F. A. 2017. "The Migration–Development Nexus in Local Immigration Policy: Baltimore City and the Hispanic Diaspora." *Urban Affairs Review* 53, no. 1: 102–37. https://doi.org/10.1177/1078087415614920.

Filomeno, F. A. 2019. "Expanding Hearts and Minds? Evaluation of an Ecumenical Educational Program on Immigration." *Journal of Applied Social Science* 13, no. 2: 152–64.

Flores, E. 2020. "Religion, Race, and Immigration in Community Organizing among the Formerly Incarcerated." In *Religion Is Raced: Understanding American Religion in the Twenty-First Century*, edited by G. Yukich and P. Edgell, 227–47. New York: New York University Press.

Fox, J. 2004. "The Rise of Religious Nationalism and Conflict: Ethnic Conflict and Revolutionary Wars, 1945–2001." *Journal of Peace Research* 41, no. 6: 715–31.

Freeland, G. 2010. "Negotiating Place, Space and Borders: The New Sanctuary Movement." *Latino Studies* 8, no. 4: 485–508.

Freire, P. 1974. *The Pedagogy of the Oppressed*. Harmondsworth, UK: Penguin.

Gadamer, H. G. 1975. *Truth and Method*. New York: Seabury Press.

Gaertner, S. L., and J. F. Dovidio. 2000. *Reducing Intergroup Bias: The Common Ingroup Identity Model*. Philadelphia: Psychology Press/Taylor & Francis.

Ganesh, Shiv, and Heather Zoller. 2012. "Dialogue, Activism, and Democratic Social Change." *Communication Theory* 22:66–91.

García Agustín, Ó., and M. B. Jørgensen. 2021. "On Transversal Solidarity: An Approach to Migration and Multi-Scalar Solidarities." *Critical Sociology* 47, no. 6: 857–73.

Garner, Steve, and Saher Selod. 2014. "The Racialization of Muslims: Empirical Studies of Islamophobia." *Critical Sociology* 41, no. 1: 9–19.

Gehrz, C. 2017. "The Need for a Comprehensive 'Theology of Diversity.'" *Patheos* (blog), March 29, 2017. Accessed April 9, 2021. https://www.patheos.com/blogs/anxiousbench /2017/03/comprehensive-theology-diversity/.

Halemba, A. 2011. "National, Transnational or Cosmopolitan Heroine? The Virgin Mary's Apparitions in Contemporary Europe." *Ethnic and Racial Studies* 34, no. 3: 454–70.

Hammack, P., and A. Pilecki. 2015. "Power in History: Contrasting Theoretical Approaches to Intergroup Dialogue." *Journal of Social Issues* 71, no. 2: 371–85.

Harris, F. C. 1994. "Something Within: Religion as a Mobilizer of African-American Political Activism." *The Journal of Politics* 56, no. 1: 42–68.

Healy, P. 2011. "Situated Cosmopolitanism, and the Conditions of Its Possibility: Transformative Dialogue as a Response to the Challenge of Difference." *Cosmos and History: The Journal of Natural and Social Philosophy* 7, no. 2: 157–78.

Herzig, M. 2011. "Fostering Welcoming Communities Through Dialogue." Cambridge, MA: Welcoming America and Public Conversations Project.

Hicks, Mark. 2010. "Building the World We Dream About: A Tapestry of Faith Program for Adults." Boston: Unitarian Universalist Association.

Hinze, B. 2006. *Practices of Dialogue in the Roman Catholic Church*. New York: Continuum.

Hobsbawm, E. 2013. "America's Imperial Delusion." *The Guardian*, June 13, 2013. Accessed April 9, 2021. https://www.theguardian.com/world/2003/jun/14/usa.comment.

Hondagneu-Sotelo, P. 2008. *God's Heart Has No Borders: How Religious Activists Are Working for Immigrant Rights*. Berkeley: University of California Press.

Hoover, B. 2014. *The Shared Parish: Latinos, Anglos, and the Future of U.S. Catholicism*. New York: New York University Press.

Hoover, B. 2021. "Still Unaccommodated: Why Are Hispanic Catholics Treated Unequally?" *Commonweal*, July 10, 2021. Accessed October 5, 2023. https://www.commonweal magazine.org/still-unaccommodated.

Houston, S., and C. Morse. 2017. "The Ordinary and Extraordinary: Producing Migrant Inclusion and Exclusion in US Sanctuary Movements." *Studies in Social Justice* 11, no. 1: 27–47.

Ignatius, of Loyola, Saint. 1987. *The Spiritual Exercises of St. Ignatius Loyola: A New Translation by Elisabeth Meier Tetlow*. Lanham, MD: University Press of America.

Interfaith Immigration Coalition. 2013. "Breaking Bread and Building Bridges Potluck and Town Hall Meeting." Accessed September 12, 2023. https://www.interfaithimmi gration.org/wp-content/uploads/2013/01/Breaking-Bread-Events-How-to-and-Pro gram-Template-FINAL.pdf.

International Organization for Migration. 2021. *The Power of Contact*. Geneva: International Organization for Migration. Accessed February 20, 2023. https://publications .iom.int/books/power-contact-designing-facilitating-and-evaluating-social-mixing -activities-strengthen.

Isaacs, W. 1999. Dialogue and the Art of Thinking Together: A Pioneering Approach to Communicating in Business and in Life. New York: Currency.

Jensen, E., N. Jones, M. Rabe, B. Pratt, L. Medina, K. Orozco, and L. Spell. 2021. "The Chance that Two People Chosen at Random Are of Different Race or Ethnicity Groups Has Increased since 2010." Census.gov. Accessed November 15, 2022. https://www.census .gov/library/stories/2021/08/2020-united-states-population-more-racially-ethnically -diverse-than-2010.html.

Jones, R. P., D. Cox, J. Navarro-Rivera, and E. Cook. 2013. "Factors Influencing Support for Immigration Reform: Analysis from the 2013 Religion, Values, and Immigration Reform Survey." Available at SSRN: http://dx.doi.org/10.2139/ssrn.2324864.

Jordaan, E. 2009. "Dialogic Cosmopolitanism and Global Justice." *International Studies Review* 11:736–48.

Juergensmeyer, M. 2000. *Terror in the Mind of God: The Global Rise of Religious Violence*. Berkeley: University of California Press.

Juergensmeyer, M. 2010. "The Global Rise of Religious Nationalism." *Australian Journal of International Affairs* 64, no. 3: 262–73.

JustFaith Ministries. 2021. "Faith and Immigration Justice: General Overview." Accessed February 9, 2022. https://justfaith.org/faith-and-immigration-justice/.

Kadayfici-Orellana, S. A. 2013. "Inter-Religious Dialogue and Peacebuilding." In *The Wiley-Blackwell Companion to Inter-Religious Dialogue*, edited by Catherine Cornille, 149–67. Hoboken, NJ: Wiley-Blackwell.

Kaufmann, E. 2019. "Why Is Secularization Likely to Stall in America by 2050? A Response to Laurie DeRose." *Institute for Family Studies* (blog). July 24, 2019. Accessed August 25, 2023. https://ifstudies.org/blog/why-is-secularization-likely-to-stall-in-america -by-2050-a-response-to-laurie-derose.

Keating, T. 2010. *Meditations on the Parables of Jesus*. New York: Crossroad Publishing.

Klages, M. 2012. Key *Terms in Literary Theory*. New York: Continuum International Publishing Group.

Klofstad, C. 2010. *Civic Talk: Peers, Politics, and the Future of Democracy*. Philadelphia: Temple University Press.

Knitter, P. 2013. "Inter-Religious Dialogue and Social Action." In *The Wiley-Blackwell Companion to Inter-Religious Dialogue*, edited by Catherine Cornille, 133–48. Hoboken, NJ: Wiley-Blackwell.

Knoll, B. 2009. "'And Who Is My Neighbor?' Religion and Immigration Policy Attitudes." *Journal for the Scientific Study of Religion* 48, no. 3: 313–31.

Koczanowics, L. 2009. "Cosmopolitanism and Its Predicaments." *Studies in Philosophy and Education* 29:141–49.

Krause, K. 2011. "Cosmopolitan Charismatics? Transnational Ways of Belonging and Cosmopolitan Moments in the Religious Practice of New Mission Churches." *Ethnic and Racial Studies* 34, no. 3: 419–35.

Latino Racial Justice Circle (LRJC). 2015. Promotional brochure. Baltimore: LRJC.

Linklater, A. 1998. *The Transformation of Political Community: Ethical Foundations of the Post-Westphalian Era*. Oxford: Polity.

Liu-Beers, C., R. Salata, and K. Gustine. 2011. "Becoming the Church Together: Immigration, the Bible, and Our New Neighbors." North Carolina Council of Churches. Accessed February 9, 2022. https://www.ncchurches.org/programs/immigrants-rights/immigration-curriculum/.

Livezey, L. 2000. "The New Context of Urban Religion." In *Public Religion and Urban Transformation: Faith in the City*, edited by L. Livezey, 3–25. New York: New York University Press.

Living Room Conversations. 2021. "Conversation Guide: Immigration." Accessed October 5, 2023. https://livingroomconversations.org/wp-content/uploads/2021/03/Immigration.pdf.

London, S., and B. Rourke. 2018. *Coming to America: Who Should We Welcome, What Should We Do?* Dayton, OH: National Issues Forum Institute.

Lulofs, R. 1994. "Cosmopolitan Communication and the Evangelical Impulse: Transcending a Paradox." Paper presented at the Annual Meeting of the Speech Communication Association, New Orleans, LA, November 19–22.

Lutheran Immigration and Refugee Service. 2021. *EMMAUS: Congregational Discernment Guide*. Baltimore: Lutheran Immigration and Refugee Service.

Maddison, S. 2015. "Relational Transformation and Agonistic Dialogue in Divided Societies." *Political Studies* 63:1014–30.

Mallon, C. M. 2008. "Dialogue and Its Discontents: Theological and Anthropological Reflections." *Missiology: An International Review* 36, no. 4: 491–503.

Marx, K., and F. Engels. 1948. *Manifesto of the Communist Party*. Accessed April 8, 2021. https://www.marxists.org/archive/marx/works/1848/communist-manifesto/.

McCoy, M., C. Flavin, and M. Reaven. 1997. "Toward a More Perfect Union in an Age of Diversity." Pomfret, CT: Study Circles Resource Center.

McDaniel, E., I. Nooruddin, and A. Shortle. 2011. "Divine Boundaries: How Religion Shapes Citizens' Attitudes toward Immigrants." *American Politics Research* 39, no. 1: 205–33.

Meintel, M. and G. Mossière. 2013. "In the Wake of the Quiet Revolution: From Secularization to Religious Cosmopolitanism." *Anthropologica* 55, no. 1: 57–71.

Melkonian-Hoover, R., and L. Kellstedt. 2019. *Evangelicals and Immigration: Fault Lines Among the Faithful*. Cham, Switzerland: Palgrave Macmillan.

Mendieta, E. 2009. "From Imperial to Dialogical Cosmopolitanism." *Ethics & Global Politics* 2, no. 3: 241–58.

Menjívar, C. 2003. "Religion and Immigration in Comparative Perspective: Catholic and Evangelical Salvadorans in San Francisco, Washington, D.C., and Phoenix." *Sociology of Religion* 64, no. 1: 21–45.

Mignolo, W. 2000. "The Many Faces of Cosmo-polis: Border Thinking and Critical Cos-mopolitanism." *Public Culture* 12, no. 3: 721–48.

Nagda, B., A. Yeakley, P. Gurin, and N. Sorensen. 2012. "Intergroup Dialogue: A Critical-Dialogic Model for Conflict Engagement." In *The Oxford Handbook of Intergroup Conflict*, edited by L. Tropp, 210–28. Oxford: Oxford University Press.

Namsoon, K. 2013. *Cosmopolitan Theology: Reconstituting Planetary Hospitality, Neighbor-Love, and Solidarity in an Uneven World*. Nashville, TN: Chalice Press.

Neufeldt, R. 2001. "Interfaith Dialogue: Assessing Theories of Change." *Peace & Change* 36, no. 3: 344–72.

Neuman, J. 2011. "Religious Cosmopolitanism?: Orhan Pamuk, the Headscarf Debate, and the Problem with Pluralism." *Minnesota Review* 77: 143–61.

Olesker, M. 2001. *Journeys to the Heart of Baltimore*. Baltimore: Johns Hopkins University Press.

Park, K. 1998. "The Religious Construction of Sanctuary Provision in Two Congregations." *Sociological Spectrum* 18: 393–421.

Paterson, I. 2017. "Love Thy Neighbour? The Impact of Political and Religious Elite Discourse on Immigration Attitudes." PhD diss., University of Glasgow. http://theses.gla .ac.uk/8642/.

Pearce, W. B. 1989. *Communication and the Human Condition*. Carbondale, IL: Southern Illinois Press.

Pearson-Merkowitz, S., A. Filindra, and J. J. Dyck. 2016. "When Partisans and Minorities Interact: Interpersonal Contact, Partisanship, and Public Opinion Preferences on Immigration Policy." *Social Science Quarterly* 97, no. 2: 311–24.

Permoser, J. 2020. "Trump, the Bible, and the Far Right's Use of Religion." *Berkley Forum* (blog). Berkley Center for Religion, Peace and World Affairs, Georgetown University. June 26, 2020. Accessed August 24, 2022. https://berkleycenter.georgetown.edu/posts /trump-the-bible-and-the-far-right-s-use-of-religion.

Petersen, L., and P. Takayama. 1984. "Community and Commitment among Catholics: A Test of Local-Cosmopolitan Theory." *The Sociological Quarterly* 25, no. 1: 97–112.

Pettigrew, T. 1998. "Reactions toward the New Minorities of Western Europe." *Annual Review of Sociology* 24: 77–103.

Pew Research Center. 2010. "Few Say Religion Shapes Immigration, Environment Views." Accessed August 24, 2022. https://www.pewresearch.org/politics/2010/09/17/few-say -religion-shapes-immigration-environment-views/.

Pew Research Center. 2015. "Religious Landscape Study: Christians." Accessed August 24, 2022. https://www.pewforum.org/religious-landscape-study/christians/christian/.

Pew Research Center. 2022. "Modeling the Future of Religion in America." Accessed August 24, 2022. https://www.pewresearch.org/religion/wp-content/uploads/sites/7 /2022/09/US-Religious-Projections_FOR-PRODUCTION-9.13.22.pdf.

Pew Research Center. 2023. "Inflation, Health Costs, Partisan Cooperation Among the Nation's Top Problems." Accessed September 12, 2023. https://www.pewresearch.org /politics/2023/06/21/inflation-health-costs-partisan-cooperation-among-the-nations -top-problems/.

Ponce, A. 2017. "Gender and Anti-immigrant Attitudes in Europe." *Socius* 3. https://doi .org/10.1177/2378023117729970.

Pope Francis. 2020. *The Encyclical Letter Fratelli Tutti on Fraternity and Social Friendship*. New York: Paulist Press.

Power, G. 1996. "The Residential Segregation of Baltimore's Jews: Restrictive Covenants or Gentlemen's Agreement?" *Generations*, Fall: 5–7.

Public Religion Research Institute (PRRI). 2023. "Religion and Congregations in a Time of Social and Political Upheaval: Findings from the 2022 Health of Congregations Survey." Washington, DC: PRRI.

Rapoport, D. 1984. "Fear and Trembling: Terrorism in Three Religious Traditions." *American Political Science Review* 78, no. 3: 658–77.

Religions for Peace. 2020. *Offering Refuge: A Discussion Guide for Faithful Americans on Immigration Policies and Practices*. New York: Religions for Peace. Accessed September 12, 2023. https://www.rfpusa.org/wp-content/uploads/2020/10/Offering-Refuge -A-Discussion-Guide-for-Faithful-Americans-on-Immigration-Policies-and-Practices -Religions-for-Peace-USA-2.pdf.

Rougeau, V. 2017. "A Cosmopolitan Church Confronts Right-Wing Populism." *Seattle University Law Review* 40:1343–58.

Saad, Lydia. 2023. "Americans Showing Increased Concern About Immigration." *Gallup*. Accessed September 12, 2023. https://news.gallup.com/poll/470426/americans-showing -increased-concern-immigration.aspx.

Sacks, J. 2002. *The Dignity of Difference: How to Avoid the Clash of Civilizations*. New York: Continuum.

Saguy, T. 2019. "Introduction: When Groups Meet—Understanding How Power Dynamics Shape Intergroup Encounters." In *The Power of Dialogue Between Israelis and Palestinians: Stories of Change from the School for Peace*, edited by N. Sonnenschein and D. Reich, 1–14. New Brunswick, NJ: Rutgers University Press.

Saldaña, J. 2009. The *Coding Manual for Qualitative Researchers*. London: SAGE.

Saunders, H. 2001. *A Public Peace Process: Sustained Dialogue to Transform Racial and Ethnic Conflicts*. New York: Palgrave Macmillan.

Schirch, L. 2001. "Ritual Reconciliation: Transforming Identity/Reframing Conflict." In *Reconciliation, Justice and Coexistence: Theory and Practice*, edited by M. Abu-Nimer, 145–63. Lanham, MD: Lexington Books.

Scully, P., and M. Leighninger. 1998. *Changing Faces, Changing Communities. Immigration & Race, Jobs, Schools and Language Differences: A Guide for Public Dialogue and Problem Solving*. Pomfret, CT: Study Circles Resource Center.

Scully, P., and M. McCoy. 2005. "Deliberative Dialogue to Expand Civic Engagement: What Kind of Talk Does Democracy Need?" *National Civic Review* 91, no. 2: 117–35.

Shapcott, R. 2001. *Justice, Community and Dialogue in International Relations*. Cambridge: Cambridge University Press.

Shimron, Y. 2022. "Religious Groups with Immigrant Members Grew Fastest over Past Decade." *Religion News*. Accessed August 24, 2023. https://religionnews.com/2022/11 /11/religious-groups-with-immigrant-members-grew-fastest-over-past-decade/.

Skirbekk, Vegard, Eric Kaufmann, and Anne Goujon. 2010. "Secularism, Fundamentalism, or Catholicism? The Religious Composition of the United States to 2043." *Journal for the Scientific Study of Religion* 49, no. 2: 293–310.

Soerens, Matthew, and Jenny Yang. 2021. *Discovering and Living God's Heart for Immigrants: A Guide to Welcoming the Stranger*. Baltimore: World Relief. https://worldrelief .org/welcoming-the-stranger/.

Sonnenschein, N. 2019. "Afterword: A Critical Analysis of the Interviews." In *The Power of Dialogue Between Israelis and Palestinians: Stories of Change from the School for Peace*, edited by N. Sonnenschein and D. Reich, 347–65. New Brunswick, NJ: Rutgers University Press.

Stern, J. 2003. *Terror in the Name of God: Why Religious Militants Kill*. New York: Harper Collins.

Stroope, S., H. M. Rackin, and P. Froese. 2021. "Christian Nationalism and Views of Immigrants in the United States: Is the Relationship Stronger for the Religiously Inactive?" *Socius* 7. https://doi.org/10.1177/2378023120985116.

Sustained Dialogue Campus Network. 2017. "How to Use Sustained Dialogue Issue Sheets." Washington, DC: Sustained Dialogue Institute.

Svensson, I., and K. Brounéus. 2013. "Dialogue and Interethnic Trust: A Randomized Field Trial of 'Sustained Dialogue' in Ethiopia." *Journal of Peace Research* 50, no. 5: 563–75.

Swidler, L. 2013. "The History of Inter-Religious Dialogue." In *The Wiley-Blackwell Companion to Inter-Religious Dialogue*, edited by Catherine Cornille, 3–19. Hoboken, NJ: Wiley-Blackwell.

Tajfel, H., and J. Turner. 1986. "The Social Identity Theory of Intergroup Behavior." In *Psychology of Intergroup Relations*, edited by S. Worchel and W. Austin, 7–24. Chicago: Nelson-Hall.

Taylor, C. 1994. "The Politics of Recognition." In *Multiculturalism: Examining the Politics of Recognition*, edited by A. Gutman, 25–73. Princeton, NJ: Princeton University Press.

Tentler, L. W. 2011. "Souls and Bodies: The Birth Control Controversy and the Collapse of Confession." In *The Crisis of Authority in Catholic Modernity*, edited by M. J. Lacey and F. Oakley, 293–315. New York: Oxford University Press.

Tropp, L., O. Ulug, and M. Uysal. 2020. "How Intergroup Contact and Communication about Group Differences Predict Collective Action Intentions among Advantaged Groups." *International Journal of Intercultural Relations* 80, no. 4: 7–16.

Turner, B. 2001. "Cosmopolitan Virtue: On Religion in a Global Age." *European Journal of Social Theory* 4, no. 2: 131–52.

U/monk2be. 2013. "Is illegal immigration a sin?" Reddit, https://www.reddit.com/r/Christianity/comments/2avmxq/is_illegal_immigration_a_sin/?rdt=51076.

United Church of Christ. n.d. "Faith and Immigration: Questions for Reflection." Accessed September 12, 2023. https://www.ucc.org/justice_immigration_worship_faith-and-immigration/.

USC Annenberg, Golin, and Zignal Labs. 2022. "The Polarization Index (Six-Month Update, October 2021–March 2022)." University of Southern California Annenberg, Golin, and Zignal Labs. Accessed July 8, 2022. https://thepolarizationindex.com/.

U/xmasx131. 2017. "Indianapolis church locks up Mary, Joseph, Baby Jesus to condemn immigration policy." Reddit, https://www.reddit.com/r/Christianity/comments/8vseeb/indianapolis_church_locks_up_mary_joseph_baby/.

Van Zanten, S. 2011. "Christian Cosmopolitanism: Reading in the Global Age." *Comment* Magazine, June 13, 2011. Accessed April 9, 2021. https://www.cardus.ca/comment/article/2826/christian-cosmopolitanism-reading-in-the-global-age/.

Vergara, C. 2022. "How Christian Nationalism Is Taking Root Across the World." *Politico*, October 27, 2022. Accessed March 6, 2023. https://www.politico.com/news/magazine/2022/10/27/global-far-right-christian-nationalists-00063400.

Vox. 2018. "68% of White Evangelicals Say America Has No Responsibility to House Refugees." November 1, 2018. https://www.facebook.com/Vox/posts/1032203446967257.

Wallis, Jim, Ched Myers, Gabriel Salguero, Sally Steenland, and Noemi Mena. 2015. *Christians and Immigration: A Guide for Personal Reflection and Group Discussion.* Sojourners Magazine. e-Book available at https://www.amazon.com/Christians-Immigration-Personal-Reflection-Discussion-ebook/dp/B010RI82AY.

Wardell, S. 2018. "'A Stranger in the Name of Jesus': Exploring Cosmopolitan Ethics in a Ugandan Christian Care Community." *SITES: New Series* 15, no. 2: 165–88.

Westoby, P. 2014. "Theorising Dialogue for Community Development Practice—An Exploration of Critical Thinkers." *Journal of Dialogue Studies* 2, no. 1: 69–85.

Whitehead, A., and S. Perry. 2020. *Taking America Back for God: Christian Nationalism in the United States*. New York: Oxford University Press.

Williams, R. H. 2020. "Assuming Whiteness in Twentieth-Century American Religion." In *Religion Is Raced: Understanding American Religion in the Twenty-First Century*, edited by Grace Yukich and Penny Edgell, 74–92. New York: New York University Press.

Winter, M. 2021. "The Fastest-Growing Group of American Evangelicals." *The Atlantic*, July 26, 2021. Accessed March 29, 2022. https://www.theatlantic.com/culture/archive/2021/07/latinos-will-determine-future-american-evangelicalism/619551/.

Wolfe, A. 2018. "Dialogue and Deliberation as Agonistic Resistance: Designing Interactional Processes to Reconstitute Collective Identities." *Journal of Public Deliberation* 14, no. 2: 1–14.

Women of Welcome. 2020. "Evangelical Leaders Wrote to President Trump Last Week to Urge Him to Reconsider Plans to Resubmit a Filing to End the Deferred Action for Childhood Arrivals (DACA) Program." July 22, 2020. https://www.facebook.com/WomenofWelcome/posts/776559233086315.

Yukich, G., and P. Edgell, eds. 2020. *Religion Is Raced: Understanding American Religion in the Twenty-First Century*. New York: New York University Press.

Zúñiga, X. 2003. "Bridging Differences Through Dialogue." *About Campus* 7, no. 6: 8–16.

# Index

**Felipe Amin Filomeno** is Associate Professor of Political Science and Global Studies at the University of Maryland, Baltimore County. He is the author of *Theories of Local Immigration Policy* and *Monsanto and Intellectual Property in South America*.